DIONYSUS

IN

LITERATURE

DIONYSUS IN LITERATURE:
ESSAYS ON LITERARY MADNESS

edited by

Branimir M. Rieger

Bowling Green State University Popular Press
Bowling Green, OH 43403

PN
56
.M45
D56
1994
~~Sept.~~ 1997

Acknowledgments

First, I am grateful to Pat Browne for her suggestion that my "Madness in Literature" panels at the Popular Culture conventions might produce a collection of essays on the topic. I am further thankful for her suggestions, editing and general Job-like patience with my forays into madness. Another debt of gratitude goes to the contributors of essays in this volume. They responded promptly to my suggestions for additions, deletions and revisions, and my onerous task was much lightened by their patience and good humor. I am thankful to the librarians at Lander University (Ann Hare, Betty Williams, Susan Going and Dan Lee) who provided me with endless articles and interlibrary loans. They also looked the other way while my leaning tower of overdue books balanced precariously in my office over the years. Thanks to John Hare for teaching me how to battle computer glitches and gritches. Great appreciation is shown toward those colleagues who read my introduction and offered valuable suggestions (Virginia Dumont, Robert Phillips, Carol Wilson and Julia Whitsitt). Special thanks to Mary Joseph who read a number of drafts and offered valuable editorial changes. And super appreciation goes to Bettie Horne who read numerous drafts with linguistic precision and frequently "nagged" me to finish my often abandoned project. I also wish to thank the Lander Foundation, the Lander University administration and my chair, Susan Guinn, for providing funds and encouragement for my research on this project. Thanks also go to the Humanities Department Secretary, Debbie Brown, whose help was invaluable, and to Linda Findley, Humanities' Administrative Assistant. I want to thank my parents, Karla and Bill Rieger, who always had faith in me and instilled in me a love of writing. I also want to thank my boys, Christopher and Andrew, for their love and support. And to Katanga, Major Tom, Baby Schnupkin, Lothar, Mookie, Nub, Baby Nub, Pockel, the Twins, Mousie, Lobotz, and Tiniest Of for their feline encouragement, and especially to Molly.

Contents

Introduction

Dionysus in Literature:
Essays on Literary Madness

Branimir M. Rieger

What exactly is meant by "Madness in Literature?" How can this thematic phrase aid in the understanding of literature? Does it refer to the writer, the abnormal behavior of the characters or some nexus? Does it refer to the writings of madmen or the actions of mad protagonists? Is literary madness similar to the clinical madness of psychology? Or is it closer to anomie, a sociological term for a type of madness in which individuals are alienated from society? How can terminology from psychology be useful in understanding literary characters? Have the concepts of literary madness changed from the ancients to today? In the opening essay of this collection, "Literary Theories and the Concept of Madness," Robert de Beaugrande discusses how literary theories have contributed to concepts of madness. To state that madness and sanity are opposites grossly oversimplifies and omits significant shades of grey. The term madness, whether used in a clinical or literary sense, is a fluid, ambiguous term encompassing many theories.

Madness is common to the human experience. We often complain that people or situations are driving us "mad," or "crazy" or "wild." The insanity of daily existence and of absurd situations can devastate tender psyches. Anger, a reaction to the insanity of the world, can be viewed as a microcosm of madness. We also have obsessions and compulsions deviating from the normal. Psychology and literature both try to explain unusual behavior, and the term "madness" seems to be a particularly useful tool in discussing certain literary characters. Strange, abnormal and deviant actions of literary characters offer an indispensable resource for investigating personality. While psychology and literature have made some significant advances in unlocking secrets of personality, it is nevertheless amazing that certain aspects of personality (What is madness and abnormal behavior? What causes it? How is it treated?) are still baffling, open to semantic debates, and laced with relativity.

1

Clinical and literary madness have many connotations. Clinical madness, for example, has a largely negative reputation because of destructive, deviant behavior of mass murderers like Son of Sam, Ted Bundy and Jeffrey Dahmer. On the other hand, R.D. Laing claims clinical madness is creative and healing. Similarly, in literary madness something both pitiful and admirable marks the actions of a King Lear or the Underground Man because both characters have journeyed to places where most of us can only dream of going. Furthermore, we often repress our mad or wilder sides in reaction to the pressures of society or pretend to be saner than we are. Literature classifies many of these situations and provides insight in understanding ourselves and others. While not everyone in society may be mad, *per se*, many have frustrations, tensions and anxieties which can lead to madness. Writers have been especially sensitive to such inner conflicts and have portrayed characters' lives with psychological realism.

Poets were thought in classical times to be divinely inspired or irrational, driven by forces beyond their control. Dionysus is the god in Greek mythology and literature who induces madness, passion, irrational behavior and frenzy; his influence and cults posed an alternative which threatened the more rational and severe Apollonian aspects of Greek thought. Plato, too, differentiated between clinical insanity and the creative insanity or Dionysian frenzy of seers and poets. For further background consult E.R. Dodds, *The Greeks and the Irrational*, and Bennett Simon, *Mind and Madness in Ancient Greece*. But in classical and later periods the clinically insane were considered criminals, outcasts, vagabonds or outlaws. During the Middle Ages mad people moved freely in everyday life, though people with "strange beliefs" were often considered to be possessed by demons or simply heretics. Medieval madness motifs are discussed in Penelope Doob's *Nebuchadnezzar's Children: Conventions of Madness in Middle English Literature*. Renaissance attitudes toward madness are covered in Robert S. Kinsman, "Folly, Melancholy, and Madness: A Study in Shifting Styles of Medical Analysis and Treatment, 1450-1675," in his edition of essays, *The Darker Vision of the Renaissance* (273-320). Michel Foucault's *Madness and Civilization* shows that the Age of Reason was a catastrophe for the insane, who were often chained and brutalized. Because madmen were antagonistic to bourgeois values and terrifying to authorities, they replaced lepers as societal scapegoats. Physicians, too, believed mental problems resulted from an imbalance of humors, and the evolution of therapies to help the insane have been horrible: induced vomits, purges and bleedings to correct imbalances of bile, blood and phlegm.

Michael MacDonald's *Mystical Bedlam: Madness, Anxiety, and Healing in Seventeenth-Century England*, explores seventeenth-century attitudes. A more sympathetic view of the insane emerges in some writers in the eighteenth century, especially in the satires of Pope, Swift and Johnson, and in the writings of the Pre-Romantics and Romantics. For the views of Neo-Classical writers, see Max Byrd, *Visits to Bedlam: Madness and Literature in the 18th Century*. Blake's reputation as an artist was long clouded by suspicions of his madness, but as Paul Youngquist shows in his essay in this volume, "Vision, Madness, Myth, and William Blake" (a portion of his book, *Madness and Blake's Myth*), Blake's myth is about the madness of forging poetry from mental suffering. Blake's furious assaults upon Urizen show how madness can lead to prophetic insights. Coleridge, in "Kubla Khan," revives the idea of the divine, mad frenzy of the writer, and the writings of Wordsworth, Byron, DeQuincey, Southey, Lamb and Clare deify the human ego and promulgate the creative, healing aspects of the insane. Some Victorian writers, especially Tennyson, suffered personal depressions and explored madness as a theme. (See Ann C. Colley, *Tennyson and Madness* and Roger S. Platizky, *A Blueprint of His Dissent: Madness and Method in Tennyson's Poetry*.) Modern convulsive therapies, including insulin, electroshock, lobotomy and drugs, which treat only the symptoms of madness, show society's primitive notions of insanity. The "talking cure" of Freud and other humanistic psychologists offered some hope for more sympathetic understandings for the causes of mental illness, but ignorance, the misapplication of Freud's theories, and a tendency toward labeling and jargon have harmed the insane. The twentieth century is filled with numerous personal breakdowns and grotesque fictions by writers like Kafka, Joyce, Pirandello, Grass, O'Neill, Tennessee Williams and Pynchon.

Deviant behavior has always both repelled and fascinated mankind. Interesting to observe are the non-conformists, the sinners or the rebels, who violate society's supposedly normal standards. Social scientists continually debate the definitions and labeling of what is deviant and what is not. But from what better source could one learn about madness, violence, murder, deceit, betrayal, lust, greed, loneliness and depression than in writers such as Sophocles, Aeschylus, Shakespeare, Dostoyevsky, Faulkner, Genet, Nabokov, Burroughs and Stephen King?

Nevertheless, one need not be a trained psychologist to identify mad or abnormal behavior. Daily, we read news of people snapping under pressures of modern life, committing violent acts (including murder), and exhibiting other bizarre behaviors. While the general public might assume that abnormal equates to "sick," "crazy" or "insane," many episodes of abnormal behavior are borderline cases between sanity and insanity, perhaps indicating, as Melville claimed in *Billy Budd*, that there is no "exact line of demarcation." Although definitions of abnormality differ and are widely debated, one current definition claims it to be: "Any behavior or state of emotional distress that causes personal suffering, that is self-destructive, or that is unacceptable to the community" (Wade and Travis 576). But under this broad definition, such common activities as smoking, drinking, gambling or overeating might be considered abnormal.

The problem with this definition and any other description of abnormal behavior demonstrates that "madness" is a semantic as well as a medical or psychological problem. People have always suffered from stress, loneliness and strange behavior. Healers attempt to classify, explain and cure such disorders. Even the commonly used terminology of such respected thinkers as Freud, Jung, Adler, Horney is extensively employed, but also is widely criticized. Today controversy still exists about which conditions are clinically classified as real mental disorders. In 1952, for example, the American Psychiatric Association published the *DSM-I* (*Diagnostic and Statistical Manual of Mental Disorders*), listing 60 types of mental illness. The *DSM-II* was expanded in 1968 to include 145 types and, by 1980, the *DSM-III* had grown to 230 disorders, accompanied by a description of their behavioral signs. Significantly, the *DSM-III* dropped the Freudian term "neurosis," showing a once widely used clinical term is currently out of fashion in the semantic battle of labeling madness. *DSM-III-R* was the revised edition, superseded by *DSM-IV*. Despite supposed improvements in the latest descriptions in the *DSM-III*, madness ("mental illness" in the clinical sense) continues as a controversial and ambiguous term because the categories are matters of clinical consensus, not science.

Critics of the *DSM-III* have compared it to a symphony written by a committee: the notes are there, but their constitution reflects the biases of the process. Critics feel the *DSM-III* is a haven for analysts who feel it their job to label observations as illness. But since the causes of supposedly abnormal behavior are often missing, *DSM-III* diagnoses may be based on complex behaviors perceived differently by different observers. As a result many disorders may not even exist, and no treatment would be warranted.

In addition to citing the semantic problems involved in identification and classification of abnormal behavior, there is criticism of the entire field of mental health. R.D. Laing, in *The Divided Self*, and Thomas Szasz, in *The Myth of Mental Illness*, both argue eloquently that mental illness is merely a term by which we designate people whose behavior deviates from the norms of society. This view is portrayed in Ken Kesey's novel, *One Flew Over the Cuckoo's Nest*, about a man institutionalized merely because he has been "disruptive." He is subjected to drugs, shock therapy and finally a lobotomy for challenging the authority of the head nurse. Both Laing and Szasz argue that "mental illness" is a term manufactured by society seeking scapegoats; Foucault, in *Madness and Civilization*, believes the mad became threats in the Age of Reason, when asylums were first built, thereby erecting a wall between the "insane" and the rest of humanity. Laing also advocates a very romantic notion of mental disorder as a state and process that can confer a deeper understanding of the world. While Laing and his followers, Artaud and Norman Brown, celebrate madness as liberation from oppressive cultural constraints, one must be careful not to glorify real clinical madness, thereby demeaning the anguish of the truly insane.

It is clear, therefore, from the controversy surrounding the *DSM-III*, as well as criticism by Szasz, Laing and others, that labeling promoted by the mental health field contributes to preserving the ambiguity of the fluid, changing term, "medical madness." How can one differentiate between literary madness and medical madness? Since the literature and research about clinical and literary madness is vast, relative and semantically confusing, one needs to state how the concept of literary madness is employed.

To date, literary madness has been used as a critical device in three ways: 1) the "mad" writer; 2) the "mad" characters of writers; and 3) the critical method by which psychological terms from the field of medical madness are applied to literary madness. Each approach has some validity in literary application, but if applied superficially, each exhibits drawbacks.

1) *The "mad" writer theory.* Advocated by Plato and other classical writers, this ancient theory claims creative writers are "mad," full of "divine frenzy" and driven by irrational, uncontrollable forces, which were the primary reasons for their creativity.

This old tradition, of viewing the literary artist as a mad and therefore interesting person, has a certain popular appeal but has been repeatedly challenged in this century by studies showing that schizophrenia, paranoia, depression and addiction can actually interfere with the creative process. See Roy Porter's summary of the literature and arguments in his chapter, "Madness and Genius" in his *A Social History of Madness*, Albert Rothenberg's *Creativity and Madness*, and Martin S. Lindauer's essay in this collection, "Are Creative Writers Mad? An Empirical Perspective."

There is no denying that many writers experience mental problems or true insanity. Insanity affected Lucretius, Nathaniel Lee, Christopher Smart, William Collins, Robert Southey, John Clare, Charles Lamb, Count de Sade, Guy de Maupassant, Ezra Pound, Nicholas Gogol, Jonathan Swift, William Cowper, Hart Crane, Jack London, Randall Jarrell, John Berryman, Virginia Woolf, Sylvia Plath and Anne Sexton. The "ancient affliction" of depression troubled William Styron (see his *Darkness Visible: A Memoir of Madness*) and countless other writers in all periods. Ironically, the best works of some writers, composed in periods of depression, might never have been completed or recognized if they had been written when the writer was more cheerful or optimistic.

The conflict between a woman's desire to be a creative artist and society's desire to restrict her to traditional female gender roles and expectations seemingly contributed to the madness and depression of such writers as Virginia Woolf, Sylvia Plath and Anne Sexton. See Nancy Topping Bazin's essay, "Postmortem Diagnoses of Virginia Woolf's 'Madness': The Precarious Quest for Truth," in this collection. This essay updates Bazin's groundbreaking work on Woolf's "madness" in her 1973 book, *Virginia Woolf and the Androgynous Vision*, while synthesizing and evaluating what has been written on the topic since then. Similarly, *The Journals of Sylvia Plath*, edited by Ted Hughes and Frances McCullough, give us a glimpse of the mood swings, painful depression and suicide wishes of the poet. More disturbing is Diane Wood Middlebrook's controversial *Ann Sexton: a Biography*, which uses tapes of therapy sessions with one of Sexton's psychiatrists. Others, like Blake, experienced visions, and many, like Poe, suffered from alcohol dependency (see Donald W. Goodwin, *Alcohol and the Writer* and Tom Dardis, *The Thirsty Muse: Alcohol and the American Writer*). One must be careful, however, not to commit the "autobiographical fallacy" of suggesting all the "crazy" elements in a work reflect the writer's "madness." Certainly, it is tempting to reinterpret a writer's works if one learns some of the personal demons, nightmares or addictions which may affect a writer. Nevertheless, because of a tendency to identify characters with the writer's supposedly unstable frame of mind, this device can produce, at best, superficial criticism, and, at worst, wrong-headed conclusions. This brings us to the second way in which literary madness is used.

2) *"Mad" characters or mad behavior of characters.* This category is general enough to encompass a very significant canon of literature dealing with some aspect of abnormal behavior. Writers endow their characters with strange behaviors for a variety of reasons. The creative artist has frequently examined contradictory motivations, inner unrest and the highly emotional impulses of mankind. Pathological experience has long obsessed writers. Some characters like Hamlet, Antigone, the Underground Man, Gregor Samsa and Edna Pontellier of Kate Chopin's *The Awakening* were defined as "mad" by their own cultural milieu. Some writers like Poe, Dostoyevsky, Browning and Beckett have adopted an "abnormal" voice and experimented with mad monologues. Since characters are sometimes considered "mad," some readers, by means of the "autobiographical fallacy," assume that artists are also demented.

There are at least three ways in which "mad" characters can operate in a literary milieu. First, a character can become mad, like an Ophelia, Lady Macbeth, King Lear, Savannah Wingo in Pat Conroy's *The Prince of Tides*, or Blanche DuBois in Tennessee Williams's *A Streetcar Named Desire*. A character can also exhibit certain psychological aberrations, like Holden Caulfield's depression in J.D. Salinger's *The Catcher in the Rye* or extreme loneliness or compulsive behavior like Mary Tyrone in Eugene O'Neill's *A Long Day's Journey into Night*. The writer frequently provides numerous clues for this breakdown, and an examination of this character's plight in light of the main ideas in the work is useful in examining the core of the work. Second, non-conformist characters can rebel against a restrictive society by either appearing to be mad or actually going mad, like Edgar's faked madness in *King Lear*, or R.P. McMurphy's struggle against the asylum in *One Flew Over the Cuckoo's Nest*. While they may plunge into a kind of Ahab-like, frenzied madness, the madness or seeming madness is an experience that provides important revelations about self or society. Third, characters can also experience a kind of anomie in which society seems intent on crushing their personalities, which results in the separation from the human community, as experienced by the woman narrator of Charlotte Perkins Gilman's short story, "The Yellow Wallpaper," by Emma in Flaubert's *Madame Bovary* or by Hamlet. For the myriad of interpretations of Hamlet's madness, see Michael Cohen's essay in this collection, "*Hamlet:* Madness and the Eye of the Reader," adapted from his *Hamlet in My Mind's Eye.*

Anomie, or sociological madness, depicts characters estranged from society's "sane," "normal" or "rational" behaviors, like Melville's Bartleby or Camus's Mersault in *The Stranger.* Frequently, a writer utilizes this literary madness to satirize the society which has produced the "mad" individual. A "mad" person, in the Shakespearean wise-fool, "reason in truth" tradition, can also utter truths that most people of a supposedly sane society would never observe or verbalize. See Alisa von Brentano's essay in this volume, "Herman Melville and 'The Sane Madness of Vital Truth,'" which points out Melville's "sane madness" in both personal experience and artistic perception, going from Ahab's sane "madness" to Vere's mad "sanity." Also see Barbara Tepa Lupack's essay, "Inmates Running the Asylum: The Institution in Contemporary American Fiction," in this collection.

Besides the paralyzed character who suffers an anomie madness, like Gregor Samsa or the Underground Man, "mad" characters can take more active steps as rebels or non-conformists to oppose society's constraints. Writers portray these characters as existing outside of the mainstream, either by choice, necessity, force or illness. Such "mad" characters portray how society's dominant cultural values are often irreconcilable with the characters' lives and convictions. Personality disorders appear to be either widespread or widely discussed in American culture. Nineteenth-century masochistic madness of Dostoyevsky's Underground Man is chronicled by Thomas C. Fiddick's essay in this collection, "Madness, Masochism and Morality: Dostoyevsky and His Underground Man."

Lilian Feder's critical work, *Madness in Literature*, deftly combines criticism about both mad artists and mad characters, analyzing the writings of mad individuals, as well as mad protagonists. Feder articulates the idea that literary madness reflects society's prohibitions and values, and that this kind of madness can be a means of self-revelation and self-knowledge. Her discussions range from classical madness, whether prophetic or Dionysian, to madness as an artistic goal, as in Theodore Roethke, Allen Ginsberg and Sylvia Plath. Additionally, Feder cites numerous cases, from

Thomas Hoccleve to Nietzsche and Nerval, to establish that personal madness may serve as inspiration, insight or escape from painful reality. Besides the critical approaches involving the writer and the characters, a third method involves psychological and medical terminology in literary discussion.

3) *The critical method by which psychological terms from the field of medical madness are applied to literary madness.* Psychological terminology can be borrowed from Freud, Jung, Horney or other modern theorists, or may be from actual descriptions, such as those from the DSM-III categories. Literature and psychology are complementary disciplines, for each contributes to an understanding of personality. As such, studying the specialized topic of "madness in literature" might actually contribute to our knowledge of human behavior.

The relationships between literature and psychology have been well documented elsewhere and only some important critics and works will be briefly noted here. Psychological criticism has been a major critical apparatus since the time of Freud, and it concentrates either on the author, the content, the formal construction or the reader. A few pivotal works in the development of psychological criticism were: Ernst Kris, *Psychoanalytic Explorations in Art*; Frederick J. Hoffman, *Freudianism and the Literary Mind*; and Simon O. Lesser, *Fiction and the Unconscious*. One must also mention the important work of Norman N. Holland, whose *The Dynamics of Literary Response*, *5 Readers Reading*, and other works followed Freud in identifying literature as a force which elicits in readers tensions between fantasies and defenses. Holland's reader-response theory combined the workings of text and personality. He produced the majority of his most important works at the State University of New York at Buffalo, which has a graduate program in Literature and Psychology and a Center for the Psychological Study of the Arts. In addition to the Freudian approaches to literature, Third Force Psychology has also been widely used in psychological criticism. "Third Force" refers to humanistic psychology and to the work of Carl Rogers, Abraham Maslow and Karen Horney who propose an alternative to psychoanalysis and behaviorism. It is more positive and optimistic than either traditional therapies or scientific psychology. An important "Third Force" critic is Bernard Paris, whose *A Psychological Approach to Fiction* and other works employ this school of criticism. His book, *A Horneyan Approach to Literature*, will appear in 1994 in NYU Press's Literature and Psychoanalysis series. He is associated with the Institute for Psychological Study of the Arts at the University of Florida.

Dangers can exist in too closely connecting literature and psychology. For example, a number of literary anthologies have highlighted fictional characters who supposedly illustrate various psychological disorders. In Alan A. Stone and Sue S. Stone's anthology, *The Abnormal Personality Through Literature*, and Charles W. Harwell's anthology, *Disordered Personalities in Literature*, the editorial commentary places the characters' lives in precise psychological categories, suggesting abnormal, clinical case histories rather than literature. The accompanying *DSM*-like labels reduce the characters to one-dimensional clinical studies if they must conform exactly to DSM-like characteristics and labels. Such critical procedures can reduce literature's complexity to trite, simplistic observations.

Psychological criticism employing Freudian, neo-Freudian, Jungian, Third-Force Psychology, Lacanian and other psychoanalytic approaches to interpret literature are numerous. Two important recent critical studies dealing with madness are noteworthy. One is Jeffrey Berman's *The Talking Cure: Literary Representations of Psychoanalysis*, which examines the use modern writers make of psychoanalysts as literary characters. Berman deals with the relationships between creative processes and therapeutic processes by examining how artists can heal themselves and others by transforming suffering into art. Berman discusses some of the major concepts of psychoanalysis, including narcissism, doubling, and transference, as he ranges through a number of post-Freudian revisionists like Kohut, Kernberg, Mahler, and Jung, to discuss Plath, Gilman, Fitzgerald, Lessing, Nabokov, Greenberg, Roth and D.M. Thomas's *The White Hotel*. Also important is Evelyne Keitel's *Reading-Psychosis: Readers, Texts, and Psychoanalysis*, which contributes to reader-response theory by providing a clear account of the paradoxical process by which some contemporary novels, like Doris Lessing's *Briefing for a Descent Into Hell*, convey analogues of borderline psychological states.

In addition to psychological critical approaches, it is evident that special topics or aspects of literary madness exist in a number of literary areas and offer productive areas for future study. For instance, madness might be studied in various national or regional literatures, geographic areas, or people, such as madness in women's writing, madness in African-American literature, madness in Southern fiction, madness in Latin American fiction or madness in postcolonial fiction. When a group or person is considered by a given society as an outsider, certain psychological pressures envelope that person. For example, Ralph Ellison, in *Invisible Man*, depicts the resulting madness of the intentionally nameless narrator, who is not considered a real person by the white, racist society. Lawrence R. Broer's essay in this collection, "Images of the Shaman in the Works of Kurt Vonnegut," adapted from his book, *Sanity Plea: Schizophrenia in the Novels of Kurt Vonnegut*, shows how Vonnegut forces readers to ponder the sanity of characters whose psychological structures make them healthier than the fragmented world has left them. In addition to Vonnegut's *Slaughterhouse Five*, other works also deal with the madness of war and its effects on characters and society; Voltaire's *Candide*, Heller's *Catch-22*, and Kovic's *Born on the Fourth of July* are a few of the numerous novels dealing with the madness of war.

The topic "Women and Madness" has been impressively covered in a number of critical texts: Phyllis Chesler, *Women and Madness*; Patricia M. Spacks, *The Female Imagination*; Barbara H. Rigney, *Madness and Sexual Politics in the Feminist Novel*; Sandra S. Gilbert and Susan Gubar, *The Madwoman in the Attic: The Woman Writer and the Nineteenth-Century Imagination*; and Elaine Showalter, *The Female Malady*. A useful deconstruction of the genealogy of women's madness is Jane M. Ussher's *Women's Madness: Misogyny or Mental Illness?* In Southern literature examinations of madness can appear either in the realistic vein, as in Lee Smith's *Black Mountain Breakdown* and Pete Dexter's *Paris Trout*, or in the Southern Gothic mode of Faulkner, Flannery O'Connor and Carson McCullers, stressing the particularly unique and often bizarre, Southern characters and customs. For an account of Faulkner's Greek view of madness, see Kenneth L. Golden's "Faulkner and the Furies," in this collection. The philosophical labyrinths of Jorge Luis Borges and the mythical madness of Gabriel Garcia Marquez's *One Hundred Years of Solitude* are just a few of the works about madness in Latin American fiction. Madness and the psychology of the supernatural is represented in this volume in Carol A. Senf's essay, "Stephen King's *Misery*: Manic Depression and Creativity." Also included in this volume are Peter H. Goodrich's, "The Lineage of the Mad Scientist: Anti-types of Merlin," as well as studies of Shakespeare, Blake, Dostoyevsky, Woolf, Melville, Faulkner, Vonnegut and Stephen King.

Hollywood's fascination with madness has taken many sensational turns, and as a result, there are few sympathetic or realistic portraits of the insane or of the asylum. Robert Coles, "Madness in Film" (*Horizon* 18-22), discusses a number of films that are thoughtful and incisive, including *Equus, Outrageous* and *I Never Promised You a Rose Garden*. Michael Fleming's and Roger Manville's essay, in this volume, "Through a Lens, Darkly." This excerpt from their book, *Images of Madness: The Portrayal of Insanity in the Feature Film*, examines how the subject of madness has been a very popular one for filmmakers, especially paranoia and the insane asylum as a locus. They analyze such films as *The Snake Pit, One Flew Over the Cuckoo's Nest, Twelve O'Clock High, Taxi Driver, Apocalypse Now* and *King of Hearts*. An interesting recent portrait of schizophrenia is Robin Williams' Grail-searching character in *The Fisher King*. Besides films dealing with mad characters and insane asylums, the image of the wacko psychiatrist, who is often loonier than the patient, is prevalent in current films. *Raising Cain* portrays a child psychologist who, for strange reasons, kidnaps his own daughter. *The Silence of the Lambs* offers us the chilling murderer, Dr. Hannibal Lecter. In *Final Analysis* Richard Gere plays a shrink who sleeps with a patient's sister. Richard Gere also plays a manic-depressive in the movie *Mr. Jones*, and his therapist falls in love with him. And Barbra Streisand, in *The Prince of Tides*, plays a therapist who sleeps with a patient's brother. For more realistic images of therapists one might view *David and Lisa, I Never Promised You a Rose Garden, Ordinary People*, and *Another Woman*. For a fuller treatment see Krin Gabbard and Glen O. Gabbard, *Psychiatry and the Cinema*. The asylum in fiction is covered in this collection by Barbara Tepa Lupack's essay, "Inmates Running the Asylum: The Institution in Contemporary American Fiction." Another recent movie, *Falling*, with Michael Douglas, portrays a white, middle-class male office worker who goes off the deep end, taking his vengeance for his failed American Dream against a group of scapegoats: ethnic groups, women and gangs. The anger in this film is reminiscent of Peter Finch's rage in the movie *Network*, when he screamed, "I'm mad as hell, and I'm not going to take it anymore."

The essays in this collection provide pluralism in psychological or psychoanalytic criticism, which the editor has selected from a wide variety of critical approaches. Like a counselor who adopts varying stances according to the needs of different patients, the editor utilizes different approaches to illuminate various types of literature. Thus, some essays analyze how a writer's personal "madness" affects the writings, some focus mainly on characters, and others deal with psychological readings of the literature, based on various clinical theories. In the final analysis the literary criticism presented by these methods is useful because it allows us to confront intelligently that which is truly important, the literature itself. The approaches offer various types of validity since the terms are adequately defined, sufficient examples are cited from the text, and the parallels between clinical and literary madness are established but never lost in absurdity.

Writers who deal with madness as a general theme reflect a deep awareness of human personality. As such, this Dionysian element in literature seems more sympathetic to mad, disturbed or agitated individuals than other literary works, but it also demonstrates that the "mad" person is often not so very different from you or me, and, in fact, illness itself is often an attempt at a cure. All clinical literature on madness merely reinforces that there is still much we don't know about mental disorders. The literary attitudes toward madness often reflect a greater awareness and understanding, as well as sympathy for, the realities of the human mind than do historical medical attitudes, thereby contributing significantly to the attempt of unraveling mysteries of personality. The oversimplified dichotomy between madness and sanity is repeatedly disputed in both clinical and literary treatments of madness and, like Wallace Stevens, one sees there is more than one way to look at a blackbird.

Works Cited

American Psychiatric Association. *DSM-III-R (Diagnostic and Statistical Manual of Mental Disorders)*. Third ed. Rev. Washington, D.C.: American Psychiatric Association, 1987.

Bazin, Nancy Topping. *Virginia Woolf and the Androgynous Vision*. New Brunswick, NJ: Rutgers UP, 1973.

Berman, Jeffrey. *The Talking Cure: Literary Representations of Psycho-analysis*. New York: New York UP, 1986.

Bootzin, Richard R., Joan Ross Acocella, and Lauren B. Alloy. *Abnormal Psychology: Current Perspectives*. 6th ed. New York: McGraw-Hill, 1993.

Broer, Lawrence R. *Sanity Plea: Schizophrenia in the Novels of Kurt Vonnegut*. Ann Arbor: UMI Research P, 1989.

Byrd, Max. *Visits to Bedlam: Madness and Literature in the 18th Century*. Columbia, SC: U of South Carolina P, 1974.

Chesler, Phyllis. *Women and Madness.* Garden City, NY: Doubleday, 1972.

Chopin, Kate. *The Awakening.* New York: Knopf, 1992.

Coles, Robert. "Madness in Film." *Horizon* 21 (1978): 18-22.

Colley, Ann C. *Tennyson and Madness.* Athens: U of Georgia P, 1983.

Conroy, Pat. *The Prince of Tides.* Boston: Houghton Mifflin, 1986.

Dardis, Tom. *The Thirsty Muse: Alcohol and the American Writer.* New York: Ticknor & Fields, 1989.

Dexter, Pete. *Paris Trout.* New York: Random House, 1988.

Dodds, E.R. *The Greeks and the Irrational.* Berkeley: U of California P, 1951.

Doob, Penelope. *Nebuchadnezzar's Children: Conventions of Madness in Middle English Literature.* New Haven: Yale UP, 1974.

Ellison, Ralph. *Invisible Man.* New York: Random House, 1963.

Feder, Lilian. *Madness in Literature.* Princeton: Princeton UP, 1980.

Fleming, Michael, and Roger Manville. *Images of Madness: The Portrayal of Insanity in the Feature Film.* Rutherford, NJ: Fairleigh Dickinson UP, 1985.

Foucault, Michel. *Madness and Civilization.* New York, Vintage, 1965.

Gabbard, Krin, and Glen O. Gabbard. *Psychiatry and the Cinema.* Chicago: U of Chicago P, 1989.

Gilbert, Sandra S., and Susan Gubar. *The Madwoman in the Attic: The Woman Writer and the Nineteenth-Century Imagination.* New Haven: Yale UP, 1979.

Goodwin, Donald W. *Alcohol and the Writer.* Kansas City: Andrews & McMeel, 1988.

Harwell, Charles W., ed. *Disordered Personalities in Literature.* New York: Longman, 1980.

Hoffman, Frederick J. *Freudianism and the Literary Mind.* Baton Rouge: Louisiana State UP, 1955.

Holland, Norman N. *The Dynamics of Literary Response.* New York: Oxford UP, 1968.

____. *5 Readers Reading.* New Haven: Yale UP, 1975.

Hughes, Ted, and Frances McCullough, eds. *The Journals of Sylvia Plath.* New York: Dial, 1982.

Kesey, Ken. *One Flew Over the Cuckoo's Nest.* New York: Viking, 1975.

Kinsman, Robert S. "Folly, Melancholy, and Madness: A Study in Shifting Styles of Medical Analysis and Treatment, 1450-1675." *The Darker Vision of the Renaissance.* Berkeley: U of California P, 1974.

Kris, Ernst. *Psychoanalytic Explorations in Art.* New York: International UP, 1952.

Laing, R.D. *The Divided Self.* Baltimore: Penguin Books, 1959.

Lesser, Simon O. *Fiction and the Unconscious.* New York: Vintage, 1957.

Lessing, Doris. *Briefing for a Descent Into Hell.* London: Jonathan Cape, 1971.

MacDonald, Michael. *Mystical Bedlam: Madness, Anxiety, and Healing in Seventeenth-Century England.* Cambridge: Cambridge UP, 1981.

Marquez, Gabriel G. *One Hundred Years of Solitude.* Trans. Gregory Rabassa, New York: Harper & Row, 1970.

Melville, Herman. *Billy Budd.* New York: MacMillan, 1975.

O'Neill, Eugene. *A Long Day's Journey into Night.* New Haven: Yale UP, 1950.

Paris, Bernard. *A Psychological Approach to Fiction.* Bloomington, IN: Indiana UP, 1974.

Platizky, Roger S. *A Blueprint of His Dissent: Madness and Method in Tennyson's Poetry.* Lewisburg, PA: Bucknell UP, 1989.

Porter, Roy. *A Social History of Madness.* New York: Weidenfeld & Nicolson, 1987.

Rigney, Barbara H. *Madness and Sexual Politics in the Feminist Novel.* Madison: U of Wisconsin P, 1978.

Rothenberg, Albert. *Creativity and Madness.* Baltimore: Johns Hopkins UP, 1990.

Salinger, J.D. *Catcher in the Rye.* Boston: Little, Brown, 1951.

Simon, Bennett. *Mind and Madness in Ancient Greece.* Ithaca: Cornell UP, 1978.

Smith, Lee. *Black Mountain Breakdown.* New York: Ballantine, 1986.

Spacks, Patricia M. *The Female Imagination.* New York: Knopf, 1975.

Stone, Alan A., and Sue S. Stone, eds. *The Abnormal Personality Through Literature.* Englewood Cliffs, NJ: Prentice-Hall, 1966.

Styron, William. *Darkness Visible: A Memoir of Madness.* New York: Random House, 1990.

Szasz, Thomas. *The Myth of Mental Illness.* New York: Harper & Row, 1974.

Thomas, D.M. *The White Hotel.* New York: Viking, 1981.

Ussher, Jane M. *Women's Madness: Misogyny or Mental Illness?* New York: Harvester Wheatsheaf, 1991.

Vonnegut, Kurt. *Slaughterhouse Five.* New York: Delacorte, 1969.

Wade, Carol, and Carol Travis. *Psychology.* New York: Harper Collins, 1987.

Williams, Tennessee. *A Streetcar Named Desire.* New York: New Directions, 1980.

Youngquist, Paul. *Madness and Blake's Myth.* University Park, PA: Penn State UP, 1989.

Literary Theories and the Concept of Madness

Robert de Beaugrande

When I was a student at Heidelberg, the professor of our lecture course in "Modern Experimental Lyrics," the late Alfred Liede, sounded quite emphatic: "Mental illness cannot be an issue for literary study—it doesn't lead anywhere." No doubt such a reservation was especially strategic when dealing with the poetry of Expressionism (Georg Heym, Georg Trakl and the like), where madness was explicitly treated as a theme, often in ways that suggested disturbing parallels between psychosis and authorship. Moreover, the prospect of exploring the mental condition of literary authors must seem highly unpromising for the traditional critical profession devoted to exalting the creative act and the author as a cultural monument.

This is an ironic twist, however, when we recall how "literary genius" "was, as early as the Greeks, conceived of as related to madness" (Wellek and Warren 81). "In folklore aesthetics," according to Ernst Kris, "the poet is the inspired, the possessed, the productively mad" (205). After all, does not the literary author speak of things that "aren't there" and "don't exist," and continually overstep the bounds of reality, committing in imagination every sort of act, however, disavowed by society? Did not Plato himself want artists banned from society for doing this?

And the view of authors and artists being "mad" is evidently quite congenial to the general public, who dotes on the countless biographies and films which emphatically portray artists being "punished" for their gifts. This may in part be a special case of the general mechanism, foreseen by ancient and widespread superstition, that any exceptional person deserves retribution, ostensibly because the gods get jealous, whence the topos of "hybris" from classical tragedy onward.[1] Frye remarks on the topos but fails to relate it properly to his classification of genres based on the relative superiority of the "hero" versus the audience.

Yet divine jealousy, apart from actual confrontations (as in the myths of Ariachne or Orpheus), can hardly apply to the mythical artist, who in some sense speaks for (interprets) the gods. So it must be the society, and maybe the audience of the art work, as well, whose jealousy is at stake. As Leslie Fiedler enjoys pointing out, society has, since the beginnings, resented the seemingly divine inspiration or possession whereby the poet was empowered to see and speak what is denied or forbidden to others (*Love*). Presumably, this ancient response provides "normal society" a recompense and alibi for its own failure to be creative: the price of creative vision is the loss of sanity.

Or, the conflict runs even deeper, namely the valence of madness as the other side, and indeed the validation, of sanity. Writing after his own "mental breakdowns," Seymour Krim hoped for a fundamental reestimation:

Until this time of complete blast-off in seemingly every department of human life, the idea of insanity was thought of as the most dreadful thing that could happen to a person [although] little was actually known about it …But in this era of monumental need to re-think and re-define almost every former presumption about madness—which has inspired a bombing way of looking at what once were considered the most unbudgeable rocks of reality—the locked door of insanity has been shaken loose and shall yet be hurled wide open. Until one day the prisoners of this definition will walk beside us, sharing only the insane plight of mortality, which makes quiet madmen of us all. (125)

But Krim's own experience confirmed no such hope, since even his artist friends shied away from him:

This struck me as…saddening, because intellectuals and especially artists should understand that insanity today is a matter of definition, not fact… An interpretation of madness is a much more real threat in a time of such infinite moon-voyaging extension to experience that the validly felt act is often fearfully jailed in a windowless cell of definition by hard-pressed authorities whose moral axis is in danger. (133)

At stake ultimately is therefore not the "essence of madness," but the criteria whereby any society views departures from its standards of conception and conduct as a mental (not merely a moral) breakdown.

Yet even the most complacent and compulsively normalized society cannot quite convince itself that art and literature are satisfactorily accounted for as side-products of madness, however useful such a facile defense may be against a particularly disturbing artist or art work. After all, a good deal of what is considered "madness" is not judged artistic or literary; and being "mad" is certainly not a sufficient or necessary criterion to make a person an artist. So even if some artists might qualify by some standard as "mad," the two conditions are obviously not linked in any direct, let alone causal, way.

Michel Foucault has attacked the problem of "madness" by showing how the notion has historically been defined or described within specific social contexts. Was it considered a disease or a punishment for sin, i.e., a medical or an ethical dysfunction? How did or does society treat its "mad" people—with reverence, as in ancient times, or with the uneasy oscillations among abhorrence, pity, curiosity, and interventionism practiced since then? And how does this treatment compare with that accorded to artists?

Though recognizing "madness" as the "other side" of "sanity" is a liberating insight, it does not necessarily bring us closer to a definition, because "sanity" itself is so seldom openly defined or described. Instead, "sanity" simply operates as a framework based on the acceptance of a prevailing world-view and its "reasonable" norms of conduct, and these are acquired more often by imitation than by indoctrination. "Sanity" usually becomes a point for discussion only as the background when some activity is judged a violation. To actually *foreground* sanity would thus be to change its status and function.

We should thus not be surprised that modern psychoanalysis, in its turn, has paid its tribute by consistently foregrounding insanity, yet refusing to see its social and political context. This too was recognized by Krim from first-hand experience:

No deep attempt was made to diagnose my "case"...My judges and indifferent captors [...] did not have the time, the patience, or even the interest because work in a flip-factory is determined by mathematics: you must find a common denominator of categorization and treatment in order to handle the battalions of humanity that are marched past your desk... What the institution-spared layman does not realize is that a sensitive and multiple-reacting human being remains the same everywhere, including a sanitarium, and such an environment can duplicate the injustice or vulgarity which drove your person there in the first place.... A mental hospital [is] just a roped-off side street of modern existence, rife with as many contradictions, half-truths, and lousy architecture as life itself.

So art and insanity at least share the factor that the standards whereby either is defined have much to do with the ways and means a society finds for regulating expression and belief. Whatever the two may share beyond that must remain open, quite simply because both are open phenomena, and this too in potentially disturbing ways.

The main question to be raised in this essay, in my estimation, is how the two might be at least circumscribed, if not defined, with respect to each other. At first blush, prevailing theories seem to offer an auspicious point to begin. For most people, Freudian theory is the most famous domain for analyzing the mind ("psychoanalysis" etymologically being a "dismantling of the soul"). Yet here already, problems abound. Recently, trenchant critiques have challenged Freudian theory on the grounds that its model of psychic functions has been derived and generalized from neurotic examples. In consequence, this theory tends to suggest that everyone is likely to be neurotic. Some people may manage to attain a fragile balance by minimizing guilt and anxiety; but a genuine, definitive escape from neurosis seems scarcely feasible.

As a corollary, we should not be surprised if Freud tended to "think of the author as an obdurate neurotic, who, by his creative work, keeps himself from a crack-up but also from any real cure" (Wellek and Warren 82). In Freud's words, "the artist" "turns from reality because he cannot come to terms with the demand for the renunciation of instinctual satisfaction," and "in fantasy-life allows full play to his erotic and ambitious wishes" (82). "He molds his fantasies into a new kind of reality," but "without creating real alteration in the outer world" (82).

Wisely, Freud himself did not make "madness" a theoretical term, no doubt because of the baggage of mystification and fear he would have had to combat. But we can validly ask about a Freudian view of how art relates to "neurosis" as a better-defined and less abhorrent subtype of "madness." Artists must after all tend to be neurotic if almost everyone does, but if so, what makes artists and their work so special? As Wellek and Warren remark, it is hardly reassuring to consider "the poet" a "day-dreamer who is socially validated"—"instead of altering his character, he perpetuates and publishes his fantasies" (82). They point out that unlike "the day-dreamer," the writer "is engaged in an act of externalization and of adjustment to society." Besides, writers "have not wanted to be 'cured' or 'adjusted'" in order to stop writing or to accept a "philistine," "bourgeois" "social environment" (83).

The most technical and thorough Freudian approach to art I know of is that proposed by Norman Holland, who underwent actual training as a psychoanalyst. In essence, he describes literature as a mode for working through submerged fantasy-content. He supports his model with instances of "clinical evidence" regarding the processes of "psychoanalysis, hypnosis, and dreaming," which involve a "persistence of adult ego-functions along with an encapsulated regression" (Holland 89). "We might well be in the same schizoid state when we are engrossed in a literary 'entertainment'; certainly, the behavioral signs of that engrossment resemble our behavior in analysis, hypnosis, and dreaming" (89). "Absurd" theatre in particular "creates in us a state approximating schizophrenia, affectlessness, concretized metaphors, klang association, depersonalization, an unclear relation of self to object"; "intellection" can then be applied as "a self-defeating way of dealing with this miniature psychosis" (177). By the same mode of comparison, Holland suggests using "motor inhibition" to explain the "basic convention" that "we do not expect to act as a result of literary or artistic experience"; "the work of art" "presents itself as divorced from usefulness" (70).

By such analogies art seems even closer to neurosis than everyday activity does. However, Holland's fantasy-model is relatively optimistic, since the working through of fantasies is considered healthy and normal enough. But I see an implicit pessimism here if all that art can offer is a form of "hallucinated gratification" (181). The reader's real state remains essentially unchanged. Neurosis is, as it were, simply made more entertaining and informative.

Leslie Fiedler, who has both Freudian and Jungian roots, proposes a more transformative account of art as a release valve. Art offers "a descent into, a harrowing of Hell," "a recourse to the dark powers in quest of salvation: a way out of the secular limbo," the "least-common-denominator consensus reality enforced in the name of sanity and virtue" (*What* 138). "All art which remains popular" "makes possible" "the release of the repressed," of "undying primal impulses" (50). In this way, "popular literature" makes us "more at home with, in tune with, the darker, more perilous aspects of our own psyches, otherwise confessed only in nightmares" (50). However, "the art which simultaneously releases and neutralizes" the "darker aspects" of "the unconscious" tends to "trigger another primeval response: the fear of the unconscious and its tyranny" (42). "Censorship" can then raise the "contention that art is incitement rather than therapy, reinforcing whatever a given era considers socially undesirable or morally reprehensible" (42).

In Fiedler's estimate, art is essentially therapeutic, yet society may readily misconstrue that function and attack the artist for revealing a suppressed, denied part of its own psyche. This account makes good sense, provided we assume that "psychic levels" form the center "from which works of art proceed and to which they seek to return" (Fiedler, *Love* 389). But this assumption is difficult to generalize in such a way. For one thing, it plainly works better for some kinds of art and literature than others. Fiedler, for instance, is quite at home with the "Gothic," which deals obsessively with repressed themes in a popular way, but he dislikes modernism, which does not (Beaugrande, *Critical*).

In recent years—another great irony—Freudian theorizing has survived better in literary theory than in psychology itself, due in part to mounting empirical evidence against certain central Freudian theses and partly to a shift in psychology toward models of information processing (Fischer and Greenberg; Beaugrande, "Freudian" and references there). Evidently, literary theorists have come to see Freud's ideas not so much as a model of what really happens in the "psyche" or "mind" or even in a person's historical life, but as a framework for a radical hermeneutics that rewrites explicit content in terms of some more hidden master code (Deleuze and Guattari; Jameson).

A contributing motive for this continuing loyalty in art theory is probably the opportunity to speculate on the "part played by the unconscious" in "the creative process" (Wellek and Warren 88). "The experience of the author" includes "the total conscious and unconscious experience during the prolonged time of creation" (148). In agreement with the old idea of being "possessed" and "productively mad" (cited above), "the poet" is thought to "speak" "out of" an "unconscious" that is both "sub- and super-rational" (81). A "special integration of perceptual and conceptual" might allow the "unconscious" to make a "central contribution" of "visual" and "auditory" "imagery" (83, 208, 188). In addition, "the Jungian thesis that beneath the individual unconscious—the blocked-off residue of our past"—"lies the 'collective unconscious,'" favored the notion that the author "retains an archaic trait of the race" (83f).

This expansion revises the encounter between psychoanalysis and art theory by shifting the emphasis away from the author as an individual personality. Wellek and Warren (207ff) declare it "mistaken" to suppose that "the poet must have literally perceived whatever he can imagine"; or that the "imagery" constitutes "a hieroglyphic report" on his or her "psychic health." Yet psychoanalysis is by no means well-suited to solving the problem of how to represent the "creative process" in its "entire sequence from the subconscious origins of a literary work to those last revisions which, with some writers, are the most genuinely creative part of the whole" (85). The inclination to see the "subconscious" or "unconscious" at work during "origins" or "inspiration" (85f) may be merely an evasion fostered by our lack of theories and data about artistic mentation. The "authors" themselves prefer to "discuss conscious and technical procedures, for which they may claim credit" (88).

In contrast to the "bleak stoicism," "despair," and "tragic view of man" diagnosed for example by Fiedler in Freudian thought (*No!* 224f, 310), "third force psychology" offers a "humanistic" alternative. Its name (created by Karen Horney and Abraham Maslow) projects it as a viewpoint that does not rely on the two "forces" of psychic drive (Freudian theory) or stimulus-response conditioning (behaviorist psychology). According to Bernard Paris, who has played a leading role in applying it to literature, this "different philosophy of human nature" projects "greater optimism" and "a more holistic approach to human behavior" (*Third* 11). Its emphatic concern is the "evolutionary constructive force" that "urges us to realize our given potentialities" (11). We should seek "self-knowledge" as a "means of liberating the forces of spontaneous growth" (Horney 15). The ultimate goal is "self-actualization," an "episode" in which "the powers of the person come together in a particularly efficient way" (Paris, *Third* 35). Freud's "pleasure principle" (focused on "lower needs") is revised to include the "pleasure and fulfillment found in the encounter with an expanding reality and in the development, exercise, and realization" of "growing capacities skills, and powers" (Schachtel 9; Paris, *A Psychological* 34 and *Third* 42).

Still, this brighter prospect of an "allocentric" realization of human potential stands opposite the darker prospect, developed by Karen Horney, of the "defensive moves" people adopt to deal with a threatening world. "In order to gain some sense of wholeness and ability to function," an "individual" "will emphasize one move more than the others" which then "operate unconsciously" and "manifest themselves in devious and disguised ways" (Paris, *A Psychological* 55f). The "neurotic" nature of "character types" results from experiencing personal episodes in ways that "overemphasize" one "element" of "basic anxiety": "helplessness," "hostility" or "isolation." In healthy episodes, experiences are used constructively to improve the scope and coherence of one's understanding of life. In neurotic ones, experiences are used destructively to show that the self and the world are somehow unable to communicate and interact.

These considerations support my conjecture that "neurosis" (or "madness" or "insanity") should be defined not merely as some syndrome or trauma brought on by a specific biographical incident (a special case the orthodox Freudians assumed to be the general one), but as a refusal of awareness, a denial of occasions for learning, knowing and evolving. Therapy would then be a process of transcending that refusal, of unblocking whatever defensive closures people deploy to ward off unfamiliar or disconcerting experiences and information. And my argument would be that art and literature offer the chance for just such a transcendence.

To pursue this argument, I would propose the general postulate that literature can only be defined with a functional description of what happens when people produce or respond to it (Schmidt; Beaugrande). The principle I consider most plausible might be called "alternativity." Participants in literary communication should be willing to use the text for constituting and contemplating other "worlds" (i.e., configurations of objects and events) besides the accepted "real world." The text need not appear "fictional" by directly colliding with everyday reality. It may fall anywhere between the extremes of the fantastic and the documentary. Yet the possibility must be left open that whatever world the text is thought to elicit should be related in some interesting and informative way to reality and should show us the latter in perspectives we might otherwise not consider. In this way, the world becomes "new and strange," as the Russian Formalists remarked.

Since, as psychologists and phenomenologists have found, every society's approved version of reality has to omit or deny certain potential aspects or perspectives, an institutionalized forum, i.e., art, for presenting and developing excluded alternatives would be necessary and useful. The limitations imposed by common sense or official consensus about how the world "really" is can be transcended there without causing widespread disorientation and conflict. Literary authors are not normally reproached for reporting things they never saw happen, or for transforming things they did. Readers are inclined to tolerate these actions as a means for sampling diverse visions.

"Poetic" texts would be those during whose use the principle of alternativity is extended to ways for organizing discourse itself.

Here, too, obvious deviation from ordinary discourse is not required, though often employed to impede the seeming transparency of language. Texts not classified as "poems" can readily be given a poetic function if the organization of their language is regarded as one among several alternatives. Ideally, just as literature as a whole sharpens our sense of the world, poetry sharpens our sense of language. Moreover, the more complex medium of poetry, renegotiating both reality and discourse, can have an especially powerful impact that enables poems to be esteemed as highly significant and enduring expressions.

The consideration of literature and poetry in numerous forms of human education over the centuries signals some hope that using texts this way could bring far-ranging benefits for the general capacities of the human mind. The danger of unduly stabilizing the appropriation of language and the world might be counteracted. Experiences could be attained that would normally be difficult, hazardous, or impossible. The human range of understanding could be expanded and refined far beyond the exigencies of individual behavior. However, we know such results face serious impediments. The theorists cited above suggest reasons why the freedom to contemplate alternatives would be mistrusted by groups who hold an unreflective allegiance to a certain order of things and see everything else as "madness."

And by virtue of this very distrust, the problematics of "literariness" can never be fully disentangled from those of "madness." We cannot maintain a genuine concern with literariness and yet ignore the commonplace defense whereby people who question established reality or propose an alternative have doubt cast on their sanity; authoritarian societies apply this principle by consigning literary dissidents to mental asylums. What for some is a healthy and insightful release from constricting givens is viewed by others as a pathological and self-deluded breaking out of reality. An American extreme of the latter view is found in the "hysterical evangelism" which, "despising everything but Grace—rejecting learning and scholarship and intelligence itself," harbors a "deep" "fear of art" (Fiedler, *Love* 430). For instance, in a recent lawsuit brought by "fundamentalist Christian" parents against a school board, *The Diary of Anne Frank* was attacked as unsuitable literature because she remarks that all religions are equal before God. This mild suggestion that alternatives exist alongside the peculiar brand of "Christianity" prescribed by the parents was deemed an intolerable affront. Equal vehemence was leveled against *The Wizard of Oz* for daring to suggest (quite facetiously, actually) that courage, intelligence and compassion are not God-given. Such extreme instances clearly show a standard trade-off: if violent enough, the very attempt to enforce a particularly restrictive kind of sanity, especially in the face of art, will flip over into insanity—a refusal of insight, just like neurosis.

A far milder, but still troubling, demand is that literature should maintain its alternatives within some frame of ethical standards. Wayne Booth, for instance, claims that "a story will be 'unintelligible'" (112) "unless the reader is made clearly 'aware of the value system which gives it its meaning'" (qtd. in Paris, *A Psychological* 17). "The author, therefore, must not only make his beliefs known: but he must also 'make us willing to accept that value system, at least temporarily'" (17). If, as Booth believes, "the rhetoric of fiction" brings about "a concurrence of beliefs of authors and readers," then authors have the responsibility to organize a work explicitly according to a valid, convincing systems of values and beliefs—thus affording an ideal aid to the critic's search for a unifying and valid interpretation (17).

The psychoanalyst Karen Horney has a similar conception (330f). For her, "art may resemble dreams" wherein "our unconscious imagination can create solutions for an inner conflict" (qtd. in Paris, *A Psychological* 128). Whether these "solutions" are "constructive or neurotic" "has great relevance" "for the value of an artistic creation" (128f). "If an artist presents only his particular neurotic solution," then the work's "general validity" may be "diminished," "despite superb artistic facility and acute psychological understanding" (129). "Artistic presentation can help many to wake up" to the "existence and significance" of "neurotic problems" and "clarify" these (129). Horney appears to demand a "consistence and healthy" "moral norm" which "identifies neurotic solutions as destructive and suggests constructive alternatives" (129).

Paris departs from Booth and Horney by uncoupling the success and value of the literary process from the author's explicit adherence to a moral norm. His argument is fully in tune with the basic insights of third force theory that one's "present position" is always "most likely an incomplete one"; and that "there is no one perspective which does not involve some distortion" (Paris, *Third* 28 and *A Psychological* 34). Hence, authors can represent the human situation much more reliably than they can assign it a complete or definitive interpretation. Even realism, the "mimetic" approach to literature, often works against total integration and thematic adequacy (*A Psychological* 9). "Mimetic characters" who are "truly alive," for example, "tend to subvert the main scheme of the book," "to escape the categories by which the author tries to understand them, and to undermine his evaluations of their life styles" (*A Psychological* 11 and *Third Force* 15).

Along these lines, psychoanalysis itself—popularly held to be the watchdog of "madness" in our times—can be enlisted to support the enterprise of literature as a mode for a constructive appreciation of values society officially rejects. Evidently, we can empathize through literature with values we do not endorse in life, without becoming—as simple-minded moralists assert—"immoral" persons. This multiplicity enables art to reveal many versions of life and our ability to understand them frees us from the inevitable limitations of any one version. For Holland, "the most basic of artistic conventions" is that "literary or artistic experience comes to us marked off from the rest of our experiences in reality," by virtue of a "far more orderly structure" and "a longer, deeper range of response" (70, 101, 283). For Fiedler, artists can "achieve" in a work "a coherence, a unity, a balance, a satisfaction of conflicting impulses" "they cannot achieve in love, family relations, politics" (*No!* 7). "Literature" is "the record of those elusive moments at which life is alone fully itself, fulfilled in consciousness and form" (*Love* 15f). The "intolerable inadequacy" of "radically imperfect human activities" is "revealed" when they are "represented in a perfectly articulated form" (7). "Telling the truth" is opening a "vision of an eternal gap between imagined order and actual chaos" (11).

In sum, art and literature offer the difficult experience of a reality that is not "real" in the everyday sense, since it belongs to and originates only through the work, and yet tells us more about reality, about its provisional and incomplete status, than any actual bit of the everyday real world can. Readers of literature can heighten their "phenomenological knowledge of reality" (Paris, *A Psychological* 23), or direct their "attention to the interaction between perception and reality" (Iser, *Implied* 210), or recover a "repressed and buried reality" (Jameson 20). And they can encounter a "disappointment of expectations" whereby "we actually make contact with reality" (Popper 102).

As if in recognition of this complex paradox, modern literary theory has come to emphasize the self-regarding problematics of literary discourse (Beaugrande, *Critical*). Paul de Man, for instance, persistently saw the literary "work" as one that "asserts, by its very existence, its separation from empirical reality" (*Blindness* 17). He accounted for this effect in terms of "figural language," whose "general" "description" centers on a "structure" wherein "the relationship between sign and meaning is discontinuous, involving an extraneous principle" (206). His chief examples are "irony and allegory," two modes for the "demystification of an organic world postulated in a symbolic mode of analogical correspondences or in a mimetic mode of representation in which fiction and reality could coincide" (222). Of the two, "irony comes closer to the pattern of factual experience and recaptures some of the factitiousness of human experience as a succession of isolated moments lived by a divided self." The self undergoes "duplication" or "multiplication," so that "irony" is "a relationship, within consciousness, between two selves" (212). "Ironic language splits the subject into an empirical self that exists in a state of inauthenticity and a self that exists only in the form of a language that asserts the knowledge of this inauthenticity" (212). "The author" "asserts" "the ironic necessity of not becoming the dupe of his own irony and discovers that there is no way back from his fictional self to his actual self" (219).

Once stated in such broad terms, "irony possesses an inherent tendency to gather momentum"; "from the small and apparently innocuous exposure of a small self-deception it soon reaches the dimensions of the absolute" and becomes "the systematic undoing" "of understanding" (De Man, *Allegories* 215, 301). "Irony" "dissolves in the narrowing spiral of a linguistic sign that becomes more and more remote from its meaning, and it can find no escape" (*Blindness* 222). On the one hand, a certain "freedom" is gained from "the unwillingness of the mind to accept any stage in its progression as definitive" (220). On the other hand, the prospect arises of a "dizziness to the point of madness"; "sanity can exist only because we are willing to function within the conventions of duplicity and dissimulation" (215f). "Once this mask is shown to be a mask, the authentic being underneath appears necessarily as on the verge of madness" (216).

Yet this is no ordinary madness, no insanity or neurosis that refuses insight—exactly the opposite. This engagement with literature constantly generates insights, even quite difficult ones, from the difference between "literary" and "real," between "language" and "world." If the principle of alternativity is allowed a dominant function, the transcendence of reality through art and literature is not pathogenic, but therapeutic (as even the Freudian critics agree, more hopeful than their master). The experience allows us to realize the irreducible multiplicity of viewpoints involved in the constitution of any "reality," whereas insanity denies all viewpoints but one that steadily narrows until a single idea seems to appropriate everything.

The world of a literary work constantly solicits our active complicity in creating it. Since the main channel of experience passes through the work itself, the writer or reader can justly feel that here at last the coherence of the world is partly his or her own achievement. Literature can frame any aspect of the world, including the very dialectic of sanity and insanity. By forcing us to deliberate on the sanity of literary characters like the Karamazov brothers or the narrator in *Notes from Underground* (who has the additional power to decide and present what we are told), or of literary authors themselves, like Heym and Trakl, involves us in the harrowing problematics of defining "sane" and "insane" and lets us alternately see each side from the vantage point of the other. Thus, we may finally be able to foreground sanity, which, as I noted, is usually the background and resists this treatment.

And thus our search for the relation of literature and madness brings us to the ultimately utopian dialectic of literature: to understand our understanding of ourselves and of our world through the unending creation of alternative worlds. The more persuasively and urgently this dialectic is implied, the "greater" a work will seem. Thus, "actual madness" would be not the release from reality through literary art, but the narrowing and closure that would supplant the work with just one predecided, constricting response to it (as in the "evangelical" or "fundamentalist" moves depicted above). As Fiedler (*What* 39) reminds us, "literary criticism" "was born of conflict, out of an attempt to dissuade those who would control or ban poetry as socially and morally dangerous." "Literature asserts," if "anything," "the impossibility of unqualified assertion, the ambiguity of all moral imperatives" (129). This function is crucial because "the burden of any system of morality becomes finally irksome even to its most sincere advocates, since it necessarily denies, represses, suffocates certain undying primal impulses" that "need somehow to be expressed" (50).

This utopian prospect comes into its own when literary theory has now attained the consensus that "a divergence of readings is more interesting than a convergence" (Culler 50f). We must repudiate an "understanding" that "reduces the surplus of meaning of the poetic text to just one" (Jauss 152). "To impose one meaning as the right, or at least the best, interpretation" is "a fatal trap" that obscures "the potential of the text" (Iser, *Act* 18). "To find complexity and value in a variety of readings" "is more relevant to literary study than the use of standards of interpretive accuracy" (Bleich 104).

Perhaps some of us will still be unsettled by the vision of a "hermeneutic 'infinitizing' that makes all rules of closure appear arbitrary" (Hartman 244). But we must not call it "madness" in the usual sense: it is, I have tried to show, rather one of our best guarantees that madness, the destructive convergence of all things on a single idea, can be counterbalanced with the freedom to make the world new and strange once again, yet giving it more sense than ever, not less.

Note

[1]A late variant might be the endless recitations in supermarket checkout counter journalism of the "miseries" of the rich and famous.

Works Cited

Beaugrande, Robert de. *Critical Discourse*. Norwood: Ablex, 1988.

____. "Freudian Psychoanalysis and Information Processing: Notes on a Future Synthesis." *Psychoanalysis and Contemporary Thought* 7/2 (1984): 147-94.

——. "Schemas for Literary Communication." László Halász, ed. *Literary Discourse* (1986): 34-68.

____. "Surprised by Syncretism: Cognition and Literary Criticism." *Poetics* 11 (1983): 83-137.

Bleich, David. *Subjective Criticism*. Baltimore: Johns Hopkins UP, 1978.

Booth, Wayne. *The Rhetoric of Fiction*. Chicago: U of Chicago P, 1961.

Culler, Jonathan. *The Pursuit of Signs*. Ithaca: Cornell UP, 1981.

Deleuze, Gilles, and Felix Guattari. *Anti-Oedipus*. New York: Viking, 1977.

De Man, Paul. *Allegories of Reading*. New Haven: Yale UP, 1979.

——. *Blindness and Insight*. Minneapolis: U of Minnesota P, 1983.

Fiedler, Leslie A. *Love and Death in the American Novel*. New York: Scarborough, 1966.

——. *No! in Thunder*. New York: Stein and Day, 1972.

———. *What Was Literature?* New York: Simon and Schuster, 1982.

Fisher, Seymour, and Roger Greenberg. *The Scientific Credibility of Freud's Theories and Therapy.* New York: Basic Books, 1977.

Frye, Northrop. *Anatomy of Criticism.* Princeton: Princeton UP, 1957.

Hartman, Geoffrey. *Criticism in the Wilderness.* New Haven: Yale UP, 1980.

Holland, Norman N. *The Dynamics of Literary Response.* New York: Norton, 1968.

Horney, Karen. *Neurosis and Human Growth.* New York: Norton, 1950.

Iser, Wolfgang. *The Act of Reading.* Baltimore: Johns Hopkins UP, 1978.

———. *The Implied Reader.* Baltimore: Johns Hopkins UP, 1975.

Jameson, Fredric. *The Political Unconscious.* Ithaca: Cornell UP, 1981.

Jauss, Hans Robert. *Toward an Aesthetic of Reception.* Minneapolis: U of Minnesota P, 1982.

Krim, Seymour. "The Insanity Bit." *Exodus Magazine.* Rpt. *The Beats,* ed. Park Honan. London: J.M. Dent, 1959.

Kris, Ernst. "Approaches to Art." *Psychoanalysis Today.* New York: International UP, 1944: 354-70.

Paris, Bernard. *A Psychological Approach to Fiction.* Bloomington: Indiana UP, 1974.

———. *Third Force Psychology and the Study of Literature.* London: Associated UP, 1986.

Popper, Karl. *Theorie und Realitaet.* Tuebingen: Mohr, 1964.

Schachtel, Ernst. *Metamorphosis.* New York: Basic Books, 1959.

Schmidt, Siegfried J. *Foundations for the Empirical Study of Literature.* Hamburg: Buske, 1982.

Wellek, René, and Austin Warren. *Theory of Literature.* New York: Harvest, 1956.

Are Creative Writers Mad?
An Empirical Perspective

Martin S. Lindauer

Are creativity and "madness" related?[1] This broad question, when posed within a literary context, actually contains several questions. Does a relationship between madness and creativity exist in writers, and if so, does it differ between novelists, poets, playwrights and other practitioners of literary expression? Further, is the madness of writers greater or more influential than it is for painters, musicians and other artistically creative types, or greater than the madness among scientists and scholars? Put another way, does the incidence of madness in writers differ from the norm? Finally, if pathology and creativity are in fact associated with one another among writers, does this mean there is a causal connection between the two? Is it that madness facilitates literary genius; is the reverse true; or is there some other factor that binds the two together, like heredity or some traumatic early experience?

These are very complicated, difficult and interconnected questions, each deserving careful analysis before any conclusion can be drawn about literary expression and pathology. What follows is a review of the positions taken on these questions in the humanities and in scientific psychology.[2]

The Perspective from the Humanities

Numerous literary essayists, historians and critics, and individual studies of "troubled" poets and novelists, like Poe, Dickinson, Woolf and Hemingway, take for granted the view that writers are, at least to some extent, "mad." Often, the pathology of a literary character is used to account for the pathology of its author. As Felman put it, there is "an inflation in discourses on madness" (205). For these scholars, there is either a stated or implied relationship between an author's mental illness—or a propensity for such—and its expression in literary creativity. Paraphrasing Wilson, the notion of "a healthy writer" is a contradiction. Mental illness, it would seem, is a necessary but unfortunate price authors must pay.

The unstable mental state of gifted writers reflects a more general view, namely, that madness and all forms of artistic creativity are linked. The morbid view of creativity is long-standing and pervasive, and is found as early as the writings of Plato. It took on scientific credentials in the nineteenth century with Lombroso, who not only found evidence that tied both madness and creativity together, but also linked the two to criminality because of a common hereditary disposition. A disease model of creativity, usually without biological overtones, has infused scholarship in the humanities, including the philosophy of art, aesthetic theory, art criticism and art history. A connection between madness and creativity, or genius, a super form of creativity, is also made by the general public.

The profile of the writer-as-mad is generally developed and amplified in the humanities by in-depth case studies of individuals, with the emphasis on describing, illustrating and quoting peculiar aspects of their lives. The scholarly approach, further, draws upon, is enriched by, and often inspired by, Freudian, Jungian, Rankian and similarly clinically oriented views of human nature which also see a close link between the abnormal personality and creativity. These dynamic perspectives generally argue that creative artists "go over the brink" of sanity because they are more in touch with, and hence more vulnerable and sensitive to, the unconscious conflicts and repressed memories of stresses from their childhood.

Less extreme clinical positions take a more positive position, holding that successful creative people sublimate, or redirect otherwise dangerous urges into acceptable expressions of aesthetic imagination. These are prized by society because its members face similar onslaughts on their sanity, but have less talent in subverting them toward higher ends. While the danger of being overwhelmed by unconscious forces is always there, the more sanguine clinical position argues, artists have a strong ego which allows them to use unconscious material constructively. "Secondary processes," like verbal abilities, controlled imagery, and reasoning, mold inchoate "primary process" material, from the primal id, the instincts and other unconscious forces, into acceptable, pleasing and outstanding artistic products. To elaborate on Kris's apt phrase, "regression in the service of the ego," artists are able to retreat safely, "dipping into" their unconscious world, using its powerful images to serve artistic ends. Thus, Martindale has shown that poets use their superior cognitive abilities to elaborate artfully otherwise unacceptable unconscious impulses.

Psychodynamic, literary and humanistic analyses of individual authors' lives and works are illuminating, interesting and provocative. They spark controversy, lead to new ways of thinking and force a re-thinking and defense of previous formulations. Armed with "deep psychology," readers can explore, find and reflect upon overlooked or overworked aspects of an author or work, and perhaps relate the outcome of this search to themselves.

The Perspective from Science

There are valuable lessons to be learned from case studies of authors and the ideas they provoke. But several questions, typically asked by scientifically oriented critics, remain unresolved. 1) Are the conclusions drawn from one, a few or a certain group of authors based on facts? Assertions about the mental life of writers are not sufficient unless they are based on objective, reliable, valid and testable observations. Since only the barest sketch, if any, is given of how the analysis of a particular author was done, including what facts were omitted, and why the facts chosen were selected, the critical reader has to accept the particular sensitivities of an expert. There is no way of replicating the method used to reach the conclusions promoted. Would another reader, given the same information, come up with the same conclusions? 2) Assuming that the facts exist, a more important question arises: Can the findings from a particular author and his or her work, or a small set of authors and their works, be applied to authors and works in general? Further, can this limited information be applied, broadly, to other areas of the arts and to creativity in any field?

Questions like these are not of primary interest to literary analyses, where they are either ignored or treated incautiously. Scientific questions are not thought to be germane to the humanities, or to literary analyses in particular, given their focus on matters related to the individual case and the uniqueness of human nature.

The search for generalities, scholars in the arts and humanities would argue, obviates the special place of their disciplines among other forms of inquiry. How then, a critic might ask, can one study specific instances, the claimed province of the humanities, and make statements about "humanity" or people in general? To do so, the critic would continue, is indeed to be concerned about empirical matters of fact and their applicability beyond the individual case. Consequently, rather than look to the individual case, as the humanities do, most scientists look primarily and exclusively to the group in order to abstract essential characteristics.[3]

Nonetheless, despite profound differences, both scientifically oriented psychologists and humanists are interested in the same problem: the existence and role of madness in the arts. Although the two disciplines follow different directions in addressing this issue, they can take advantages of their individual strengths, and compensate for their limitations, by combining some aspects of their respective positions.

The opportunity for an interdisciplinary exchange lies in the topic of creativity and madness. The exacting methods of science could be informed and broadened by humanistic scholars. Literary experts could direct empirical researchers on what to look for and where to look for it, supplement quantitative facts with qualitative information and illustrative material, place statistical analysis into a larger context, and through interpretive commentary, offer scientific studies broader meaning.

This idealized picture of cross-disciplinary cooperation, unfortunately, is rare. There are large and complex reasons for the almost insurmountable barriers between science and the humanities, but these cannot concern us here.

What assistance does a scientific approach to the madness-genius issue provide? There are several suggestions. 1) Collect and study many rather than one or a few examples of authors, their work and their lives. 2) Emphasize observable kinds of information, such as interviews, and questionnaires, as well as tests, ratings, frequency counts and content analysis. Wherever possible, translate as much of the available material into empirical assertions that lend themselves to proof or disproof. 3) Recognize that the goal of research is not to explain everything, or to prove or disprove an idea with absolute certainty. Instead, scientific studies search for probabilities and likelihoods, and these depend on the accumulation of many studies, not just one or two.

These general values translate into more specific procedures. As applied to the theme of "literary madness," science offers the following strategies: 1) Look for, question, doubt, be skeptical about and evaluate the facts, if any, that support assertions about madness. A critical literature review serves this purpose. 2) Suggest ways in which some of the uncertainties and questions raised by the critical review might be reduced. This is the point at which one restates a problem so that it is testable, or takes the form of an hypothesis, a guiding statement that results in a research design to guide the collection of data. 3) Collect data by doing a study. 4) Subject the results of the study to the same critical scrutiny which initially began this sequence. The rest of this paper will pursue steps 1) and 2).[4]

The Empirical Evidence

A number of scientifically reliable facts about creativity have been found, and some fairly good generalizations can be made about the madness-creativity connection in literature, the other arts and in general. Some studies, beginning with Galton in the late nineteenth century, and followed up by Cox, Lehman, Dennis and Simonton, among others, have concentrated on historical figures. They have relied on statistical extrapolations from biographical and other records of the past. Other researchers have applied a longitudinal life-span perspective to intellectually gifted children, as Terman most notably did, or studied artists intensively, as Barron and others did.

These studies, with few major exceptions, contradict prevailing literary, scholarly and popular thought: Creative persons as a group are healthy, not only in physical terms, but in their personality and intellect as well. They are successful and fulfilled in lives that are long-lived and productive.[5]

Some of the findings and their conclusions are mixed, open to other interpretations, or use a methodology that might be questioned. Nevertheless, the main conclusions are fairly clear: 1) Creative people are healthy; 2) creative people in the arts are healthy; and 3) writers are healthy.

The case for writers is somewhat blurred, though, by certain findings. Leaving aside the many individual case studies and anecdotal accounts of "writers in distress," statistical tallies appear to show a large number of "sick" artists, as determined by such measures as the number who have been hospitalized for mental illness. For example, Ellis found that 4.2 percent of a large sample of eminent British writers were psychotic. A more recent survey by Juda concluded that nearly 30 percent of the artists in his sample (of biographies) were either psychotic or psychopathic, compared to about 23 percent of scientists; the latter were more likely to be either psychopathic or manic-depressive. These oft-cited studies are summarized and evaluated in Winner (357).

These surveys, however, did not include living writers, and are limited in other ways, such as depending on written accounts whose biases are unknown. Winner has questioned the value of these statistical counts on other grounds. For example, the figures by Ellis, although "perhaps slightly higher than the average population [are still] low" and well within "normal bounds" (357). Winner adds that the clinical-type labels are rather vague, and may actually be descriptions of eccentric behavior rather than representative of valid diagnoses. The terms have also been questioned by Andreasen (see her article, "Creativity and Mental Illness").

The biographical information used in these studies has other ambiguities. Creative writers who became schizophrenic, Winner points out, could have been affected in different ways—i.e., either their style or the content of their work was "disturbed." Thus, it is not clear where the "psychotic" in literature is to be found. Another questionable strategy, used with living artists, has been to search for parallels between psychotic artists and non-artists, and to ignore all other differences between them (and with authors who became schizophrenic after they became established writers).

For these and other reasons, Winner concludes that there is no good evidence that artists become manifestly psychotic at an above average rate. "[T]here is only meager support for the hypothesis that schizophrenia is associated with an enhancement of artistic powers in the artist" (362). Mental illness, if it does anything, Winner suggests, blocks rather than facilitates writing. Wilson adds that "Writers are on the whole as different from one another as they are from nonwriters. There appears to be no single or simple dynamic mechanism that drives people who create literature" (129). If mental illness is a factor in writers' lives and works, he adds, it is one of many contributors.

In the face of these severe criticisms of the earlier work, the studies by Andreasen stand out: She found strong evidence for a high incidence of madness in creative writers. Her seminal studies, beginning in 1975, have been updated and are frequently referred to in the current literature. The work is exemplary in several regards: It relies on scientific procedures, such as the important one of including a control group, and it uses statistical analyses in support of its conclusions. Hence, an in-depth review of the study is warranted.[6] The highlighting of her prototypical 1975 study, including both its strengths and weaknesses, serves as a model of how to advance the issue empirically.[7]

Andreasen studied 30 famous writers, faculty members at a nationally known writer's workshop. They were between 26 and 48 years old, and she claims that they represented "a reasonably valid cross-section of contemporary American writers" (1288). The writers were subject to a structured interview on their history of mental illness. They were asked questions such as "Have you ever had a period of mental illness in your lifetime?...[or] received psychiatric treatment?" Another group of non-writers, hospital administrators, equivalent in age, sex and educational status to the writers, were similarly interviewed. They served as the control group. The interviews took place over a 15-year period, from the mid-1970s to 1980s.

The writers, compared to the controls, reported a higher incidence of affective disorders (i.e., manic-depression); 80 percent vs. 30 percent, respectively. Andreasen suggests that the difference between the two groups may be even greater than indicated, since the illness rate among the control sample was "somewhat higher than [the population norm]" (1289). Although Andreasen did not do so, the point could also be made that the controls were not representative of the general population. Andreasen did not find, contrary to expectations based on the psychiatric literature, an unusual number of self-disclosed cases of schizophrenia among the writers. She does not make much of the fact, perhaps even more unexpectedly, that there were few diagnoses of schizophrenia in the control group. Thus, the question of the control group's representativeness is again raised. Also somewhat unexpectedly, given the image of the addictive and suicidal writer, Andreasen found that the two groups did not differ on other pathological measures, such as alcoholism, drug abuse or suicide. Additional evidence, taken from the reported incidence of mental illness in family members, suggested to Andreasen that the writers' affective disorder was "a hereditary trait" (1292).

Andreasen's study of the mental health of writers is a solid empirical achievement. Unresolved, though, are several important questions. A detailed analysis of six of the study's major problems or omissions indicates the complexities of the topic, and the empirical efforts that remain to be undertaken.

1) The sample studied. One group of writers, especially if it is chosen for accessibility, rather than randomly, is not representative of writers. Consider the fact that there were only three women among the writers. Questions about the control group as representative of the general population have already been raised.

2) Comparability of the writers and non-writers. The pathological profile of the writers was compared to a non-writing group. But the basis for matching them—age, sex and education—

is probably not sufficient. In order to distinguish the two groups on the basis of their rates of mental illness alone, both the writers and the non-writers have to be equivalent on many other relevant dimensions. While it is not easy to know what dimensions are most relevant, a reasonable case can be made for matching them on such variables as personality, e.g., introversion or extroversion, as well as insuring their comparability on other dimensions, including such remote but still relevant possibilities as their familiarity with or acceptance of the "Freudian literature" on madness and creativity.

3) The measure used. The psychiatric interview is just one of several ways of determining pathology, among several that might have been chosen (for example, the MMPI, the Rorschach and Cattell's "16 PF"). An interview may not be either a sufficient or even the best measure. Self-reports can be self-serving, incomplete and ambiguous. A battery of tests would have been corroborative, although not necessarily sufficient either. In addition, objective behavioral indicators would have been helpful, such as the documented incidence of treatment by psychiatrists, or periods of institutionalization in mental hospitals. These would have supplemented the subjective reports, as well as any tests, had they been given.

4) Generalizing. Consideration of the above three points leads us closer to the goal of ascertaining the mental health of these particular writers—but not of writers in general. What more is needed?

In order to determine if there is in fact a higher incidence of mental illness in writers as a group, a random sample would have to be selected from a complete list of writers of different kinds who make up the "population" of writers: novelists, short story writers, poets, playwrights and others (film writers).

To insure that only first-rate professionals were included, experts might rank the names on a list. For example, the writers' "fame" might be judged by editors of publishing houses.

Ideally, the best writers would then be given a battery of tests, interviewed and observed at work and in real-world settings. They would complete a life history questionnaire. Documentation would also be obtained from psychiatrists, other clinicians and hospitals. Finally, some of the writers' associates, friends, family and colleagues would be questioned.

The task is not quite finished. Converging evidence on the writers' mental health, taken from several sources, would then be classified by the type of pathology they demonstrated (e.g., affective, schizophrenic, anxiety disorder and so on), and then cross-indexed by type of writer, among other personal variables, like gender. The tabular results for writers would then be compared against carefully selected samples of other types of creative people, in and out of the arts, and the general population. Each sample would have been carefully matched with the writers on specified dimensions and tested in the same way as the writers.

Yes, quite a program of research! It is an ideal to be striven for, yet some research comes close to the ideal—e.g., the work of MacKinnon and Roe. Assuming that such heroic efforts resulted in an acceptable correlation between madness and creativity, the task is not yet complete.

5) The possibility of alternative explanations. Assume that correlational evidence for the pathology of writers was found, such as a higher incidence of psychiatric treatment, as Andreasen determined. Yet this association may not actually reveal mental illness. Instead, there may be more benign ways of accounting for the correlation.

Consider the following likely chain of possibilities: Two key characteristics of writers are probably a high degree of introspectiveness and spending a lot of time on self-analyses. These traits, one imagines, are an integral part of writers' personalities and the way they work. They are likely to be contemplative, self-conscious and curious about their inner life, including its vulnerabilities and weaknesses. Some consequences of these obsessions are that writers could be more likely than others, including people with different or no creative abilities, to be excessively open and brutally frank about revealing themselves, in both their work and in their relationships with others. Thus, writers express themselves in highly noticeable ways, they say more about themselves and they reveal a great deal of themselves in conversations and in their semi-autobiographical work. This free expression may encourage concerned family members, friends, colleagues and even neighbors to insist that writers seek therapeutic help, or lead them to forcibly bring writers to clinics. These remedial actions, perhaps with the acceptance of the writers themselves, may be exaggerated by the belief in the prevailing myth about "madness and literature."[8]

The self-revelatory nature of writers may have another consequence. They might seek out professional help because they are more curious than others about their "inner voice." In seeking assistance in charting unknown waters, writers purposefully recruit psychiatric help in order to sharpen their own analytical skills, and to increase their self-knowledge. Hence, the apparent link between madness and creativity among writers.

6) Confusing correlation with causation. Assuming that alternative ways of accounting for an association between "writers and madness" have been ruled out, finding a correlation does not end the matter there. The factors responsible, the causes, need to be determined. Three possibilities for a correlation exist: 1) the "literary way of life" caused the madness; 2) the madness led to writing as a profession; or 3) the association between the two is the result of some third undisclosed factor. The latter includes heredity, certain childhood experiences, major life crises ("traumas"), the impact of a mentor or model, innate intelligence, an unusual imaginative ability and so on. A formidable task, indeed.

Conclusions

1. If there is a link between writers and pathology, it has not been proven. And even if there were a link, it might reflect a bias that leads people (including writers) to hold a stereotyped view of their mental health. Expectations about writers can be either selectively confirmed, or worse, self-fulfilled. Further, even if madness is found among writers, it may hold only for the minority. These exceptions, because of their dramatic and newsworthy prominence, falsely serve as a general model.

2. Creative authors may only *appear* to be more abnormal— but they are not. That is, writers *show* signs of madness, such as a high degree of impulsivity, playfulness, childishness and spontaneity. These outward signs of eccentric behavior may serve the writers' art for reasons that are obscured by making them synonymous with madness. Writers may indeed have a potential or a latent capacity for psychosis. But writers may be able to better handle malevolent tendencies because of their ego strength, an ability reflected by extreme self-confidence and an extraordinary sense of self-worth, qualities which may further exaggerate their eccentric profiles.

Observers of writers, and their biographers, may therefore be overreacting to their nonconformity, iconoclasm and other outward signs of "madness." But unlike the truly mad, these are signs of a freed yet constrained unconscious, one that has been harnessed and exploited for creative ends.

3. A case can be made that the production of great works, in any field, cannot be the result of, or accompanied by, severe

emotional handicaps. If writers are indeed mentally disturbed, and they are still able to write masterpieces, then they must do so *despite*, not because of their handicap. If writers were "crazy," it hardly seems possible that they could reach, accomplish and maintain a high creative level over a lifetime. If madness is found, it could have occurred before such people became professional writers, or after they had stopped writing, when they had "burned out."

4. Why then the fascination, indeed preoccupation and strong feelings about "the mad writer?" One can only guess. Perhaps a "Freudian" hypothesis will suffice, useful as it may be, as a last resort when simpler reasons are unavailable or unsatisfactory. Extreme explanations can justifiably be called upon in accounting for the otherwise unaccountable, the maintenance of a strong belief in the face of contrary or a dearth of information, the acceptance of facts which are questionable, limited or incomplete, and the neglect of alternative accounts.

The public, of which scholars and researchers are also a part, may be unconsciously envious and jealous of the success creative writers and creative people of all kinds have. To attack the mental stability of authors, in effect, is a rationalization, a way of saying, "You may be talented, but look at the price you pay." Authors bear the brunt of this attack, compared to other creative people in the arts or elsewhere, because they write about themselves, and do it so well and honestly. Hence, writers are more exposed. Writers may also encourage and enjoy "playing" with their audience.

5. There are many connections between psychology and literature. Both disciplines examine the mind, heart, soul and spirit, and their translation into outward or behavioral consequences. Consequently, psychology has studied many aspects of literature: 1) a work's content and structure; 2) the readers' cognitive and affective reactions; 3) the context in which writers work, including the impact of other writers, the audience, market forces and institutions that bring the writer and public together; and finally, 4) the writers themselves, including their personality, motivation, intellect, productivity and creativity. Pathological characteristics, the "madness and literature" theme, falls within the last of these multiple areas. Even then, pathology is only part of a larger concern with creativity, since there there are also "normal" processes of personality that play their part. (See, for example, the treatments by Guilford, McCurdy, MacKinnon, and Taylor and Getzels.)

There are therefore many facets of literature, authors and writing that have received and deserve equal if not greater attention than the preoccupation with madness. A fascination with madness is just one of many possible and useful interdisciplinary challenges. Unfortunately, other options have not been adequately explored because of a less than fruitful overconcern with "madness."

Notes

¹The term "madness" is a popular word that is more appropriately expressed in clinical ways, where it refers to psychotic states, such as schizophrenia, or affective disorders, like depression.

²The issue is presented from an empirical (scientific) perspective. No attempt is made to summarize the huge literature on this subject, both empirical and non-empirical. Greater details and additional references are in several sources by Lindauer, including *The Psychological Study of Literature* (Ch. 2, 7), "Applying Empirical Research Methods to the Psychology of Literature," "Psychology and Literature" and "The Short Story." Other useful sources are in Winner (Ch. 1, 13) and the various studies of Andreasen and her colleagues. For an update, see the Afterword.

³For a fuller discussion of the empirical method, and its application to literature, see Lindauer in Natoli.

⁴For examples of Steps (3) and (4), see footnote 3.

⁵For a review, see the 1992 and later articles by Lindauer.

⁶Other recent studies are alluded to in Holden, but these seem to be "works in progress," since a careful literature search failed to find them. They are therefore not available, unlike Andreasen's, for a complete and critical review. For an update, see the Afterword.

⁷Andreasen herself, to her credit, lists many of the studies' shortcomings.

⁸For a history of changing views of creativity, see Porter.

Works Cited

Andreasen, Nancy C. "Creativity and Mental Illness: Prevalence Rates in Writers and Their First-Degree Relatives." *American Journal of Psychiatry* 144 (1987): 1288-92.

Andreasen, Nancy C., and Ira D. Glick. "Bipolar Affective Disorder and Creativity: Implications and Clinical Management." *Comprehensive Psychiatry* 29 (1988): 207-17.

Andreasen, Nancy C., and Pauline S. Powers. "Creativity and Psychosis: An Examination of Conceptual Style." *Archives of General Psychiatry* 32 (1975): 70-73.

Andreasen, Nancy J.C. "Creativity and Psychosis." *Archives of General Psychiatry* 32 (1975): 70-73.

Andreasen, Nancy J.C., and Arthur Canter. "The Creative Writer: Psychiatric Symptoms and Family History." *Comprehensive Psychiatry* 15 (1974): 123-31.

Barron, Frank. *Artists in the Making.* New York: Seminar P, 1972.

_____. "The Creative Personality: Akin to Madness." *Psychology Today* July 1978: 42-44.

_____. *Creativity and Psychological Health.* Princeton, NJ: Van Nostrand, 1963.

Cox, Catherine. *Genetic Studies of Genius.* Vol. 2. Stanford: Stanford UP, 1926.

Dennis, W. "Creative Productivity Between the Ages of 20 and 80 Years." *Journal of Gerontology* 21 (1966): 1-8.

Felman, Shoshana. *Writing and Madness.* Ithaca, NY: Cornell UP, 1985.

Galton, Francis. *Hereditary Genius.* London: Macmillan, 1892.

Guilford, J.P. "Creativity: A Quarter Century of Progress." *Perspectives in Creativity.* Eds. Irving A. Taylor and J.W. Getzels. Chicago: Aldine, 1975.

Holden, Constance. "Creativity and the Troubled Mind." *Psychology Today* Apr. 1987: 9-10.

Kris, Ernst. *Psychoanalytic Explorations in Art.* New York: International UP, 1952.

Lehman, H. *Age and Achievement.* Princeton: Princeton UP, 1953.

Lindauer, Martin S. "Applying Empirical Research Methods to the Psychology of Literature." *Psychological Perspectives on Literature: Post-Freudian and Non-Freudian—A Casebook.* Ed. J.P. Natoli. NY: Anchor Books/Shoestring, 1984.

_____. "Art In Old Age." *Creativity and Aging: Theoretical and empirical perspectives.* Ed. Carolyn Adams-Price. NY: Springer, forthcoming.

_____. "Creativity in Aging Artists: Contributions from the Humanities to the Psychology of Old Age." *Creativity Research Journal* 5 (1992): 211-31.

_____. "The Old Age Style and Its Authors. *Empirical Studies of Aesthetics* 11.2 (1993): 135-41.

_____. *The Psychological Study of Literature.* Chicago: Nelson-Hall, 1974.

_____. "Psychology as a Humanistic Science." *Psychocultural Review* 2 (1978): 139-45.

_____. "Psychology and Literature." *Psychology and Its Allied Disciplines.* Ed. Marc H. Bornstein. Hillside, NJ: Erlbaum, 1984.

____. "The Psychology of Literature and the Short Story: A Methodological Perspective." *Literary Discourse: Aspects of Cognitive and Social Psychological Approaches*. Ed. Laslo Halasz. Berlin: de Gruyter, 1987.

____. "The Span of Creativity Among Long-Lived Historical Artists." *Creativity Research Journal* 6.3 (1993): 221-39.

Lombroso, C. *The Man of Genius*. London: Walter Scott, 1891.

MacKinnon, D.W. "IPAR's Contribution to the Conceptualization and Study of Creativity." *Perspectives in Creativity*. Eds. Irving A. Taylor and J.W. Getzels. Chicago: Aldine, 1975.

____. "Personality and the Realization of Creative Potential." *American Psychologist* 29 (1965): 273-81.

Martindale, Colin E. *The Romantic Progression: The Psychology of Literary History*. NY: Hemisphere, 1975.

McCurdy, Harold G. *The Personality of Shakespeare: A Venture in Psychological Method*. New Haven: Yale UP, 1953.

Porter, Roy. *A Social History of Madness: The World Through the Eyes of the Insane*. New York: Weidenfeld & Nicolson, 1987.

Roe, Anne. *The Making of a Scientist*. Boston: Dodd, Mead, 1953.

____. "Painters and Painting." *Perspectives in Creativity*. Eds. Irving A. Taylor and J.W. Getzels. Chicago: Aldine, 1975.

Simonton, Dean. *Genius, Creativity, and Leadership*. Cambridge: Harvard UP, 1984.

Taylor, Irving A., and J.W. Getzels, eds. *Perspectives in Creativity*. Chicago: Aldine, 1975.

Terman, L.M. *Genetic Studies of Genius*. 4 vols. Stanford, CA: Stanford UP, 1925-59.

Terman, L.M., and M.H. Oden. *Genetic Studies of Genius*. Vol. 4. Stanford, Stanford UP, 1947.

Wilson, R.N. *Exercising Creativity*. New Brunswick: Transaction Books, 1986.

Winner, Ellen. *Invented Worlds: The Psychology of the Arts*. Cambridge: Harvard UP, 1982.

Afterword

Since this essay was written, the uncritical promotion of the thesis that "writers are mad" continues unabated, and remains embedded within a larger context that holds that madness is found in all artists, as well as among creative people and geniuses in all professions, at least to some important degree. I have found only a few who object, as I do, to this thesis among authors. (See Leon Edel, *Literary Biography*, Garden City, NY: Anchor/Doubleday, 1959.)

The methodological questions raised in my essay—such as the habit of overgeneralizing from limited samples, and focusing on so-called abnormal personality traits in authors without comparing their incidence among "normal" controls—remain unaddressed and unrecognized. The belief in the link between creativity and madness, for reasons discussed in the essay, is evidently too strong to be weakened by qualifications.

The larger issue remains popular, as indicated by its application to musicians on the front page of a widely read semi-professional psychological publication (see Tori DeAngelis, "Mania, Depression and Genius," *The American Psychological Association Monitor*, 1989, 20 [1], 1, 24). Objections to the piece have been raised, however (see the letters by Bruce E. Kline and Carol L. Patrick, "A Disservice To the Gifted," *The American Psychological Association Monitor*, 1989, 20 [4], 2). One letter writer, though, faults the article for restating the obvious (S. Wiegersma, "Old News," *The American Psychological Association Monitor*, 1989, 20 [5], 2).

Since the original manuscript was written, the published literature on the alleged madness of creative artists and writers continues and increases. The Andreasen data, reviewed in this chapter as pivotal, continues to be quoted and referred to. Additional supporting evidence by Kay R. Jamieson was mentioned in a semi-professional publication addressed to a wide academic audience, although the research has not, as far as I can tell, been published and therefore could not be evaluated ("Researchers Link Manic-Depressive Illness and Artistic Creativity," *Chronicle of Higher Education*, 21 June 1989, A4, A6). Indicative of its popularity, the research was also reported on Public Broadcasting, 29 November 1988.

The larger issue of creativity and health was covered in a special issue of the *Creativity Research Journal* 3.2 (1990): 81-149, which itself was reviewed (see Ruth Richards, "Everyday Creativity, Eminent Creativity, and Health," *Creativity Research Journal* 3.4 1990: 300-26). I would also recommend an older historical and scholarly work by Becker. He surveyed the uses and misuses of the label of madness, although he did not evaluate its validity, or single out either artists in general or writers in particular (G. Becker, *The Mad Genius Controversy*, Beverly Hills: Sage, 1978).

Although my intent has not been to provide an extensive bibliography, especially of the scholarly literature, several non-empirical works deserve to be noted:

Hershman, D. Jablow, and Julian Lieb. *The Key to Genius: Manic-depression and the Creative Life*. Buffalo: Promethus Books, 1989.

Pollock, George H. "Introduction: Aging and Creativity." Eds. J.E. Gedo and G.H. Pollock. *Psychoanalysis: The Vital Issues. Vol. 1. Psychoanalysis as an Intellectual Discipline. Emotions and Behavior Monographs*. No. 2. New York. International P, 1984: 257-75.

Prentky, Robert. "Creativity and Psychopathology: Gamboling at the Seat of Madness. *Handbook of Creativity*. Eds. J.A. Glover, R.R. Ronning, and C.R. Reynolds. New York: Plenum, 1989.

Rothenberg, A. *Creativity and Madness*. Baltimore: Johns Hopkins UP, 1991.

Schneiderman, Leo. *The Literary Mind: Portraits in Pain and Creativity*. New York: Insight, 1988.

With only one exception (excluding the unavailable Jamieson report), I have not uncovered any empirical evidence to support the presumed tie between creativity and madness. The single empirical study (Dean K. Simonton, "Political Pathology and Societal Creativity," *Creativity Research Journal* 3.2 [1990]: 85-99) deals with the effects of societal madness, like war and civil disobedience, on creative output. It too, though, has its detractors (Sharon Beilin, "Societal Creativity: Problems with Pathology," *Creativity Research Journal* 3.2 [1990]: 100-03).

Through a Lens, Darkly

Michael Fleming and Roger Manvell

Film, even from its silent days in the 1920s, has proven to be an art form particularly suitable for handling intimate psychological subjects. It is a medium of observation, the almost clinical recording of human behavior, with every nuance of expression and gesture enhanced in the close-up. As a highly controlled flow of images, film is uniquely able to reflect the flux of mental and emotional experience. And madness, which raises basic questions about the nature of these experiences, has been a very popular subject for filmmakers.

For the film artist, madness is a subject that probes the darkest and most hidden side of our being. For the psychologist, madness is something to be understood, then treated. Although every age has produced those who were held to be mad, there are many conflicting theories about what madness is or what causes it. The perception of madness has not been a single one but a combination of perceptions overlapping past and present and reflecting both popular and scientific views.

We have found that the images of madness presented in film have a unique relationship to fluctuations in psychological and psychiatric theory and practice. Particular elements of a film, such as plot, characterization of the visual text, reflect clinical impressions of madness in the psychological and psychiatric literature. Broader social and cultural factors have also played a part in this relationship.

We have selected certain films that highlight some of the more interesting changes, as well as the continuities, in these views of madness. There are certain themes that continue to reappear, including society and madness; war and madness; paranoia and madness; and madness as sanity. Here, we contrast an earlier film with a later one that depicts the same theme, arguing that the

Reprinted from *Images of Madness*, 1985, Fairleigh Dickinson University Press, with the permission of Associated University Presses.

differences and similarities over a 20- to 40-year range point to the subtle interaction between popular and clinical views.

The history of madness is tied closely to the history of the institutions that have cared for the afflicted. At first it was the family or village that cared for the mad individual, but by the seventeenth century mental hospitals had become a fixed part of European society as the mad were increasingly seen as a threat to the normal functioning of society. By the end of the nineteenth century, large state hospitals were built in this country but could offer little except custodial care until the late 1940s and early 1950s.

In the late 1940s, state hospitals became the object of professional and public concern, largely due to the prospect of serious overcrowding by World War II veterans with various neuro-psychiatric disorders. Up to this time, Hollywood had taken some interest in madness but had done so primarily in mysteries, romances and horror films that paid little attention to the plight and symptoms of those confined in psychiatric institutions. *The Snake Pit* (1948) was produced at a time when the United States first began to recognize the serious deficiencies of these institutions. The film, based on a popular novel, was a partly autobiographical account of a young woman's harrowing experiences in a state mental hospital.

When the film opens, Virginia (Olivia de Havilland), confined in a hospital after a breakdown, is having difficulty responding to the questions of Dr. Kik, her psychiatrist. Kik is portrayed as a humane man who is devoted to the care of the lost souls at the institution. Unlike the other staff psychiatrists, he believes in one-on-one treatment, and though this treatment is never directly labeled psychoanalytic, he constantly appears in line with a small picture of Freud on his office wall. Kik also administers electroconvulsive therapy and hydrotherapy, which were sometimes used together with psychotherapy in the 1940s and reflected the belief that madness involved problems of both mind and body.

The villains in the film are the institution and some of the people who work in it. Overcrowding is stressed as a problem, and two staff members are depicted as enjoying, in almost a sadistic manner, their power over the patients.

Through flashbacks, we find that as a little girl Virginia was angry at her father about the attention he paid to her mother. When her father died, Virginia unconsciously associated his death with her angry wish for his destruction. A later flashback shows that the final cause of Virginia's nervous breakdown was the death of a suitor who resembled her father—an incident that reawakened Virginia's distorted feeling of responsibility for her father's death.

At the end, Kik explains to Virginia the reasons for her repressed fears; taking a classic psychoanalytic position, he declares that from earliest infancy the child has oral feelings that are tied to being helpless. The film flashes back to a newborn child, squirming in swaddling, and Kik's explanation ends with the words: "You have learned that husbands and fathers can't be the same thing."

Though it adopted a simplified explanation of madness, *The Snake Pit* was effective in presenting the forms of treatment and the institutional problems faced by state psychiatric hospitals in the 1940s. It revealed that problems come from overcrowding and the cruel attitudes of some staff, and it portrayed electroconvulsive therapy and psychotherapy as highly effective. The final message seems to be that the doctor knows best how to help the patient, and despite overcrowding and the occasional sadist, the psychiatric hospital can provide a cure for the mentally ill.

By the 1960s, this attitude had changed. Psychiatry was attacked as a political institution, used for the repression of individual differences, and madness was viewed as a label attached to those who were rule-breakers. This idea found its best-known advocate in R.D. Laing, a British psychiatrist seen as the major proponent of "antipsychiatry." "Madness need not be all breakdown," Laing wrote, "it may also be breakthrough. It is potentially liberation and renewal as well as enslavement..." His writings were quickly adopted by the anti-establishment movements of the 1960s, which included Laing among a host of gurus (Timothy Leary, Baba Ram Dass, Maharishi) and authors (Norman O. Brown, Herbert Marcuse, Kurt Vonnegut, Jr., Ken Kesey) who became the evangelical seers of a new age.

The film *One Flew Over the Cuckoo's Nest* was based on Kesey's very popular book published in 1962. The novel's action is presented through the eyes of Chief Broom, a giant Indian who has received numerous electroconvulsive "treatments." His account of the hospital revolves around the work of Nurse Ratched, who runs the hospital for the Combine, the prime power center of society. Patients are sent to the hospital by the Combine because they are nonconformists. R.P. McMurphy, the book's hero, comes into this hell and through his actions assumes a Christlike role, dying so his followers can be saved.

The movie version of *Cuckoo's Nest* wasn't made until 1975. By then, antipsychiatry was considered to be an extreme position.

Although deinstitutionalization and advances in the use of antipsychotic drugs dramatically decreased the population of large state hospitals, readmission rates were higher because the discharged patients were not receiving adequate care in the community. The great hopes of the 1960s for change had not been realized and by the late 1970s were considered to be misguided.

In the film, the hospital ward is no longer just a symbol for the establishment, and the political nature of the Combine and McMurphy (Jack Nicholson) has been exchanged for a simpler story of the great American hero, the Western gunfighter type, who is always ready to take up a dare, even if it means giving up his life. While in the book McMurphy's actions allow his fellow patients to realize that they are sane, the film ducks these issues; the patients remain patients, except for the Chief, who escapes. The film version fits the view of psychiatry dominant in the mid 1970s, which, though it realized that institutions needed humanization, considered patients to be mentally ill, not visionary.

Changing views of madness are also reflected in Hollywood war films. Most films depicting war have done so in a highly stylized, romantic manner, but those that have become classics usually represent explorations into the personal experience of war. Such films probe the inner, psychological responses of individuals in combat, and frequently they focus on madness.

In the early days of World War II the clinical term for soldiers' madness was traumatic "war neurosis," which had obvious physical symptoms such as paralysis and blindness. These were thought to stem from one explosive incident of overpowering intensity in combat. Later psychologists adopted a more complex view of war symptoms and their origins and began to use the term "combat fatigue." They began looking at the cumulative effect of stress and realized that, while there might have been an incident that finally triggered the madness, a series of previous events had lowered the soldier's emotional resistance. This cumulative effect of stress was one of the major issues portrayed in *Twelve O'Clock High* (1949), a film that depicted the psychiatric casualties of aerial warfare.

It opens with a bomber sliding uncontrollably across a landing field. When it finally settles to a stop, the captain crawls out of the bullet-ridden cockpit area, stands frozen for a moment and then turns aside and vomits. His copilot, who saw a crewman's head blown off, wanders aimlessly around, disoriented. The flight surgeon says the copilot needs to be sedated immediately but should be back in action within a matter of days.

The film presents a sketchy approximation of the psychiatric view of madness in the early part of the war, which vacillated between a social and a medical model. Drug-induced "sleep therapy" was in limited use at the time, and, while the short beginning sequence emphasizes this approach, the rest of the film focuses on social bonding and modeling and their effect on morale.

The squadron morale, after months of combat, is shaky: Discipline is lax and drinking is a problem. General Savage (Gregory Peck) is sent by headquarters to restore order, and he pushes his men relentlessly. Though they hate his guts at first, he finally succeeds in welding them into a proud, efficient and, above all, disciplined team. However, Savage himself has a temporary nervous breakdown the day after his wing commander is shot down. The flight surgeon speculates that this is probably a momentary condition, triggered by the events of the previous day. The film ends with Savage lowering himself to his cot as his officers, gravely concerned, look down at him.

Vietnam was a different war and gave rise to a different, longer-lasting madness. The U.S. soldier was in a situation where he could be killed both in the front lines and in the back lines. The boundaries of the war and the identity of the enemy became increasingly vague, and the soldier seemed to be able to depend on fewer and fewer people. For many, Vietnam became a private war as they retreated further and further into themselves.

The type of madness described in the clinical literature and depicted by many films on Vietnam involved soldiers who isolated themselves in interior worlds, where reality and hallucination were indistinguishable. The individuals most adaptable to this war appeared to be people with a personality disorder, such as sociopathic loners who were poorly adapted to "normal" society. They had given up trust and had become experts in avoidance and detachment. They were people of impulsive violence who were mildly paranoid, who developed a compulsive need to test the feeling that power and mastery determine what is right. For the drug abuser in *Who'll Stop the Rain?* (1978), the volatile protagonists in *The Deer Hunter* (1978) or *Taxi Driver* (1976) and finally the Kilgores and Kurtzes of *Apocalypse Now* (1979), madness had a survival value.

While paranoia was part of the madness of Vietnam, the idea that one is being persecuted and plotted against has often been thought of as a symptom of madness outside of war. In the middle of this century, Freud's notion that paranoia can be linked to repressed homosexuality was dominant in psychoanalytic circles. It is not surprising to find that paranoid film characters of the 1930s, 1940s and 1950s were often diminutive, weak, effeminate and unpredictable people who exuded lurking sadistic malevolence, such as Joel Cairo (Peter Lorre), one of Sam Spade's antagonists in *The Maltese Falcon* (1941).

By the mid 1950s, there was increasing evidence against Freud's theory of paranoia as a response to unacceptable homosexual wishes. Clinical literature of the time introduced the notion of "pseudohomosexuality." The problem in paranoia was no longer being perceived as fear of homosexuality but a fear of social powerlessness. Nonmasculine feelings were associated with a loss of power and assertiveness, which was the real threat to an individual. For Hollywood, the theme of power and paranoia was dominant in films like *The Caine Mutiny* (1954), in which the military trappings of supermasculinity were explored as a defense against feelings of failure, incompetence and loss of power. In *Reflections in a Golden Eye* (1967) and The *Sergeant* (1968) military machismo was shown to hide grave conflicts over masculinity.

As the United States reeled from the assassination of its leaders and the eruption of street violence in the 1960s, a certain uneasiness developed about whether the order of society was as well-structured as previously thought. These beliefs reached their zenith with the Vietnam War, the Watergate conspiracy and the revelations about the use of government intelligence services for spying on United States citizens. The thinking about paranoia began to move away from a sexual perspective to include the idea that paranoia might be a legitimate response to the political insanity that seemed to be gaining dominance in the country.

The reality core of paranoia became a major focus in the clinical literature. Sociologist Edwin Lemert, an advocate of this view, maintained, "We make an explicit break with the conception of paranoia as a disease, a state, a condition, or a syndrome of symptoms." Attention shifted to factors in the environment that could create a feeling of paranoia. The new "conspiratorial model of behavior" pointed to the ways in which people are driven into madness not only by the family but by social forces as well. The work of sociologists such as Erving Goffman and Thomas Scheff in this area resulted in a greater willingness to view the paranoid individual as a victim.

Beginning with *Dr. Strangelove* (1964), and including films such as *The Parallax View* (1974), *Three Days of the Condor* (1975),

Marathon Man (1976), *All the President's Men* (1976) and *The China Syndrome* (1979), the basis for paranoia came to be viewed as the external political reality rather than the repressed homosexual drives of the neurotic. The problem was a real one, which lay not in fantasies about persecution but in the actual megalomaniacal strivings of others. In numerous films the hero was accused of paranoia for suspicions that in the end were shown to be justified. A popular saying of the 1960s, "Just because you're paranoid doesn't mean they're not after you," illustrates this mentality.

Reversals like this, where madness appears to be sanity, become popular in times of great social crisis, such as the 1960s. Another period when the world seemed to come unglued was the Great Depression. In the 1930s, the United States, the land of plenty, suddenly became unable to provide the goods and resources needed to maintain a subsistence level for each citizen, and the rich and powerful appeared pitted against the little man. Democratic values suddenly seemed to disappear as the hired muscle of big business broke heads and twisted arms in picket lines and farmers lost their land to banks.

Artistic visions of a world cut asunder easily found their way into the cinema of this period, in the form of the screwball comedy. Frank Capra directed films that exemplified this genre, such as *It Happened One Night, Mr. Deeds Goes to Town, Mr. Smith Goes to Washington* and *You Can't Take It with You.* His films all presented wacky characters who experienced profound reversals which, as Capra said, always resolved themselves into a comedy of uniting opposites and left the audience with "a glow of satisfaction." Opposite factions were shown to be, beyond their superficial appearance, similar.

Throughout these films, joyful, childlike delusions were shown to have greater merit than the ordinary thinking of so-called sensible, rational adults who, caught up in the world of commerce, forgot the importance of the individual. Capra seemed to say that delusion and fantasy must be nourished and are at times even preferable to "realistic" pursuits.

This theme reappeared in the 1960s, but without Capra's optimism about the unity of opposing views, most notably in *King of Hearts* (1966). Appealing primarily to college-age adults, this film enjoyed sell-out status throughout the late 1960s and early 1970s. The film conveyed a sense that the adult world was corrupt and that the old order had to give way to a new, youthful vision of reality.

The film is set in the closing years of World War I. Private Plumpick (Alan Bates) is pushed into accepting a perilous mission to defuse a bomb that will blow up a town from which German troops are retreating. In the town, Plumpick finds a group of citizens who treat the world with delightful indifference: Their world is one of play, and pleasure and love are the only criteria for establishing what is real. What Plumpick does not know is that the ordinary townspeople have fled after being told about the bomb. His new friends are really inmates of the local insane asylum, which was accidentally left unlocked.

While Plumpick tries in vain to make them see the peril they face, their main focus seems to be on persuading him, whom they crown the King of Hearts, to marry one of their number. Though resistant at first, Plumpick gives up his search for the bomb when he falls in love with his preselected bride; but a moment before the bomb is to go off, he figures out where it is and stops it from detonating.

Soon afterward, Plumpick's commander arrives, a caricature of the self-serving, conceited militarist, whose own antics do not allow him to recognize the madness of the townsfolk around him. The difference, of course, lies in his aggression, and he and his German counterpart confront and destroy each other and their troops. Other forces arrive, along with the original townsfolk, and the old order of things is quickly restored. Plumpick is ordered back to the front lines, and the inmates, having had enough of the sanity of the outside world, gladly retreat back into their cells.

As Plumpick passes the asylum, however, he leaps from the truck and, appearing nude before the gate, seeks admission into the sane world of the insane. The new king, the King of Hearts, or emotion, has finally arrived, and he has brought nothing of the old order but himself, reborn.

King of Hearts demonstrated the victory of humanity over technology and war, the power of youth and the birth of a new order, all orchestrated within a psychological interpretation of madness popular in the 1960s: that it was not a bad thing but was in fact a special journey, a journey of potential enlightenment into the true nature of things. *King of Hearts* was followed by films such as *Marat-Sade*, *The Magic Christian*, *The Ruling Class* and *Harold and Maude*, which clearly emerged from this particular social, political and psychological worldview of madness as a positive experience and sanity as an uptight, bourgeois state of mind.

These alternative concepts of madness—as human nature gone awry, as responses to social injustice, as enlightenment—have been repeated, interwoven and maintained throughout history and are all still held in some measure today. The expression of these ideas in the medium of our times, the film, illustrates how contemporary explanations of madness and its treatment are derived from a long history of ideas about what is not normal and how it should be set right. An understanding of madness can be richly enhanced by looking at this history, which in spiraling fashion continues to reiterate earlier concepts and to reintegrate them with later ones.

A Horneyan Approach to American Literature

James R. Huffman

This essay is related to a psychological study of American life, tentatively titled *In Sickness and in Health: A Psychological Approach to U.S. History and Culture*. This book-in-progress goes beyond works that are founded on biology-based psychology (Freudian psychoanalysis), using theories that take cultural influences more strongly into account. I am using Karen Horney's theory of anxiety neurosis in particular, carrying her insight that anxiety neurosis defines "the neurotic personality of our time" more broadly into American history and culture than she or sociologists have done. Although American Psychological Association manuals from *DSM-III* on use the term "personality disorder" rather than "neurosis," Horney's insights remain accurate in connecting the psychological phenomena she describes in the original theory.

I believe that the personality disorders Horney identifies as psychologically connected have not only affected many individuals in the United States in the twentieth century but have materially affected the course of American history and culture. Horney has described not only "the neurotic personality of our time" (the title of one of her early books) but of several eras; she has found a root not only of American psychological trends, but of those in several cultures. These are huge claims, and more than one book would be required to do full justice to them. For this paper, I am limiting myself to the task of beginning to apply them to American literature, particularly American fiction. Nevertheless, an outline of the overall argument of the book should be helpful.

My basic claim is that Americans have been suffering on a massive scale throughout the existence of the nation from the personality disorders Horney identifies. These disorders have helped determine the course of American history and, to the extent that this controversial entity exists, the formation of American character. The prevalence of the basic symptoms of these personality disorders in American attitudes and behavior, high art and popular art, intellectual and social history, religion and government suggests that its quantity has been more than sufficient to affect the quality of

American life. (See the outline of Horney's observations to follow my application of it to American culture.) All the symptoms are present. From its own perspective, the nation has lived in an almost constantly threatening environment from the beginning. That threatening environment has affected American identity deeply, from the tendency toward violence to the struggle against charges of cultural inferiority. To counteract such pressures, much of American history reveals a grandiose search for glory and an incredibly idealized image of American character. Americans began to believe that the United States would be the greatest nation on earth, then that it already was and always would be. Americans had a "Manifest Destiny" and were, as Abraham Lincoln described them, an "almost chosen people." Americans are caught in a vicious circle: fearing inferiority, they must prove themselves superior; and if they fail to live up to perfection, they feel inferior once again.

All the major unhealthy strategies show up in Americans, from resignation and isolationistic withdrawal to self-effacing compliance and conformity. But most notably, Americans—particularly their leaders—behave expansively and aggressively. Several Presidents, including Lyndon Johnson, show strong signs of this disorder; government, economic and business systems, religion and popular culture all show major symptoms. (See my essay on "Young Man Johnson" in *The American Journal of Psychoanalysis* 49.3: 251-65, for one sample.) Fortunately, healthy forces are also at work, though I must neglect them in this essay due to space. My book traces the nation's history and culture in sickness and in health, with the hope of diminishing the one and reinforcing the other.

American literature shows the presence of these symptoms just as most of our other cultural artifacts do. With most of Europe telling the young nation that it was an inferior colony during its early history, it is not surprising that many American writers would deal with our alleged inferiority. "Who reads an American book?" English reviewers contemptuously asked even in the early nineteenth century. Literary critics in English periodicals were notorious for their scathing attacks on what claimed to be literature in America, and their contempt did not stop at our pretensions to culture; Americans were branded "servile copyists and imitators" (like the Japanese in the mid-twentieth century) and even presumed by some to be biologically inferior. Nor has this attitude totally disappeared. Only 20 years ago a colleague of mine visiting a French university which was trying to establish a program in American culture overheard an old professor mutter, "American culture? *Il n'y a pas."* Some of us in departments of "English" pick up similar attitudes toward American literature among our colleagues in British fields, and the feeling is even stronger in Canada.

As a result, early American literature reveals an identity crisis. The first problem was forming any identity at all which differed from European roots. The next problem was making that identity at least equal, and hopefully superior, to European identities. But our writers came through. Crevecoeur's question, "What is the American, this new man?" is nearly as old as the country, and most of the answers to it include an idealized image that served the unhealthy need of some Americans to compensate for fears of inferiority. R.W.B. Lewis, for example, in his well-known book *The American Adam* traces the use of this "American Adam" myth among numerous important spokespersons such as Hawthorne and James—a clearly idealized image of American character and glorified sense of American destiny, seeing Americans as new Adams with a divine second chance to recover Eden. (Lewis's "Party of Hope" particularly glorifies Americans, though his "Party of Irony" helps establish a healthier perspective.) Brother Jonathan, an Adamic symbol of U.S. national character before Uncle Sam, may have been a country bumpkin, but he was presented as intelligent and honest and pure, unlike Europe. Our writers turned the deficiencies of American life into positive virtues, as in making the lack of intellectual cultivation into an ideal like Cooper's Leatherstocking hero. They participated, in the early nationalistic period of American history, in the creation of idealized images that could make Americans feel proud.

Popular literature, of course, pandered the most in this enterprise. The threatening environment of the frontier produced a search for glory and an idealized self that is hard to surpass in the Western hero. Similarly, Southern fiction helped protect the South temporarily from the threatening environment that led to the Civil War by idealizing the Southern lady and gentleman and the Southern version of pastoral life. Works like *Uncle Tom's Cabin* implied Northern superiority. And though some of our writers decried the shame of our cities in their threatening environments, others like Horatio Alger preached to American boys what they wanted to hear: that even the poorest and most threatened American could rise to riches and heroic stature, or at least to the middle class. The appeal of that myth to those afraid of inferiority can hardly be exaggerated. Virtue and hard work (and Horneyan "shoulds") would turn Ragged Dick into Richard Hunter, Esquire, with a little bit of providential luck. (Americans have always believed that Providence helps those that help themselves; and we help ourselves to as much as possible.) Unfortunately, the plan did not work fully even for Alger himself. His devastating childhood and bouts with religion created abysmally clear unhealthy tendencies in his personality, eventually making him the victim of his never-achieved goal of becoming the Great American Novelist—an idealized self and search for glory shared by many, including even Snoopy (as Erich Beagle) in the *Peanuts* comic strip. Outside popular literature, looking at Thomas Wolfe's ambition to read the whole Harvard library as just one example, it is difficult to ignore a search for glory in the quest of many twentieth-century figures to write the Great American Novel.

And it is mainly on the twentieth century that I would like to focus. Since Horney felt that she had discovered "the neurotic personality of our time" and place in her early book (1937), it is particularly appropriate to center on twentieth-century American literature for illustration, though the phenomenon she was describing goes beyond the twentieth century and American culture. A number of Horneyan studies of American works have already been completed, though more of English literature has been dealt with than our own, and there have even been excursions into French, German, Spanish, Russian and Indo-English novels. Indeed, the International Horney Society recently formed under the direction of Bernard J. Paris of the University of Florida at Gainesville due to international interest in her work. Several of its members are literary critics, including figures such as Norman Friedman and Jay Martin, who are known in the field of American literature.

A mostly chronological overview of Horneyan studies in American literature should be a helpful start. Doris V. Falk uses Horney to approach *Eugene O'Neill and the Tragic Tension* (1958). Bernard J. Paris, one of the first literary critics to use Horney widely and the most eminent Horneyan literary critic, has an early analysis of Bellow's *Herzog* (1976). My own essay, "A Psychological Redefinition of William Styron's *Confessions of Nat Turner*," appeared in *The Literary Review* in 1981, reprinted in Bernard J. Paris, ed., *Third Force Psychology and the Study of Literature*. Karen Butery includes an analysis of James's *Portrait of a Lady* in "The Contributions of Horneyan Psychology to the Study of Literature" (*AJP* 1982) and analyzes "From Conflict to Suicide: The Inner Turmoil of Quentin Compson" in Horneyan terms (*AJP* 1989).

Marjorie Haselswerdt has published an Horneyan analysis of Joe Christmas and *Light in August* from her dissertation on psychology and character in Faulkner. Abroad, Ineke Bockting of the University of Amsterdam has published on psychological aspects of Faulkner novels, and has completed a book entitled *Character and Personality in the Novels of William Faulkner* that uses aspects of Horney personality theory. In literary biography the monumental, Pulitzer Prize-winning study of Robert Frost by Lawrance Thompson (1966, 1970) was heavily influenced by Horney though without attribution, as pointed out by Donald Sheehy recently in *American Literature* (1986). Kristin Lauer is completing a study of relationships in Edith Wharton's fiction to be called *Gallery of the Damned: Understanding Edith Wharton's Pessimism*, and has published other Horneyan character studies in *The Journal of Evolutionary Psychology*.

Similarly, there are works not specifically Horneyan which nevertheless reveal things Horney understood probably as well or better than these later writers. John J. Clayton, in a work-in-progress called "Gestures of Healing," argues that much of modernist literature in Europe as well as America reveals similar symptoms. Examining the canon of British and American modernism, in pre-publication publicity, Clayton states that great novels by Henry James, Joseph Conrad, Ford Madox Ford, E.M. Forster, James Joyce, Virginia Woolf, D.H. Lawrence, F. Scott Fitzgerald, Ernest Hemingway and William Faulkner expressed "anxiety and the need to defend against anxiety...expressed anxieties and defenses that grew to be shared by most people in the intelligentsia." Moreover, most modernist writers "came from similar families, families with controlling mothers and shattered fathers...families offering little support to the developing self." Modernism, then, "was shaped by a common pain from a common source and from a common attempt to cope with pain." Clayton sees these writers "expressing, hiding, and coping with anxiety that derives from a failure of self." "Pathologies of the self, failures in the structure of the self, disintegration of self" abound in these writers, and Clayton sees "their novels and their lives as attempts at healing this failure of self." Without realizing it, I believe, Clayton provides evidence of how much of modernism shows the influence of the anxiety in American culture which Karen Horney discovered and defined so well in her descriptions of personality disorders.

Similarly, Julius Rowan Raper in an unpublished paper titled "An Emerging Model of Southern Culture" finds parallel personality structures throughout Southern fiction and history. Raper sees a "pattern of shame and arrogance" parallel to Kohut's model of the bipolar self at work in Southern culture, and cites Eugene Gant's swings between shame and arrogance as a good literary example. Similarly, "Eva Birdsong's violence...Thomas Sutpen's grandiose design, Rosa Coldfield's rage, Lancelot Lamar's plan for a Third Revolution" are all seen by Raper as part of the same underlying psychological patterns, part of the "mind of the South" taken "as a collective and historical psyche," partly applicable to both blacks and whites. As a result, "the South responds to blows to the nation's self-esteem...with greater outrage and defensive righteousness than other regions." I think Raper is right, like historian Bertram Wyatt-Brown, but fails to see that the same patterns appear in national behavior, not just in the South. And the behaviors he is describing with the Kohut model are better understood through Karen Horney. For example, Raper argues that Eugene Gant of Wolfe's *Look Homeward Angel* "very clearly erects a grandiose and false self as a barrier against the sense of shame and hollowness that so often threatens to overwhelm him." This view is parallel to the Horneyan one in that Eugene has adopted an idealized self to compensate for his feelings of inferiority in response to his threatening environment, but at times feels ashamed because his actual self cannot live up to his idealized image. (Clayton and Raper rely mainly on Heinz Kohut and similar analysts in shaping their models, a position criticized effectively by Jack Danielian in *"Karen Horney and Heinz Kohut: Theory and the Repeat of History," American Journal of Psychoanalysis* 48.1 [1988]: 6-24.)

Both these studies aim mainly at the early twentieth century, and I would add the literary movement known as naturalism to them as evidence of similar phenomena. In particular the career and writings of Theodore Dreiser show the patterns of personality disorder. The threatening environment is of course prevalent in naturalistic writing, since the movement was predicated as a form of realism that reveals the "seamy side" of life, the most Darwinian and threatening of human environments. It is not difficult to see a search for glory even in *Sister Carrie*, though the expansive/ aggressive tycoons that Dreiser admired and portrayed in such novels as *The Financier* and *The Titan* are more obvious manifestations of the need for and worship of power. Even Carrie is more attracted to men with money and position than to men with great bodies. Poor Clyde Griffiths of *An American Tragedy* is a very weak individual, yet even he is driven in his own way into a search for glory and the attempt to become his idealized self through marrying glitter and wealth.

In the brief space that is left, let me just describe what a Horneyan approach reveals about some of our major novels and writers. Several novels contain characters that reveal symptoms of personality disorder, such as Nathaniel West's *The Day of the Locust*. Harry Greener, small-time vaudevillian, has a search for glory that centers around some producer putting him "into a big revue against a background of beautiful girls and glittering curtains." But it never happens. Instead, as Greener himself puts it, "his life had consisted of a lightning series of 'nip-ups,' 'high gruesomes,' 'flying-W's' and 'hundred-and-eights' done to escape a barrage of 'exploding stoves.' An 'exploding stove' was any catastrophe, natural or human...." At the heart of *The Day of the Locust* is the threatening environment that eventually causes the eruption of human emotions in violence which ends the novel and which is represented by Tod Hackett's painting, "The Burning of Los Angeles." Expansive people such as Harry and Faye Greener come to California with impossible dreams and desperate searches for glory, and find self-effacing people like Homer Simpson who have never had lives and who want to live vicariously through the dreamers. Very few achieve their dreams. Harry clowns as his "sole method of defense" against reality. His daughter Faye wants to be a film star, and tells Tod that she can "love" only men with money and looks who can further her career. She has a whole pack of dreams, some of which she realizes are absurd, such as her ideas on writing scripts for films. She ends up in prostitution and sponging off poor Homer, who has no looks and only enough money to help her get by. Homer has no hope for a better life, and simply lets Faye use him. He is one of the crowd who come to California to die, who are desperate enough to set the city on fire if provoked, the "pick of America's madmen" if not "typical of the rest of the land." Hollywood is symbolized by the studio lot, a "dream dump" history of American civilization, and California is not the paradise of dreams but more the graveyard of them, as in Steinbeck's *Of Mice and Men*. In West's short novel personality disorders define the state of American culture.

Similarly, Hollywood novels like Budd Schulberg's *What Makes Sammy Run?* center on characters like Sammy Glick, desperately climbing from the slums of New York to the heights of Hollywood. He is compulsive, and ruthless, but ultimately is a victim of people just like himself:

...what was coming to him was not a sudden pay-off but a process, a disease he had caught in the epidemic that swept over his birthplace like a plague; a cancer that was slowly eating him away, the symptoms developing and intensifying: success, loneliness, fear. Fear of all the bright young men, the newer, fresh Sammy Glicks that would spring up to harass him, to threaten him and finally to overtake him. (New York: Penguin Books, 1978: 246)

Schulberg realizes that Sammy's expansive psychological solution is "a way of life that was paying dividends in America in the first half of the twentieth century" (247)—in Hollywood, in business and in government.

F. Scott Fitzgerald records his view of similar people in *The Great Gatsby*. The poor James Gatz becomes his idealized self, Jay Gatsby, and tries to realize his dream, represented by Daisy Buchanan and the light on the dock across the bay. Nick Carroway obviously sympathizes with Gatsby more than the callous Buchanans, even though Gatsby teams up with organized crime to reach his goals. But Fitzgerald clearly sees an American malady here, as in the famous lyrical ending he describes Americans chasing their dreams as if they are in boats borne ever backward into the past.

A number of Southern novels also reflect anxiety neurosis in American culture. Marjorie Haselswerdt sees Joe Christmas of *Light in August* as responding to his threatening environment and identity with neurotic solutions, and Julius Raper sees both Thomas Sutpen and Rosa Coldfield of *Absalom, Absalom!* as responding with "overwhelming rage and grandiose posturing" to blows against their egos. With a poor-white alcoholic father and an absent mother, Sutpen responds to being told to go to the back door of a Virginia mansion by embarking on a tremendous search for glory. He must create a plantation that outweighs the mansion he was spurned from. Rosa Coldfield, with a cold, withdrawn father and an absent mother as well, reacts with "sterile outrage...in which her life hangs suspended for forty years" to Sutpen's proposition to marry her only if she produces a male heir first. Raper adds Eva Birdsong of Ellen Glasgow's *The Sheltered Life* and Walker Percy's *Lancelot* to his list of similar psychologically defective Southern characters.

I would like to add some characters of Carson McCullers and Robert Penn Warren to the list of those reflecting Horneyan personality disorders, in addition to Styron's Nat Turner whom I have already analyzed. At the very heart of "The Ballad of the Sad

Cafe" and *The Heart Is a Lonely Hunter* is an unhealthy conception of love clearly explicable by Horney. The truth in the famous statement in the "Ballad" that "the beloved fears and hates the lover" is the fact that in unhealthy love the lover creates an idealized version of the beloved and loves that rather than the actual person. For that reason "most of us would rather love than be loved," and "the state of being loved is intolerable to many." The lover, who is often self-effacing on the surface in relationship to the beloved, in effect remakes the beloved. The beloved, often expansive/aggressive in personality at least in relationship to the lover, fears and resists being remade and may even despise the lover for trying to do so. Expansive personalities often dislike self-effacing ones anyway, thinking they are weak and dependent, and self-effacing personalities often wish they could be like the expansive personalities they admire. But as in the case of Marvin Macy's love of Miss Amelia, Miss Amelia's love of Cousin Lymon, and Cousin Lymon's love of Marvin Macy—a complicated triangle—each of these personalities rejects being loved because none wants to surrender any autonomy in determining the nature of the self.

The same basic phenomenon is recorded in *The Heart Is a Lonely Hunter* in the love of Mick, Jake Blount, and Benedict Mady Copeland for the mute John Singer, and in Singer's love for the mute and unintelligent Spiros Antonapoulos. Each one thinks that Singer is what he or she needs—an understanding father, or a fellow-radical, a sympathetic listener who will agree and not contradict. Each one creates a Singer to talk to, not with. And meanwhile Singer himself idealizes Antonapoulos as wise and understanding: "Sometimes he thought of Antonapoulos with awe and self-abasement, sometimes with pride—always with love unchecked by criticism, freed of will." And of course Antonapoulos cannot criticize Singer either, just as Singer is basically unable to communicate with the people who make an idealized figure out of him. At the heart of this unhealthy conception of love is an idiocy well symbolized by the fat inarticulate Greek. It is a conception of love which McCullers never seems to overcome and outgrow in her writing.

Robert Penn Warren portrays a very expansive Willie Stark in *All the King's Men*, of course, and this model could certainly be used to approach many aspects of the novel. Warren is frying more than just this one fish here, however, and I think the clearest Horneyan case in his work is Jeremiah Beaumont of *World Enough and Time.* From early in his childhood Beaumont wants to be a gallant hero, and eventually goes on a quest to redeem the dignity and honorable reputation of a woman he has never met. He is obsessed with doing "justice" for her, and failure to accomplish that would mean the failure to be his idealized heroic self. Killing Colonel Cassius Fort is Rachel's condition for Jeremiah marrying her and accomplishing justice for her, so when Fort refuses to duel with him, Beaumont must murder the man. Nothing else can give him the grandiose sense of self which he needs to feel adequate. But the way he ends up having to kill Fort violates his idealized self as well. When he kills the Colonel, suddenly all exaltation is gone, and he feels a "deadly emptiness and weariness. For what had he striven? For what did men strive?" The judgment of the outside world which he fears so constantly is nothing to his judgment of himself. His trial and conviction lead him mostly toward resignation and detachment, and he and Rachel become completely distanced from each other. He escapes from jail, but not from himself. And since Fort is dead, Rachel no longer plays the role of unavenged lady in his search for glory, and so she loses her previous glamour. She sinks deeper into her own unhealthy state, centered around her compulsive desire to have a child, and finally commits suicide.

Like Ecclesiastes, which expresses the philosophy of resignation much as in *The Sun Also Rises*, the theme of *World Enough and Time* becomes vanity, vanity, all is vanity. Jeremiah realizes that vanity in the sense of self-absorption was the major cause of his actions, that "The crime for which I seek expiation is never lost. It is always there. It is unpardonable. It is the crime of self, the crime of life. The crime is I." Even his view of his crime is grandiose, and his resignation will not be without its grand gesture, to try to return to face expiation. Unfortunately he does not make it. The bounty-hunter One-Eye overtakes him and cuts off his head in the wilderness, and wild pigs leave nothing but his bones. The other meaning of vanity comes in now, not self-absorption but futility. "Was all for nought?" asks not only Jeremiah Beaumont but the historian-narrator who "can show you what is left" after the "pride, passion, agony and bemused aspiration...the scraps of newspaper," the diaries, the documents, the yellow letters, and Beaumont's manuscript written in his cell and on the escape trail which gave no escape. The answer to the question is clear to the philosopher prepared by Ecclesiastes and to the psychological critic of Beaumont: yes, all was for nought. And Warren's novel joins several of Hemingway's, and perhaps Barth's *Floating Opera*, in depicting detachment and control as all. Unfortunately many of our writers have not recognized that detachment and control can be unhealthy. (How refreshing that Macon Leary, at least, in Anne Tyler's *The Accidental Tourist*, chooses life and health rather than detachment and resignation for a change!)

Willy Loman of *Death of a Salesman* could of course be added to the list of characters showing clear signs of Horneyan personality disorders, as could some of Saul Bellow's creations, a few of Henry James's, Styron's Nat Turner and assorted characters by black writers such as Rufus Scott in Baldwin's *Another Country*, Francie Coffin in Meriwether's *Daddy Was a Number Runner*, the early Bigger Thomas in Wright's *Native Son* and the early Meridian Hill in Alice Walker's novel. Some of these move toward health; most do not. Sometimes the authors realize the shortcomings of their characters, and sometimes they do not. Like writers of most nations, ours are better at depicting unhealthy behavior than at diagnosing and curing it.

Popular literature such as the Harlequin romance also shows similar defects in its characters, again most often without recognizing that these are psychological defects. Most Harlequins show self-effacing women extravagantly admiring expansive men, yet even while admiring expansiveness the novels partly validate a self-effacing value system in that these women win the men and often improve them. Similarly, westerns and detective fiction aimed mainly at men tend to validate expansive value systems without ever realizing the full psychology involved.

Whole books could be written on these elements in American popular and critically accepted literature. But I have enough of a catalogue and probably enough brief analysis to establish my main point: the personality disorders described by Karen Horney have had a significant impact on American culture, and not least upon its literature.

NOTE: This essay was first presented in 1989 at the initial meeting of members of the MLA forming a new organization of specialists in American literature. It presumes a basic knowledge of the field and its criticism, and so does not footnote the obvious. Further bibliographic information on Horneyan analyses can be obtained from the International Karen Horney Society, c/o Bernard J. Paris, English Department, University of Florida, Gainesville, FL 32606, in the list of members, and in the abstracts and bibliographies put out by IPSA (Institute for Psychological Study of the Arts) at the same university.

ANXIETY NEUROSIS

Based on
Karen Horney, *Neurosis and Human Growth:*
The Struggle Toward Self-Realization
New York: W.W. Norton & Company, Inc., 1950

A. The vicious circle

1. Threatening environment as cause of neurosis leads to
   a. "basic anxiety" and
   b. fear of inferiority
2. Result: a search for glory to compensate for fear of inferiority and
   a. formation of an idealized self and very vulnerable pride system,
   b. the making of neurotic claims on others to grant one higher status,
   c. and the "tyranny of the should," in which goals must be set so high to try to realize the idealized self that failure occurs.
3. Alienation from the real self results, accompanied by self-contempt because the idealized self despises the actual self in its perceived present state, and so represses its potential development.
4. Leads to a more threatening sense of environment, more anxiety, more fear of inferiority, and the cycle starts over.

B. Strategies for coping with a threatening environment:

	Moves	Values	Idealized Image
1. Self-effacing/compliant	toward people	love	Christlike
		service	martyr
2. Expansive/aggressive	against people	power	Napoleonic
		mastery	powerful
Specifically, expansive persons may tend to be:			
a. arrogant vindictive		power	powerful
		revenge	wealthy
b. narcissistic		beauty	charismatic
		popularity	charming
c. perfectionistic		perfection	meticulous
		cleanness	just
3. Resigned/withdrawn	away from people	solitude	unperturbed
		independence	aloof

The Lineage of Mad Scientists: Anti-types of Merlin

Peter H. Goodrich

How does a popular literature generate its icons?[1] In *Billion Year Spree: The True History of Science Fiction*, Brian Aldiss implies that the origins of the science fiction genre and the mad scientist figure are coeval in Mary Shelley's *Frankenstein: or, The Modern Prometheus*. In *Trillion Year Spree: The History of Science Fiction*, the revision of his earlier study, he affirms this idea by stating that while there was no word "scientist" in 1816, the year of *Frankenstein's* genesis, "the world has adopted Frankenstein as the model of the irresponsible scientist" (51).

Aldiss's claim for Shelley's novel is carefully considered and influential, yet it cannot settle speculation about science fiction "before science fiction" or about earlier forms of the mad scientist figure that appears, fully realized, in Victor Frankenstein. In fact, when Aldiss's "true" history discusses how Shelley's creation grows out of romanticism, the Gothic literary vogue, and the beginnings of the industrial revolution, he implicitly explodes the claim that *Frankenstein* is "more than a new story, a new myth" (*Billion Year Spree* 30). Such "newness" connotes more radical innovation than these deeply rooted influences can justify. While continuing to argue for the primacy of Mary Shelley's first novel, Aldiss has since acknowledged that origins "can never be definitively settled," for "the more a subject is studied, the further back its roots are seen to go" ("A Monster for All Seasons" 14, 17). Consequently, his most recent claim is less extravagant and more specific: "Frankenstein's is *the* modern predicament, involving the post-Rousseauvian dichotomy between the individual and his society, as well as the encroachment of science on that society, and mankind's dual nature, whose inherited ape curiosity has brought him both success and misery" (*Trillion Year Spree* 51).

A shorter version of this essay originally appeared in *Extrapolation* 27.2 (Summer 1986). Reprinted with permission.

Aldiss's gradual retrenchment is instructive, for Frankenstein's predicament may not even be as modern as he thinks. If the absence of the word "scientist" from the vocabulary of the early nineteenth century does not disqualify *Frankenstein* from consideration as the first science fiction novel, then the dualities of the individual and society or of man's two selves need not be considered as essential determinants of the modern, either. Aldiss is really observing that *Frankenstein* is modern and science fiction because it was timely: it memorably explored at the outset of the industrial era problems that we have come to identify with the machine culture of the past two centuries. That timeliness doesn't mean that such problems didn't exist earlier, in relation to scientific or other technologies like magic, or that such dualities as he invokes haven't always been important to us. It means only that Mary Shelley's novel galvanized popular culture to evaluate these fundamental problems and dualities in a new context.

As Aldiss admits, literary conceptions do not generate their materials spontaneously but develop over a long period of time, shaped by both historical and imaginative influences. After all, as Rome was not built in a day, neither were genres and popular icons like Victor Frankenstein and his monster. Instead, each genre or icon is constituted, like Rome, in concatenated "houses of fiction" erected by author-architects out of material quarried from their cultural environments or left by other authors. In turn, these "houses" often double as self-catering accommodations for the readers who throng the fictional streets and who occasionally take architectural tours with urbane building inspectors called scholars, teachers, or literary critics. The problem is, as Jonathan Culler observes, that "if one attempts to identify any utterance or text as a moment of origin one finds that they depend upon prior codes" (103)—literary as well as building codes.

In this light, we should inquire further into the origins of the mad scientist. Brian Stableford correctly notes that mad scientists "inherited the mantle and the public image of the medieval alchemists, astrologers, and sorcerers" (533), a mantle which Victor Frankenstein first adopts and later rejects. The medieval image, however, lingers. And even when Frankenstein makes a claim for empirical, applied science as opposed to alchemy and magic, modern readers and critics in the heat of commending historical innovation are all too easily disposed to overlook earlier claims like it.

For example, the Arabic protoscientist Alhazen (965-1038 A.D.) asserted that he could build a machine to control flooding on the Nile River. Taken at his word by al-Hakim, the Egyptian Caliph—whom Isaac Asimov calls "the most dangerous crowned madman between the times of Caligula and Ivan the Terrible" (78)— Alhazen could not produce the machine and saw no alternative but to feign madness himself until the caliph died in 1021. In the 1679 chapbook *The famous historie of Fryer Bacon*, a popular legendary biography of the thirteenth-century philosopher and protoscientist Roger Bacon, the learned friar explains to the king, "I will speak only of those things performed by Art and Nature, wherein shall be nothing magical: and first by the figuration of Art, there may be made Instruments of Navigation without men to row in them, as great ships to brook the Sea, only with one man to steer them and they shall sail far more swiftly than if they were full of men" (np). And on he goes, describing additional devices which resemble those we know today as aircraft, diving suits, holograms, telescopes and lasers. Bacon is also renowned in legend for creating a talking brass head, as was the thirteenth-century philosopher Albertus Magnus for building a robot. According to the work of Derek de Solla Price and Patricia Warrick, automata preceding Frankenstein's monster had in fact been designed from ancient times in a variety of cultures. Frankenstein differs primarily from the creators of these automata and their fictional counterparts like E.T.A. Hoffmann's Coppelius because he works with human flesh instead of machinery or clockwork.

Jonathan Swift, for his part, turns such inventions upside down in Part III of *Gulliver's Travels* by savaging the Royal Society's academicians as the cuckolded cloud-dwellers of Laputa, whose creations are of no use whatever to society. Darko Suvin regards the Laputans, not Frankenstein, as "the first 'mad scientists' in SF" and as a bourgeois character type used to satirize middle-class, dominated society's obsession with "counting, weighing, and measuring" (109).[2] Therefore, I would like to reenter the "mirage of citations" by focusing on the lineage and nature of the mad scientist before, as well as after Frankenstein. Three models predominantly influence the convention, and this essay's title proposes a fourth.

The first model for the mad scientist is named in the subtitle of Frankenstein itself—"The Modern Prometheus." The story of this Titan is not a "new myth" at all, but one of our most ancient. Prometheus ("fore-thinker") is a divine craftsman and trickster, famous for creating the first human out of clay and for disobeying Zeus by bestowing what the gods regarded as their exclusive property upon this lesser order of being. Fire and all it symbolizes for both poetic and scientific imaginations resembles the fruit urged upon Eve by another "light-bringer"—except that fire does not contain knowledge of good or evil. In his quest for insight into the laws of nature, the mad scientist, too, tends to envision himself as a titan, yet misinterprets or altogether fails to perceive the full moral and ethical dimensions of his experimentation. His failure in foresight radically flaws his power of forethought. The gift's giver and its recipient both suffer unforeseen and mortal consequences. As Zeus's revenge for the theft of fire, Prometheus is chained and his liver is gnawed until Hercules releases him, while human society acquires the "gift" of Pandora and her box.

In the Promethean mode, both magic and empirical science are morally ambivalent; one may be equally saved or damned by their application. And they are particularly dangerous because they provide power, which, as Patrick Callahan puts it, "deteriorates moral sensibility" in humans (42). The mad scientist, therefore, proves that the power to create is as inherently entropic as the universe itself. Both Promethean and humanly vulnerable, Victor Frankenstein admonishes us to "Learn from me, if not by my precepts, at least by my example, how dangerous is the acquirement of knowledge" (52).

The second, Faustian approach to the lineage of mad scientists is also prominent within Frankenstein's narrative. Its earliest direct ancestor may be St. Augustine's Manichaean tutor Faustus, who reportedly possessed heretical knowledge about the dualistic nature of God (Warrick 33). Victor Frankenstein repeatedly mentions the works of alchemists and reputed magicians like Albertus Magnus, Cornelius Agrippa, and Paracelsus; he rejects them when his experiments with their methods fail repeatedly and his Ingolstadt professors Krempe and Waldman propose empirical science as the only efficacious alternative. Yet he continues his research in the same ethically questionable spirit that was often attributed to the medieval and Renaissance practitioners, led on by his curious and power-hungry intellect. His pride in his discoveries leads him to unspeakable acts of grave-robbing.

In this Faustian mode, discovery is not merely ambivalent or presumptuous, but damnable; the corruption of the bodies secretly exhumed by Frankenstein signifies the corruption of his activity. Frankenstein becomes his own Mephistopheles, like Dr. Jekyll after him, and being imperfect, devilishly abuses the secret of creation itself from society's point of view. This devilishness is passed on, as so many commentators have noted, to his monster. Initially innocent, the monster catches his maker's disease, an Adam created in a fallen garden by a fallen god.

The Faustian ambition of the mad scientist has become a commonplace of grade B (not to mention C through Z) science fiction and horror thrillers. In English tradition, powerfully influenced by Christopher Marlowe's rendition of the German legend, characterizations of the ambitious knowledge-seeker tend to portray a scurrilous individual who, operating apart from his fellows, discovers some fundamental truth of the natural order. This scenario is ultimately derived from the shaman's homeopathic magic in which the application of both natural and supernatural forces corresponds to the manipulation of their signs, and is brought into play through the shaman's unique charismatic ability to identify with both worlds. However, Faust demeans this power. He discovers the true importance of his soul, which gives him this shamanistic ability, only after he has consigned it to Lucifer. The only actual magic he wields is that of summoning a demon to fulfill his desires. Like Faust's heavily qualified insight, the mad scientist's discovery of some arcane power is also paradoxically blind and self-centered. Although nominally rational and empirical, it links him to the world of magical practitioners like Agrippa, and especially to black magic or sorcery because the blind application of his principle threatens human society. Warrick comments that "Faust appears in SF as the contemporary magician, the man of science whose discoveries lead him to the secrets of the universe. Some of the stories also suggest that the tragic consequences of Faust's quest for knowledge may also be the consequences of the quest of modern science for knowledge" (33).

In his treatment of Hawthorne's fascination with the mad scientist figure, Taylor Stoehr has described this Promethean and Faustian heritage as "utopian" and "gothic": "While the utopian scientist may be either a model of self-sacrificing idealism or a self-deluded figure of fun, the gothic scientist is almost invariably a Faustian experimenter, sacrilegiously meddling with the souls of his victims and thereby forfeiting his own innocence" (252-53). From society's viewpoint, condemnation of the scientist as mad is typically justified when his insight is revealed to be perilously incomplete or tainted by self-seeking lusts, and therefore dystopian. In this way, magic and empirical science are alike, manipulations of a preordained cosmic order by signs (as in astrological or mathematical formulae) and substances (as in alchemical or laboratory experiments). The supernatural may be redefined by science as the unknown or unperceived natural order of things; however, both kinds of knowledge are often judged by society as belonging properly to God alone—as stolen fire.

Shakespeare's Prospero, conceived partly as a counter-figure to Marlovian portraits of Renaissance magician-scientists like England's own John Dee (1527-1600), has been proposed as the third literary origin of the mad scientist. In *The Emotional Significance of Imaginary Beings*, Robert Plank demonstrates that both Prospero and the mad scientist are outcast through their volatile interaction of hubris and blasphemy (the Promethean and the Faustian) with society's psychological defenses against them. His analysis also stresses that *The Tempest* contains a romance motif frequently associated with the mad scientist of contemporary popular culture: namely, his daughter's marriage to a young man who represents the scientist's enemies and is destined to save everything. Consequently, Prospero's mode is essentially Utopian. The "new Eden" which the scientist anticipates as the result of his research must have its Eve (or Lilith), yet the Adam which the motif presents is initially seen by the would-be "god" as an intruder or saboteur. He supplants the scientist in a Freudian "family romance," either murdering him as in an Oedipal conflict, or reconciling him, through the daughter's mediation, with society (Plank 157).

Plank's hypothesis is persuasive in its own terms and as a tool for analyzing such varied fictions as Hoffmann's "The Sandman," Hawthorne's "Rappaccini's Daughter," the science fiction movie *Forbidden Planet*, and Robert Bloch's parody of literary, cinematic and comic book formulas "The Strange Island of Dr. Nork." However, it clearly does not extend to all plots centering on mad scientists for the simple reason that not all mad scientists, literary or otherwise, *have* daughters (unless one wishes to consider the invention or discovery itself as "daughter"). Indeed, like Victor Frankenstein or Hawthorne's Aylmer in "The Birthmark," some have peer love interests. Others, like Hawthorne's Owen Warland in "The Artist of the Beautiful," have given up a woman for the obsessive pursuit of a craft or ideal, or like Stanley Kubrick's Dr. Strangelove, have no interest in love at all.

Yet Plank's scheme need not be applied so literally. *Frankenstein* also displaces Prospero's story through the monster's murder of Victor's intended bride Elizabeth, and then applies it in reverse when Victor creates and subsequently destroys a bride for the monster. In this interpretation, the monster or putative son replaces the daughter figure and thwarts the father's intended marriage; then the roles are exchanged as the scientist thwarts the marriage of the son. Victor's failure to provide a mate for his monster is presented not as an act of madness, however, but of social responsibility—despite its effect of ensuring his persecution. Similarly, Prospero himself may have merited his exile through overinvolvement in his arcane studies and neglect of his ducal affairs, but is no longer "mad" or misguided when *The Tempest* begins. Still, Frankenstein must die before his monster will disappear, and Prospero must acknowledge the passage of his fortunate star to Miranda and Ferdinand and abjure his magic, both to preserve his humane equilibrium (in which the interests of society supersede those of the individual) and to avoid offending Providence.

All three figures mentioned so far build upon one another and accumulate characteristics associated with the wizard or magus— one who possesses magical knowledge (or empirical knowledge interpreted as magical). Francis Yates's suggestion that both Marlowe's Doctor Faustus and Shakespeare's Prospero are counter-images of the historical Elizabethan magus John Dee (120, 160) is not idle speculation, therefore, but appropriate to the popular conception that all human wizards are morally suspect. Society has always tended to view magic with profound ambivalence. In English and French culture, the figure who has been the primary model for wizards since the Middle Ages is Merlin, King Arthur's legendary prophet and mastermind. Like Prospero and many other mad scientists, Merlin has the predominantly good intentions that helped to motivate the Western embrace of technology and empirical method. Yet he also retains a significant potential for evil; for both his conception and his eventual death or disappearance are tainted in literary tradition by demonic lust. This fruitful ambivalence, which I believe to be one reason for Merlin's continuing popularity as a cultural icon, also makes him an important if previously unacknowledged forerunner of the mad scientist.

Merlin has always been designed to tantalize us with his superior insight or intellect, and to employ it for the fulfillment of our wishes. First, he possesses the knowledge and power to improve our natural and social environment—to shape the phenomenal world to our wills. This ability to order phenomena grows out of the lesser ability to foresee or foretell it, which produces a fascinating development in the wizard's character.[3] Historically, Merlin develops from the widespread medieval wild man convention; his oracular inspiration is irrational rather than empirical, attributed by early Welsh poetry to possession *by* rather than *of* knowledge. Because the condition of the wild man is "separation from wonted or due status" both socially and mentally, it appears schizophrenically as insanity coupled with second sight (O'Riain 184). Merlin's insanity drives him to separate himself from society, which simultaneously seeks him out for his insight or foresight. Yet his supernatural perception can also be an unwelcome gift, since it repeatedly leads to the discovery of flaws in society (such as adultery) and his re-expulsion from human companionship.

In medieval terms, the wild man's power of insight and foresight also initiates him into supernatural or divine knowledge; in more modern terms, it serves as entry into the Jungian collective unconscious, or substratum of cultural archetypes. In medieval romance and most subsequent literature, Merlin's power eventually reintegrates his personality when his story is connected to King Arthur's and becomes dedicated to a new chivalric order. Consequently, he is portrayed as the servant of divine will and soon as the master of events rather than remaining at their mercy. This movement from neurosis to integration characterizes not just the wild man figure alone, but the whole literary development of Merlin as he becomes the master magician of English fiction.

Yet Merlin is also introduced in chronicle and romance as the son of a devil who intends him to be the Antichrist that will doom mankind. Because of his half-human status, as incomplete prophet, trickster and lustful old man, he retains the tension between neurosis and integration—and ironic treatments of him emphasize this tension. In addition, the flaws of the Camelot he advises suggest his ultimate failure as counselor and artificer and signal an oscillating rather than a linear movement, because neurosis is the human condition in a fallen world that nevertheless aspires to redemption. As dealers in illusion and reality, intermediaries between secular and sacred ontologies, all wizards share this equivocal movement between neurosis and integration. It is the foundation of their appeal.

A whole succession of late medieval and renaissance legends which culminate in Faust expand upon this ambivalence. The popularity of stories about Virgil the Necromancer (an imaginary figure based upon the Roman poet, whom John Spargo has called the "Medieval Wizard of Oz"), Roger Bacon, Robert Grosseteste and others gradually darken Merlin's essentially good characteristics, thus preparing audiences for figures like Faust and Victor Frankenstein. The Reformation audience responded to protoscientists like Agrippa, Paracelsus and Robert Fludd (whose largely symbolic methods were attacked by early empiricists like Kepler and Mersenne) with fascinated repulsion. Edward Peters has shown that "it was largely by lifting the portrait of the magician and the traits attributed to him out of their original contexts, and placing them in new contexts, that the sixteenth-century onslaught against magic and witchcraft was accomplished" (90-91). Peters concentrates on the doctrinal attack spearheaded by Protestantism and the Inquisition; but the movement in secular circles towards capitalism and empirical methods which de-emphasized spiritual influences were at least as important.

The mad scientist figure develops from this darkening lineage through stages in which the evil influence is considered as hereditary, then external and finally internal to the self. Merlin's legend reports that an incubus demon has engendered him; Faust summons Mephistopheles from hell; Frankenstein, Dr. Jekyll, *Forbidden Planet's* Doctor Morbius, and Marvel Comics's Victor von Doom all father their own inner demons through their lust for unlimited knowledge. Thus Donald Lawler can describe the methods of Frankenstein and Jekyll and Hyde as "a gothicized science, which subverts rational science by allowing direct access to the unconscious or preconscious self," and "a new way of expressing science as a human force" (251). Eventually the fruit of the wizard's labor is not a cultural savior for an oppressed people, like King Arthur, or even an absurd homunculus or talking head, but a monstrous double who is rejected by everyone and who persecutes his creator as he himself is persecuted. The quasi-religious quest for the Holy Grail of scientific revelation turns into a mutually destructive hide-and-seek battle with the nemesis loosed by the scientist's breakthrough discovery.

Merlin plays an important part in this development because he connects the Promethean, Faustian and Utopian modes. In *The Psychoanalysis of Fire*, Gaston Bachelard perceives in "the unconscious of the scientific mind" (10) a Prometheus complex which overcomes social prohibitions and "includes all those tendencies which impel us to know as much as our fathers, more than our fathers, as much as our teachers, more than our teachers"—an Oedipus complex of the intellect (12). For Bachelard, this knowledge is metaphorically identified with fire, and the "fire world" is intermediate between heaven and earth, divinity and mortality. The Celtic Merlin is driven mad by a fiery vision in the sky, and Geoffrey of Monmouth proposed that he was sired on a sleeping nun by a lustful incubus demon or fire spirit who lived between the earth and the moon. Robert de Boron and his French continuators strengthened the Faustian element by instituting this demon in Satan's entourage, and rationalizing Merlin's birth as a plot to counter Christ's harrowing of hell that is foiled only by the fortunate intervention of the nun's confessor Blaise and by God's grace. At the end of Merlin's life in Malory's interpretation, this heredity reasserts itself as he falls into dotage on a lady of the lake. Since the intellectual passion has decayed into a carnal one, he is shut up by her in a subterranean prison of his own making.

Merlin is often portrayed as an overachiever as well as a devil's son. His avowed purpose in romance is to reinstitute a golden age of British sovereignty through King Arthur, and he indisputably becomes the mastermind of Camelot. Nevertheless, his creative demiurge fails and Camelot falls from within. For all his prophetic ability, Merlin seems unaware to what extent the devil creates him and the homoerotic undercurrents of Arthurian society. Psychoanalyst Arthur Kimball has described this tendency in terms of Malory's own traumatic experience in the War of the Roses as a "repetition compulsion" which works out contemporary medieval history through legend (28). Yet long before Malory, it had been extended metaphorically to Merlin, who together with Arthur represents the highest creative forces in society. The compulsion appears most clearly in the wizard's arrangements of illicit sexual trysts that produce worthy knights (of which Arthur is the chief instance) as well as his lust for Vivian or Nimuë. The intrigue of his own birth, and of Arthur's, is replayed especially in Mordred's conception; the mage's neglect to inform Arthur of his relationship to Morgause compounds adultery with incest. In this sense, Merlin is perhaps as much Mordred's "uncle" as Arthur is. Initially, Merlin's aim is to reconstruct the dismembered corpse of British power into a new political creature of chivalry. But if Camelot is largely his creation, then the sexual undertow that corrupts it in treatments like Tennyson's *Idylls of the King* and Robert Nye's *Merlin* also corresponds to Frankenstein's "filthy workshop of creation," and Mordred's rebellion to the monster's. Merlin pursues Nimuë and Mordred Guinevere, Frankenstein's monster strangles Frankenstein's younger brother and bride, Hyde tramples a young girl and bludgeons an inoffensive old man to death. So much for chivalry. The grail quest for life's secret is succeeded by a hard fall from grace.

Thus Faust's and Prospero's human fallibility eventually demythologizes Merlin. This negative potential appeared from Merlin's beginning as a man punished by madness for his transgressions, and as the influence of Arthurian romance waned he was occasionally portrayed as wholly evil. In Lewis Theobald's *Merlin: or, The Devil of Stonehenge*, the mage actually takes the role of Mephistopheles; the hero, named Harlequin, succumbs to the sexual blandishments of Merlin's demonic handmaidens and is renamed Faustulus in hell.

More recently, the developing image of the mad scientist has itself refertilized portrayals of Merlin. While the wizard himself is portrayed in Twain's *A Connecticut Yankee in King Arthur's Court* as an anachronistic charlatan, Hank Morgan, the representative of the capitalistic and industrial age, is not only his replacement but his double. This new Merlin's schemes also go horribly wrong in a holocaust which destroys all of Arthur's knights—not only because of the imperfections and abuses of medieval society but because of Hank's increasingly self-righteous pride in his technological innovations and blind meddling in the feudal order.

Roger Zelazny's Nebula Award-winning story "He Who Shapes" introduces an even more up-to-date Merlin analogue, the psychiatrist Charles Render, who applies future technology, archetypal images, and the repetition compulsion (which Render calls "autopsychomimesis") to manipulate his patients' dreams. The danger of this therapy is that the doctor may become too personally involved in the dream world and contract the patients' psychoses. This happens to Render when he treats and falls in love with another psychiatrist, the blind and suggestively named Eileen Shallot (for Tennyson's "The Lady of Shalott," which retells the story of Elaine of Astolat who conceives Galahad and dies for love of Lancelot). Render is driven mad and imprisoned in an Arthurian dreamworld as surely as Merlin is imprisoned by Nimuë. In "The Last Defender of Camelot," Zelazny portrays Merlin himself as an insane idealist who can animate a suit of armor, and whose reawakening from Nimuë's spell threatens the fragile equilibrium of twentieth-century diplomacy. The sorcerously preserved Lancelot and Morgan Le Fay must battle him in Stonehenge, a prehistoric scientific marvel which Geoffrey of Monmouth first attributed to Merlin. Lancelot tells him, "You say that your ends are noble...but I do not believe you. Perhaps in the old days they were. But more than the times have changed. You yourself are different" (288).

The theme of a maladjusted Merlin reawakening is also developed in Peter Dickinson's *The Weathermonger*, in which the wizard is a mutant whose bias against machine technology and its pollution of the environment reverses the mad scientist's devotion to technical progress by returning England to the Dark Ages. In K.W. Jeter's ingenious *Morlock Night*, a Doctor Ambrose (for Ambrosius, one of Merlin's medieval names) must enlist the help of a reincarnated Arthur named Edwin Hacker to thwart an invasion of Morlocks into 1982 London. The Morlocks, who have killed H.G. Wells's Time Traveller and taken over his machine, are masterminded by Ambrose's evil counterpart Dr. Merdenne (developed from Merlin's Welsh name, Myrddin). By contrast, David Drake's *The Dragon Lord* reimagines the wizard in the Dark Age rather than in a modern context. There, Merlin's magical technology summons a wyvern to aid Arthur in his battles, but the monster grows too large and he eventually loses control of it. As the seeress Veleda accuses him, "You're a man who rolls a rock down a mountainside and expects to run with it, Merlin. You can't control a landslide just because you had the power to begin it. There are no fools in the world so great as the ones who think themselves knowing" (148-49).

Thus, the mad scientist is in one sense a technologized Merlin as well as a Prometheus, a Faust, a Prospero. Metaphorically and historically speaking, the mutating figure of Merlin has come to include these three traditional models of the type, thus becoming master trope or icon. He is like Prometheus in his half-divinity, cunning and foresight, his intermediary status as light-bringer to a benighted society and his interminable imprisonment. He is like Faust in his unquenchable curiosity and human imperfection, penchant for tricks, susceptibility to erotic desires, and damnable connection to the demon world. And he combines these similarities with the positive example of Prospero, who learns through bitter experience to reconcile his own appetites and attainments with the workings of Providence and the demands of society.

These conventions are attributed to the mad scientist by a populace which does not share his special expertise, and which therefore views it alternately with admiration and suspicion. His genius has been individually determined as a natural gift of heredity, grace or study—Merlin's abilities in medieval romance come from both the devil, who gives him his knowledge of what has been, and from God, who gives him knowledge of what is and is to come; in modern treatments they are as often the product of hard work and study to develop his innate talent. However, his "madness" is socially determined because all extraordinary genius provokes doubt in ordinary mortals—a doubt confirmed in the literature by events. Whereas the mad scientist is Promethean or concerned chiefly with discovery and innovation, society is typically Epimethean or concerned with consequences after they occur. This ambivalence is one reason why so many mad scientists are presented as doppelgängers: Merlin and Arthur decay or split into Merlin and Mordred, Faust and Mephistopheles, Frankenstein and his monster, Jekyll and Hyde, Ambrose and Merdenne, Ben Kenobi and Darth Vader, Yoda and the Emperor, Doctor Who and the Master.

The mad scientist icon therefore depends upon a social perspective, which is justified in two main ways. First of all, the scientist becomes isolated from society; either he distances himself from others in order to pursue his investigations with less chance of interruption, or others distance themselves from him because they perceive him as "strange" or threatening. Physical isolation connotes mental isolation, and implies madness because it removes the figure from the behavioral norms and consequences which define "sanity." His isolation also encourages the scientist's functional abuse of his abilities. Perhaps this is one reason why the popular image of the scientist or inventor is of a person working alone, whereas most scientific work is actually performed in social collaboration. Zelazny's Merlin becomes mad, for example, because his vision of Camelot has become detached from social realities and his idealism has become oppressive. Intellectual isolation and detachment from society create a vicious circle that spirals to disaster.

Second, the mad scientist is usually seen as initially rational in respect to his discovery or creation, but subsequently irrational in respect to its uses or consequences. His identification with it becomes both narcissistic and atavistic. These urges may originate a desire to protect and nurture a younger generation, as Merlin protects and nurtures the young Arthur, but eventually they degenerate into self-love or sexual lust and even murder or genocide. The mad scientist compels popular imagination, then, because despite his great abilities he comes to grief through some transgressive act—either his own, or the savage response of a horrified society, or both. Most of all, his narcissism and atavism arise from the uncontrolled and jealous nature of his own ego turned inward upon itself. This is another reason for the frequency of doppelgängers in the literature. With such motifs, stories of mad wizards or scientists confirm society's urge to reveal the monstrous id lurking behind the intellect, to discover the light-bringer as Satan and to confirm its hard-won communal or tribal conventions. This habit contradicts the myth of control in science and technology and the illusion that they are value-blind, for all discoveries eventually have applications, and those applications have consequences which are judged in terms of human and social values.

According to most Arthurian romances, Merlin contains and masters his devil until Nimuë or Vivian sinks him, as in *The Tempest* Prospero sinks his book, deeper than a plummet sounds. Nevertheless, Merlin's and the mad scientist's fall does not leave society blameless. Despite a wizard's role in its creation, Camelot as a shared and approved social vision pays the price not only for his faults but for his absence and its own faults. Similarly, Stevenson's Dr. Jekyll and Wells's Dr. Moreau only seem to place the moral burden on the mad scientist rather than on society by externalizing their own inner hideousness through their more limited creations: the murderous Hyde identity and the pathetic, essentially subhuman Beast People. These anti-Hippocratic doctors share their identities with their nemeses—and most people still confuse Frankenstein's identity with his monster's. This irony permits them (and us) to identify the isolating obsession with the scientist rather than the culture or nation, and to displace guilt for the unsavory consequences of radical innovation. The mad scientist reverses Merlin's essentially positive character by illustrating action and thought divorced from morality and ethics, and reverses Merlin's literary evolution from savage beast to sophisticated superman by releasing the destructive power of his own repressed desires. Characters like Prospero and Doctor Morbius eventually join the good Merlin by reason of their benevolent goals (the pursuit of responsible utopianism and knowledge beneficial to mankind) as well as by their willingness to atone for their errors and to abjure the power they dare no longer wield. Yet all of these characters are subject to dooms of their own making, just as Merlin's *fine amour* imprisons him in a cage of his own design.

Consequently, the figure of the mad scientist continues to question both individual and cultural causes of Merlin's ambiguous end even while diverting attention from the societies which produce him and his successors. Modern images of the mad scientist can range from relatively harmless and only inadvertently destructive absent-minded putterers in basement laboratories to powerful intellectual megalomaniacs in control of nuclear arsenals. Established in popular tradition by a paradoxical liaison between creative idealism, technical innovation and corrupting lusts gone awry through isolation and overweening absorption in scientific research, the mad scientist or anti-Merlin embodies visions of what can happen to the white wizard when the demons within (or without) him are released through the alchemical interaction of divine knowledge, human fallibility and demonic ambition.

I do not wish to recreate the overstatement of Aldiss or Plank by proposing Merlin himself as the originating figure of the mad scientist (after all, which Merlin would that be—the Celtic wild man, Geoffrey of Monmouth's wonder child sired by an incubus, King Arthur's wise counselor, Nimuë's senile pursuer, or Zelazny's reawakened madman?). Many figures contribute to the lineage of the mad scientist. These prototypes, both mythic and historical, extend back even before literature to an irrecoverable era when humankind may not yet have recognized itself as knowledge-bearing or knowledge-producing. Merlin is the most imaginatively flexible and one of the most culturally significant of such figures, drawing upon and mediating among their manifold characteristics. His early conceptual roots as oracle, religious heretic, holy or unholy wild man or the woods, Indo-European shaman and mythical trickster or overachiever are undoubtedly those of the mad scientist as well. He links the pre-Christian context of Prometheus, which presupposes the sinful nature of the gods, with the Christian context of Faust, which presupposes the sinful nature of man. And like literary mad scientists, his figure develops by assimilating new modes of knowledge. Scientific or technical knowledge itself is not necessary for such development, only exemplary. The entire cultural history of ideas forms an imaginative continuum out of which popular wizards like Merlin and subsequent wizardly offshoots like science fictional mad scientists emerge. Without Prometheus, Merlin, Faust, Prospero and, yes, Frankenstein—and without the fascinating lineage of prototypes comprehended by Western societies through them—the personality of the mad scientist would elude modern conception.

Notes

[1] This essay is a revised and expanded version of a paper initially written for the 1983 Popular Culture Association Annual Meeting in Toronto, Canada, and published in *Extrapolation* 27.2 (Summer 1986): 109-15.

[2] Suvin's tendency to interpret mad scientists as an elite but abstracted product of mercantile society interestingly mirrors Walter Hirsch's earlier description of SF scientists between 1926 and 1950. He observes that the scientists of that period decline under the influences of the social sciences, "magical or charismatic" mental powers, and the figure of the alien; the real "mad scientist" of the quarter century seems to have been the narrow-minded or manipulative businessman like Sinclair Lewis's George Babbitt. The mad scientist and the evil capitalist (as in today's junk bond wizards) are thus analogous character types in western culture.

[3] The development summarized in this paragraph and the next is treated at greater length in my article "The Metamorphosis of a Mage" and *The Romance of Merlin*.

Works Cited

Aldiss, Brian W. "A Monster for All Seasons." *Science Fiction Dialogues*. Ed. Gary Wolfe. Chicago: Academy Chicago, 1982.

——. *Billion Year Spree: The True History of Science Fiction*. New York: Schocken Books, 1974.

Aldiss, Brian W. with David Winfield. *Trillion Year Spree: The History of Science Fiction*. New York: Atheneum, 1986.

Asimov, Isaac. *Asimov's Biographical Encyclopedia of Science and Technology*. Rev. ed. Garden City: Doubleday, 1972.

Bachelard, Gaston. *The Psychoanalysis of Fire*. Trans. Alan C.M. Ross. Boston: Beacon, 1964.

Bloch, Robert. "The Strange Island of Dr. Nork." *Mad Scientists: An Anthology of Fantasy and Horror*. Ed. Stuart David Schiff. Garden City: Doubleday, 1980.

Callahan, Patrick J. "Frankenstein, Bacon, and the 'Two Truths.'" *Extrapolation* 14.1 (Dec. 1972): 39-48.

Culler, Jonathan. *The Pursuit of Signs*. Ithaca: Cornell UP, 1981.

Dickinson, Peter. *The Weathermonger*. New York: DAW, 1968.

Drake, David. *The Dragon Lord*. New York: TOR, 1982.

Famous Histories of Fryer Bacon. London: M. Clark, 1679.

Geoffrey of Monmouth. *History of the Kings of Britain*. Trans. Lewis Thorpe. Harmondsworth: Penguin, 1966.

————. *Vita Merlini*. Ed. and trans. J.J. Parry. Urbana: U of Illinois P, 1925.

Goodrich, Peter. "The Metamorphosis of a Mage." *Avalon to Camelot* 2.4 (1987): 4-8.

Hawthorne, Nathaniel. *Nathaniel Hawthorne's Tales*. Ed. James McIntosh. New York: W.W. Norton, 1987.

Hirsch, Walter. "Image of the Scientist in Science Fiction." *American Journal of Sociology* 43.3 (Mar. 1958): 506-12.

Hoffmann, E.T.A. "The Sandman." *Selected Writings of Hoffmann*. 2 vols. Eds. and trans. Leonard J. Kent and Elizabeth C. Knight. Chicago: U of Chicago P, 1969.

Jeter, K.W. *Morlock Night*. New York: DAW, 1979.

Kimball, Arthur Samuel. "Merlin's Miscreation and the Repetition Compulsion in Malory's Morte d'Arthur." *Literature and Psychology* 25.1 (1975): 27-33.

Lawler, Donald. "Reframing *Jekyll and Hyde*: Robert Louis Stevenson and the Strange Case of the Gothic Science Fiction." *Dr. Jekyll and Mr. Hyde after One Hundred Years*. Eds. William Veeder and Gordon Hirsch. Chicago: U of Chicago P, 1988.

Malory, Sir Thomas. *The Works*. Ed. Eugene Vinaver. 2nd ed. 3 vols. Oxford; Clarendon, 1967; rev. 1973.

Marlowe, Christopher. *Doctor Faustus*. Ed. John D. Jump London: Methuen, 1965.

Nye, Robert. *Merlin*. New York: G.P. Putnam's Sons, 1979.

O'Riain, Padraig. "A Study of the Irish Legend of the Wild Man." *Eigse* 14.3 (Summer 1972).

Peters, Edward. *The Magician, the Witch, and the Law*. Philadelphia: U of Philadelphia P, 1978.

Plank, Robert. *The Emotional Significance of Imaginary Beings*. Springfield: Charles C. Thomas, 1968.

Price, Derek de Solla. *Science since Babylon*. Enl. ed. New Haven: Yale UP, 1975.

The Romance of Merlin. Ed. Peter H. Goodrich. New York: Garland, 1990.

Shakespeare, William. *The Tempest*. Ed. Northrop Frye. *The Riverside Shakespeare*. Ed. G. Blakemore Evans. Boston: Houghton Mifflin, 1974.

Shelley, Mary. *Frankenstein*. Ed. James Rieger. New York: Signet, 1983. (Since this is an article about origins, I have chosen to cite the 1818 text, although many now consider the 1831 text, Ed. M.K. Joseph. [Oxford: Oxford UP, 1971], to be definitive.)

Spargo, John Webster. *Virgil the Necromancer: Studies in Virgilian Legends*. Cambridge: Harvard UP, 1934.

Stableford, Brian. S.v. "Scientists." *The Science Fiction Encyclopedia*. Ed. Peter Nicholls. Garden City: Doubleday, 1979.

Stevenson, Robert Louis. *The Strange Case of Dr. Jekyll and Mr. Hyde and Other Stories*. Ed. Jenni Calder. Harmondsworth: Penguin, 1979.

Stoehr, Taylor. *Hawthorne's Mad Scientists: Pseudoscience and Social Science in Nineteenth-Century Life and Letters*. Hamden: Archon, 1978.

Stuart, W.J. *Forbidden Planet*. Boston: Gregg, 1979.

Suvin, Darko. *The Metamorphoses of Science Fiction: On the Poetics and History of a Literary Genre*. New Haven: Yale UP, 1979.

Swift, Jonathan. *Gulliver's Travels*. Rev. Ed. Robert A. Greenberg. New York: W.W. Norton, 1970.

Tennyson, Alfred Lord. *Idylls of the King*. Ed. J.M. Gray. New Haven: Yale UP, 1983.

———. *The Poems of Tennyson*. Ed. Christopher Ricks. London: Longmans, 1969.

Theobald, [Lewis]. *Merlin; or, The Devil of Stonehenge*. London: John Watt, 1734.

Twain, Mark. *A Connecticut Yankee in King Arthur's Court*. Ed. Bernard L. Stein. Berkeley: U of California P, 1983.

Warrick, Patricia S. *The Cybernetic Imagination in Science Fiction*. Cambridge: MIT P, 1980.

Wells, Herbert George. *The Island of Dr. Moreau*. London: Heinemann, 1896.

Yates, Francis A. *The Occult Philosophy in the Elizabethan Age*. London: Routledge and Kegan Paul, 1979.

Zelazny, Roger. *The Last Defender of Camelot*. New York: Pocket Books, 1980.

Madness, Masochism and Morality: Dostoyevsky and His Underground Man

Thomas C. Fiddick

Fyodor Dostoyevsky may well have been the greatest "psychological novelist" of the nineteenth century, or even of all time. His themes and characters prefigured many of the terms and insights coined, or discovered, by Freud and other founders of modern psychiatry. His characters, especially the Underground Man, are fictional examples of the terminology used to describe deviant behavior and madness in the twentieth century. This essay will examine how the strange behaviors and unconscious impulses in *Notes from Underground* parallel numerous modern notions about mental illness, especially the concepts of the obsessive-compulsive, masochist, paranoid, schizophrenic, epileptic and "detached neurotic," but also the sadism of displaced hostility.

Freud, of course, saw proofs of his Oedipus complex in the family conflicts of *The Brothers Karamazov*. But other works by the Russian can be read as "case studies" of various psychic disorders. *The Gambler* was a semi-self-portrait of an "obsessive" personality. *The Possessed* (also translated as *The Devils*) has been called the greatest political novel ever written, and as a psychological study of political fanaticism it was a forerunner of Harold Lasswell's *Psychopathology and Politics*. *The Idiot* pictured the "divine madness" to be found in those "holy fools" who dotted the landscape of Orthodox Russia. *Crime and Punishment* can be variously interpreted. It might be seen as a portrait of a "split personality" with its protagonist, who struggles with his dual nature, named Raskolnikov, from the Russian word for split, or schism—*Raskol*—while the more normal, integrated personality is named for the Russian word *Razum*, meaning "reason." But Raskolnikov might also be seen as an intellectually motivated psychopath, trying to prove, before Nietzsche ever wrote his works, that he was "beyond good and evil"—a "superman" whose "will to power" was on a par with that "Anti-Christ," Napoleon.

The infamous German philosopher once "admitted" (or bragged) that Dostoyevsky was the "only psychologist...from whom

I had something to learn." The intensely Christian Russian would probably have been amazed and appalled to have learned that the champion of anti-Christian morality and master-race theorist had so misread him and his intentions. (Perhaps it is the occupational hazard of genius to be misunderstood.) For Nietzsche apparently thought that Dostoyevsky, "deep down," admired criminals. He lauded "this profound human being, who was ten times right in his low estimate of the superficial Germans," and pointed out that, during his imprisonment and exile, he "lived for a long time among the convicts in Siberia—hardened criminals for whom there was no way back to society—and found them very different from what he himself had expected: they were carved out of just about the best, hardest, and most valuable wood that grows anywhere on Russian soil" (Kaufmann 549-50).

What Nietzsche was referring to, and may have just read, was *Notes from the House of the Dead*, which Dostoyevsky wrote after a decade of forced labor and exile in Siberia, followed by forced service in the Russian Army in the Far Eastern province. Far from idealizing the criminals with whom he came in contact, he was disturbed by the lack of conscience he observed among the "deprived and depraved," and became fascinated by criminal psychology after that harrowing experience. While retaining his earlier interest in those innocent "poor folk" who felt "insulted and injured" by an oppressive social system, he became increasingly concerned about the evil men do and the question of guilt and redemption for tormented, twisted souls who commit crimes. Seven years after Nietzsche's death in 1900, a book appeared with the title *The Semi-Insane and the Semi-Responsible*, which paid quite a different tribute to Dostoyevsky's work than the German paid it: "Fifty years before the appearance of criminal anthropology he described types of criminals in *The House of the Dead* among which there is not one single character that has not been confirmed by the...laborious investigations of...criminologists" (qtd. in Kravchenko 160-61).

Maria Kravchenko, who cited this passage in her excellent survey of psychological interpretations of Dostoyevsky's works, also pointed out that the Russian novelist, whatever his contribution to criminal anthropology, avoided a rigid "dosiometry," that method of classifying types, or "pigeon-holing the human personality." She also noted that Dostoyevsky concluded that punishment fails to "reform" the criminal; on the contrary, isolation and punishment often "achieve the very reverse of their intended purpose" by hardening the convict, eliminating any sense of guilt. She further used an interesting term to describe the psychic state of the criminals populating the "house of the dead"—"moral insanity"—as originally coined by the psychologist and student of Dostoyevsky, Chizh. The modern-day term which corresponds most accurately to "moral insanity" is the mental "state of a psychopath"—a person "devoid of moral sensibility" (Kravchenko 161, 81).

Actual insanity was explored by the early Dostoyevsky in his book, *The Double*, in which the hero, Goliadkin, is literally "taken away" at the end as completely mad. Lawrence Kohlberg has argued that, though this work "is a striking portrayal of the paranoid attitude, it is not the portrayal of a genuine paranoid psychosis." This is because, "While the typical paranoid concept is one of spotless self-blame being unjustly tortured and blamed by others who are evil, Dostoyevsky's hallucinatory Doubles...persecute their creators by asserting their identity with them." Although "Goliadkin's behavior...with his delusions of persecutory...figures" would appear to betray symptoms of paranoid-schizophrenia, especially when his personality splits in half and drives him insane, Kohlberg disputes such a diagnosis. He suggests that the character lacks a necessary "delusion of grandeur" to accompany his delusion of persecution. He suffers instead from low self-esteem and shame, and, like other "doubles which appear in later works"—Stavrogin (in *The Possessed*) and Ivan Karamazov—displays "classical symptoms of the obsessive-compulsive character," struggling "between autonomy of will and shame." Kohlberg also maintains that this "psychoanalytic notion helps us understand the literary structure of *Notes from Underground* in which the first part of the book contains the ideological assertion of free will...while the second part...makes excursions into self-degradation," expressive of the "'shame-humiliation' syndrome" (Kohlberg 346-62; Kravchenko 144-45).

Concerning this latter book, Kravchenko has written that it is Dostoyevsky's "greatest essay on the human will and the psychological basis of inferiority, and since it expounds the bankruptcy of reason it places the psychological center of gravity in the emoto-volitional field" (162). Such a view is confirmed by the foremost scholar to have written on *Notes from Underground*. Robert L. Jackson, in his monumental treatment of that work and its impact on Russian (and world) literature, wrote: "In this living image of solitude and despair, Dostoyevsky reaffirms the absolute value and integrity of the single, separate individual.... In its irrationalist spirit, its critique of reason...its scepticism...its offended idealism" and "its defense of the individual and despairing confession of impotence and error," it is "a work of modern consciousness." The famous, and nameless, "anti-hero"—well-known as The Underground Man—"is in permanent rebellion. This is his tragic status—his metaphysical misery and his metaphysical freedom" (Jackson 13-15).

The internationally respected literary critic George Steiner has likewise argued that "it was in *Notes from Underground* that he resolved most decisively the problem of dramatizing through a single voice the many-tongued chaos of human consciousness.... No other text by Dostoyevsky has exerted more influence on twentieth century thought or technique" of writing. Referring to the passages in which the anti-hero confesses that he "could not even become an insect," Steiner points to Franz Kafka's portrait of a man who *did* become an insect, in *Metamorphosis*, and asserts that since this underground man appeared "we know that the insect is gaining on the part of man. Ancient mythology dealt with men who were half-gods; post-Dostoyevskian mythology depicts roaches who are half-men." Concerning the man from the underground and his "bilious masochism," the critic notes that he not only "affects a sense of self-loathing" but "is genuinely odious" (Steiner 220-28).

The view of the Underground Man as repugnant will not be universally accepted by those who admire his individualism and refusal to bow down to "reality"—even the mathematical reality that "two times two is four." But Steiner appreciates what that character tells us about ourselves and our age. Calling *Notes* a "Dostoyevskian *summa*—even if we grant that the narrator's views cannot be identified with the novelist's," he praises the anti-hero because he "expresses through his acts and language a final 'No.'" And, given the history of the twentieth century, it is a pity that more people did not say nyet! "Our times—the world of death camps—confirms beyond denial Dostoyevsky's insights into the savagery of men, in their inclination, both as individuals and as hordes, to stamp out within themselves the embers of humanity. The subterranean narrator defines his species as 'A creature which walks on two legs and is devoid of gratitude'" (Steiner 228-30).

Steiner's keen insights, so long ignored by other critics and analysts, are valuable for both their psychological and sociological, not to mention their historical, perspective. He argues that "Dostoyevsky stands out as one of the foremost students of the schizophrenic"—implicitly comparing the nineteenth century Russian with that twentieth century American "student of the schizophrenic," Kurt Vonnegut. Like the famous Hoosier novelist, Dostoyevsky, or his narrator, "recounts his abject experiences 'as a well-merited punishment'"—like Kilgore Trout becoming a "jailbird." He embodies "both a philosophic myth—the rebellion against positivism—and a psychological myth—the descent of man into the darkness of the soul." Also like Vonnegut, and another American author, Walker Percy (*Lost in the Cosmos*; *The Second Coming*), the Russian novelist was engaged in "polemics against spiritual nihilism" and the erosive, disintegrating effects of modernity on the soul. As Steiner observed, Dostoyevsky, along with "Engels and Zola," was "one of the first to realize what factor labour" and other institutions, such as bureaucracies, "can do to eradicate individual traits or the play of intelligence on a man's face," for "capital and bureaucracy" have "left him without an overcoat" (216, 235).

The question of how the Underground Man came to be the strange "paradoxicalist" he described himself as being has been addressed by several writers who are more interested in explaining his evolution than in just describing or defining him. One Danish scholar, who explored the relationship between that character and the later figure of Raskolnikov, has suggested that they are similar in that they both lived literally beneath the ground, in cellars. He also pointed out in his study that the Russian term for the character is *podpolnik*, derived from the title, *Zapiski iz podpoliia*, and the peculiarities of his ideas, attitudes and life style largely stem from his "living quarters" (Villadsen 14). And thus when Dostoyevsky suddenly has his *podpolnik* say, "Incidentally, there is a whole psychological system in this," he is suggesting that an underground mentality is the byproduct of a physically underground existence.

Another attempt to explain the *podpolnik* and his attitudes or behavior has been made by Bernard Paris. Suggesting that the psychological system that best does this is that of Karen Horney, he cites many oft-overlooked details about the anti-hero's own past, as related both to the reader and to a prostitute he visits in Part II. Pointing to the "singularly bleak and loveless childhood" experienced by the *podpolnik*, Paris argues that the character opted for a "compliant" or "I don't care" strategy for "coping with his environment," becoming in Horney's terms a "detached neurotic" (Paris 511-12).

Regardless of the psychological terminology used to analyze, or perhaps peg and pigeon-hole, the *podpolnik*—obsessive-compulsive, masochist, paranoid, schizophrenic or detached neurotic—there remains the question, why did Dostoyevsky create him? One of the most recent, and controversial, studies of the artist and his work has been done by James L. Rice, who has tried to relate the novelist's epilepsy to his creations. His thesis is that the man's "greatness lies not in the denial of illness but in its acceptance and mastery, and in the discovery...of polymorphous and polyphonic values precisely within his pathological condition, which he consciously and ingeniously negotiated through art. What he rejected for the sake of artistic productivity was by no means his epilepsy but on the contrary—medical science and the therapeutic methods which it offered" (Rice 234).

Rice's contention challenges all Dostoyevsky readers and scholars to reconsider, and reread, that master through altered lenses. "As all readers of Dostoyevsky's novels should be aware," he has pointed out, "what can be called an epileptic emotional state, with plunges in and out of consciousness, sudden shifts of mood, and swings from exaltation to guilt, is common in many of his fictional characters. In addition, there is hardly a novel in which 'illness,' whether physical or mental, does not play a prominent role." Indeed, the opening words spoken by the *podpolnik* are: "I am a sick man...a spiteful man...an unpleasant man. I think my liver is diseased." Even consciousness itself is called a "disease."

One criticism of Rice's work argues that it, and he, "tend to entitize Dostoyevsky's epilepsy. That is, he views it as a cause in its own right, an inner 'illness' whose periodic eruption" (once every three weeks on the average) was "itself the source of anxiety. This view is apparent when he speaks of 'real mental illness' or traces anxiety to the fear that epilepsy might progress to 'insanity' or that death might result from an 'apoplectic stroke.'" Rice has suggested that the first truly psychological novel, *The Double*, which the initial admirer and "discoverer" of Dostoyevsky, literary critic Belinsky, denounced as belonging "in a mad-house," actually reflected anxieties about his epilepsy—that "Goliadkin's splitting in half is the literary counterpart of his creator's death anxiety." However debatable that specific interpretation may be, this critic concludes that "Rice presents a model—Dostoyevsky as his own doctor-therapist" (Breger 735-37).

Notes from Underground partly supports this view of Rice's *Dostoyevsky and the Healing Art*. Although there are no epileptics in that work, as there are in four others he wrote, and it is *hyper-consciousness*, rather than a lack of consciousness, which he and his narrator fret about, the author's distrust of the medical profession is apparent. He implies that it is "superstitious...to respect medicine," and refuses to see a doctor about his alleged liver ailment, saying "I refuse to treat it out of spite," knowing full well that "I only injure myself.... My liver is bad, well then—let it get even worse." This initial reference to a "liver" ailment is misleading, of course, for it soon becomes apparent that the *podpolnik* suffers from a personality, not a physical, disorder. And Dostoyevsky may well have been referring to the medieval superstition which attributed character traits to "humors," which in turn were supposedly related to parts of the body. The liver is the source of "bile," and thus the personality which corresponds to that organ is "bilious"—choleric and irritable.

Steiner implicitly suggested his understanding of this connection by referring to the "bilious masochism of the underground man." And Joseph Frank, the most thorough of all students and biographers of Dostoyevsky, has noted the "inverted irony" of the liver symbolism. Moreover, in his translation of two key sentences from the work, Frank revealed the actual source of the *podpolnik*'s "bilious" resentments and what makes him "abnormal." In describing the "normal" man of action, symbolized both by a "bull" and by a military officer named Zverkov (whose name derives from the Russian word for "beast"—zverk), the "anti-hero" confesses: "I envy such a man till my bile overflows" (translated by some as "till I am green in the face.") And, as if to drive the point home, the novelist has his character repeat several pages later: "I envy the normal man to the last drop of my bile" (Frank 235, 321, 331).

Notes from Underground is partly a study in the rancor of resentment and suppressed revenge, showing how the effects of envy eat away at the soul. It is also a study of masochism, for the *podpolnik* confesses to feeling pleasure from pain—the pain of his body (a toothache) and the pain to his psyche caused by petty humiliations and jealousies. He confesses that a "nasty desire to repay with spite whoever has offended" his mousy ego "rankles," but soon becomes a sensual pleasure and he enjoys "lacerating and irritating himself." He even tries to stage a scene in which an officer he hates, or envies, will throw him out of a tavern window. As one of the foremost students of the subject, Theodor Reik, observed, the "masochist...conjures up what he fears, staging scenes of pain and humiliation." His "ego not only is willing to pay the high price of discomfort and humiliation, but even longs for pain and humiliation" (Dostoyevsky 10-11; Reik 119).

Another example of his apparent delight in self-inflicted pain is the scene in which the *podpolnik* describes the ordeal of simply walking down Nevsky Prospect in class-ridden, or rank-ridden, St. Petersburg—an experience which perhaps only blacks in America, walking the streets of race-conscious Southern cities in the "bad old days," can appreciate. "I did not stroll so much as experience innumerable torments, humiliations and resentments.... I used to wriggle like an eel among the passers-by...continually making way for generals, for officers of the Guards and the Hussars, or for ladies." Yet, ironically, he admits that this "was no doubt just what I wanted," and he experienced a "regular martyrdom," even though it made him feel like "a fly in the eyes of the whole world.... Why I inflicted this torture on myself...I don't know. I felt simply drawn there." Yet Dostoyevsky's pathetic *podpolnik* also made this profound observation about the pervasiveness of a system of "dominance-submission," to use Erich Fromm's term: nearly everyone else also felt inferior to someone in the pecking order of Russian society. The officer he resented "made way for generals and persons of high rank, and he, too, shifted among them like an eel." Yet, when approaching someone of lesser, or no, rank, "he simply walked over them" as though "there was nothing but empty space before him, and never, under any circumstances, moved over" (Dostoyevsky 46).

This seemingly insignificant scene, or observation, was in reality a key to understanding the novel and at least one of the many "messages" Dostoyevsky hoped to convey. In modern psychological parlance, any hierarchical social system based on dominance and submission tends to create the sado-masochistic character type. Dostoyevsky is not usually seen as a social critic, especially after his imprisonment for reading forbidden literature and being a utopian socialist in 1849. But Geoffrey Kabat has convincingly argued that, upon his return from Siberia, the novelist "presents both a critique of society" as well as "a criticism of...the excesses of the critics themselves" (8). Although *Notes from Underground* contains a polemic against the utopian, utilitarian novel *What is to be Done?*—by Chernyshevsky—Dostoyevsky was in a sense presenting an even more radical revelation, or exposé, about the nature of the Tsarist, bureaucratic political and social system.

This interpretation is borne out in the opening scene, in which the anti-hero as a civil servant admits that he was "rude and took pleasure in being so" toward his petitioners. "After all, I did not accept bribes, so I was bound to find compensation in that, at least." And he adds, parenthetically, "(A bad joke, but I will not cross it out.)" This innocuous passage was actually a daring criticism of the system, suggesting that all *chinovniki*, or officials (literally, people with "rank"), were either bribe-takers or petty sadists who enjoyed lording it over civilians. He grows to resent an officer who clanked his sword "in a disgusting way," and after he resigns from the civil service he gnashes his teeth at nearly every military officer he encounters. The intense conflict between "civilian and official Russia" which was so pervasive in nineteenth-century Tsarist society (and is also pervasive in Russian society today) has never been explored so well as by this novelette.

The process whereby people in a class society must submit to superiors while being free to bully inferiors will encourage the phenomenon which psychologists call "displaced hostility." Having to "take it" from the stronger, people tend to "take it out" on those who are weaker. Dostoyevsky noticed this process once when a coachman he had witnessed being humiliated by his "master" began beating a luckless horse *he* controlled. The scene made an indelible impression on him, and in *Notes from Underground* he created a parallel scene, which has been overlooked by most if not all the many analysts of that work.

The *podpolnik* had just been humiliated at a party thrown for a former school chum, Zverkov. Although feeling snubbed he decided to join the group on a trip to a house of ill repute. He hired a coach, or "sledge," and while dwelling on his insulted ego suddenly "punched the sledge-driver on the back of the neck...'What are you hitting me for?' the poor man shouted, but he whipped up his nag so that it began to kick out" (Dostoyevsky 75). This minor scene is a dramatic foreshadowing of the final, climactic confrontation between the "anti-hero" and the prostitute, Liza.

His first encounter with the girl is tender, and the *podpolnik* seems out of character. He has a heart-to-heart conversation with her, reminiscing about his own sad childhood and commiserating with her unhappy past. He tries to talk her into quitting her profession by describing in dark detail the destitution and degradation that await her as she grows old, mistreated by both her customers and her madame, eventually dying from consumption and buried in a swampy grave. By contrast, he paints an idyllic picture of what family life can be. In one extended, often ignored paragraph he uses the word "joy" or "happiness" a dozen times and the word "love," either as a verb or a noun, a total of 18 times (84-86).

It is now known that the Tsarist censors cut out part of the manuscript of *Notes from Underground*, and, judging from Dostoyevsky's angry denunciation of that excision, it had to do with the Christian message he hoped to deliver. One scholar has speculated that the novelist intended to demonstrate that his anti-hero's "salvation would come...through the acceptance and appreciation of the ideal of compassion and self-sacrifice embodied in the prostitute, Liza." This "happy" outcome, although it did not actually occur, was implicit in "the moral dialectic of the novel" (Rosenshield 325, 337).

It could also be argued, however, that the author initially meant to see his despicable *podpolnik* undergo a conversion and then "save" Liza. For in this first, tender scene the protagonist conjures up an image worthy of Russia's best icon artists—though with a modern touch: it is a picture of a mother, father and a child suckling its mother's breast. And the anti-hero asks Liza: "Is not all that a joy when they are all three together.... One can forgive a great deal for the sake of such moments. Yes, Liza, one must first learn to live oneself before one blames others." This, I would suggest, was the essential, Christian message Dostoyevsky hoped to get across—forgiveness is divine, and "judge not lest you be judged" (Dostoyevsky 86). It has been asserted that this work is "unique...in its consistently *secular* analysis of the human situation," since it allegedly does not "raise a religious issue," nor mention "the Deity...not any symbols of Christian dogma" (Menut 18). Yet, during the *podpolnik*'s preachy peroration about the evils of prostitution, he says that a happy family life is possible "if the blessing of God is upon it." And later he assures her: "Love is a holy mystery" (84-85).

But this message of deliverance is destroyed when Liza later returns to tell him that she is quitting her "profession," as he had urged. Instead of sharing her joy, he feels shame—over his own poverty, and because his manservant, Apollon, refuses to do as he is told. The *podpolnik* denies that he really meant any of the high-flown sentiments he had spoken before, insisting that he was just toying with her emotions and tyrannizing her with his imperious ethical superiority. In words which prefigure Nietzsche's insights about the "will to power" and the tyranny of morality, he shouts: "Power, power was what I wanted then. Sport was what I wanted, I wanted...your humiliation." And to himself he admits his sadism, which Fromm and others have defined as the desire to exercise total control over another being: "I cannot get on without domineering and tyrannizing over someone...with me loving meant tyrannizing and showing my moral superiority" (108, 111).

But this angry, aggressive outburst was not directed at her so much as at himself. She, like the sledge-driver and his horse, just happened to be at hand, a convenient object for his *displaced hostility*. "I was angry at myself, but, of course, it was she who would have to pay for it." And to her he says:

I had been insulted just before, at dinner, by the fellows.... I came to you, meaning to thrash one of them, an officer; but didn't succeed. I didn't find him; I had to avenge the insult on someone to get my own back again; you turned up; I vented my spleen on you and laughed at you. I had been humiliated, so I wanted to humiliate. I had been treated like a rag, so I wanted to show my power. (107)

This process whereby a victim becomes a tyrant victimizing another has been called a "Dostoyevskian inversion of the dominance hierarchy" (Cox 90); but W.H. Auden best expressed it poetically in "September 1, 1939": "Those to whom evil is done / Do evil in return." A poet whom Dostoyevsky knew and admired, Grigoryev, wrote of "the mad happiness of suffering." To the psychologist this would seem to be masochism. For the Russian novelist and poet, however, such "sufferings of the soul," when accompanied by "forgiveness and love" for others, are "capable of passing over into a sense of beatitude" (Frank 46, 128). Directly opposed to the "divine madness" which is genuine Christian morality is the "moral insanity" of Nietzsche's "will to power," which makes one "power-mad" or "power-crazed."

Works Cited

Breger, Louis. "Dostoyevsky and Medicine." *Slavic Review* 45.4 (Winter 1986): 735-37.

Cox, Gary. "Dostoyevskian Psychology and Russian Cultural and Political Identity." *Mosaic* 17.3 (Summer 1984): 87-102.

Dostoyevsky, Fyodor. *Notes from Underground & The Grand Inquisitor.* Trans. Ralph Matlaw. New York: E.P. Dutton, 1956.

Frank, Joseph. *Dostoyevsky: The Stir of Liberation, 1860-1865.* Princeton: Princeton UP, 1986.

Fromm, Erich. *Escape from Freedom.* New York: Avon Books, 1965.

Jackson, Robert L. *The Underground Man in Russian Literature.* The Hague: Mouton, 1958.

Kabat, Geoffrey C. *Ideology and Imagination: The Image of Society in Dostoyevsky.* New York: Columbia UP, 1978.

Kaufmann, Walter. *The Portable Nietzsche.* New York: Viking, 1954.

Kohlberg, Lawrence, "Psychological Analysis and Literary Form: A Study of the Doubles in Dostoyevsky." *Daedalus* 92.2 (1963): 346-62.

Kravchenko, Maria. *Dostoyevsky and the Psychologists.* Amsterdam: Bibliotheca Slavonica, 1978.

Menut, A.D. *Dostoyevsky and Existentialism.* Lawrence: Coronado, 1972.

Paris, Bernard. "*Notes from Underground*: A Horneyan Analysis." *PMLA* 1973 (May 88): 511-22.

Reik, Theodor. *Masochism in Sex and Society.* New York: Grove, 1941.

Rice, James L. *Dostoyevsky and the Healing Art: An Essay in Literary and Medical History.* Ann Arbor: Ardis, 1985.

Rosenshield, Gary. "The Fate of Dostoyevsky's Underground Man: The Case for an Open Ending." *SEEJ* 28.3 (Fall 1985): 324-39.

Steiner, George. *Tolstoy or Dostoyevsky.* New York: Alfred A. Knopf, 1971.

Villadsen, Preben. *The Underground Man and Raskolnikov: A Comparative Study.* Odense UP, 1981.

Hamlet:
Madness and the Eye of the Reader

Michael Cohen

When Olivier made his Academy Award-winning movie of *Hamlet* in 1948, he loaded the spectator's response at the beginning by announcing in a portentous voice-over: "This is the tragedy of a man who could not make up his mind." Stephen Booth, writing "On the Value of *Hamlet*" in 1969, turns the formula around. "*Hamlet*" he says, "is the tragedy of an audience that cannot make up its mind." I want to take Booth's point of view to what you may well think is an absurd length by insisting that the madness in *Hamlet* is never really a problem about the main character, but rather always about the audience.[1] In order to do that I have to show you a way of reading the play which you may see as, if not completely mad, at least very much like the willful adoption of a multiple personality disorder.

I

Hamlet first appears in the second scene of his play, and after several exchanges between him and Claudius, he is asked, first by Claudius and then by Gertrude, to remain with them rather than returning to Wittenburg. Hamlet's reply is directed to Gertrude:

I shall in all my best obey you, madam. (1.2.120)

How does Hamlet read this line? Does he stress the *you*, implying that he is not about to obey *Claudius*? Does he stress the *best*, implying that Gertrude is directing him to do ill? Does he stress the *obey*, implying that though he will do her bidding, his heart is not in it? Or does he stress the *madam*, drawing attention to the formal address and the fact that he is not calling her *mother*, with whatever that may imply about the way she is acting? All these possibilities are there, but on the stage only one will be given voice.

Adapted from *Hamlet in My Mind's Eye*, Michael Cohen, University of Georgia Press, 1989. Reprinted with permission.

Every production of *Hamlet* is another interpretation. The person who directs the play, the men who play Hamlet and Claudius, and the woman who plays Gertrude must all decide on readings of the main characters which are convincing and consistent. And each reading pushes out other possible readings. If Claire Bloom plays Gertrude as fearful and clinging, she cannot also play her as lusty and independent. This exclusiveness of interpretation creates fewer problems for some parts than for others: the range of possibilities for playing Osric extends only so far, regardless of the actors' maxim that there are no small parts. But as the parts get larger and we approach Hamlet himself, the necessity for one consistent interpretation becomes very limiting.

There would be no problem if there were only one *right* interpretation of Hamlet's role and each of his speeches. Some criticism in the past has indeed argued for such a single view. Psychological approaches, historical approaches and textual approaches (Coleridge, Bradley, Jones, Wilson) have often implicitly asserted that those who find mystery or ambiguity in the play simply do not understand some crucial fact about the main character's personality, the social, political, or aesthetic background of the play or its printing history. Few critics would take such a position now; most have accepted the plurality of *Hamlet*, though that acceptance has not always led to favorable critical judgments. One group of critics, which Paul Gottschalk has called the evolutionary school, sees the play's ambiguities as resulting from its sources (Gottschalk 14). Such writers as Stoll, Robertson, and T.S. Eliot, believing Shakespeare's *Hamlet* to be an unresolved combination of disparate elements deriving from several sources, judge the play to be less than a success. Other critics do not find ambiguity or multivalence an obstacle to dramatic success (Schlegel, G. Wilson Knight, Traversi, C.S. Lewis, Mack, Harbage). They may write, as L.C. Knights does, about "the stubborn way in which the play resists attempts at consistent interpretation," but they find such resistance enriching rather than confusing or artistically weakening (Knights 82).

The problem of production remains. Each individual reading of a line contributes to a general effect. A director must choose *one* reading of an individual line, and his choices for readings of all lines must be as consistent as possible for a unified and coherent interpretation of the play.

But for the reader the play is always in rehearsal. I, as reader, can hold all four readings of Hamlet's line above in mind at once. I can keep many interpretations of Hamlet's character in mind as I move through the play and think not only of how his lines would be read to support one or the other, but how other characters' lines would change and be changed by such interpretations. I can play *Hamlet* in my mind's eye. As an example, Hamlet's first scene (act 1, scene 2) can be read in this way, from the beginning until Hamlet's first soliloquy.

II

The second scene works by a series of shocks. Claudius begins by telling us that his brother's death is so recent that he and the whole kingdom should still be in mourning. Then he admits to a technically incestuous marriage with his brother's wife, his "sometime sister." This quick remarriage of Gertrude seems to be what has enabled Claudius to climb onto the throne. But we are not informed how the succession actually worked and whether Claudius's marriage to the queen influenced the nobles to cast their votes for him in the normal process of an elective monarchy or whether his marriage short-circuited any elective process. Claudius also confirms what has been said in 1.1 of the country's danger from without by referring to Denmark as "this warlike state."

Why does Claudius admit these things? It should be pointed out that he goes on to deny them, either explicitly or implicitly, by what follows. That his brother's death is still so recent that it deserves mourning is denied by Claudius's exhortation to Hamlet to stop mourning, that the proper term for "obsequious sorrow" is over:

> to persever
> In obstinate condolement is a course
> Of impious stubbornness. (92-94)

That his marriage to Gertrude violates any moral codes is implicitly denied by Claudius's words to the assembled nobles about how they have freely gone along with this affair. That any serious threat exists to the country is denied by the way Claudius handles the whole matter of Fortinbras's challenge. *Young* Fortinbras has "a weak supposal" of Claudius's worth, which is presumably strong; the state is *not* "disjoint and out of frame;" Fortinbras's plan is a "dream;" and, rather than a threat, he is a pest. So much for him.

Claudius may be reminding everyone of the unsavory details of his assumption of the throne merely because he *can*, demonstrating a kind of sleaziness of character dramatically calculated to turn us against him from his first words. He may also just be ineptly babbling about what has happened without realizing the effect his words may have. The latter interpretation goes along with a reading of Claudius as drunkard, taking off from what Hamlet says about him at the beginning of 1.4. Claudius is rarely played as a drunkard, but much in the text can support this reading. Anthony Hopkins's Claudius, in Nicol Williamson's 1969 film version of *Hamlet*, came as close to this interpretation as has been done in any modern production. But the whole speech of Claudius here seems nothing if not conscious, deliberate.

Part of what Claudius says here is necessary exposition: we need to have other people besides Hamlet talk about how soon his mother's remarriage followed his father's death. Hamlet tends to be confused about it—is it a month, two months, two hours (3.2.121) or the twice two months Ophelia replies to the two hours? Horatio confirms that "it followed hard upon," but he is a friend and of Hamlet's way of thinking. Here the antagonist himself confirms the haste. It was quick enough to have the appearance of unseemly haste, quite apart from the unseemliness of its uniting of sister and brother-in-law.

The readings that are left concern *policy* or sheer pleasure in exercise of *power*, the one not necessarily excluding the other. For policy, Claudius opens the discussion in order to close it. Once he has announced that those present "have freely gone / With this affair along," he has made it so, even if there was no agreement before. It may even be that there was no formal election of Claudius, in which case he boldly preempted the throne and has now averted the possibility of an election as well. The matter is closed. There will be no further discussion of technical incest or Claudius's right or lack of right to the throne. Now on to other business.

Certainly the handling of the Fortinbras threat seems like carefully controlled policy. The impression Claudius intends to convey is one of control and strength: "Fortinbras is not strong enough to present a serious threat; we *are* strong, and moreover prepared; not only can we defend ourselves but we can nip the plan in the bud by exercise of diplomacy; even here we are firmly in control and our ambassadors will do only exactly what we instruct in 'these delated articles.'" We cannot forget on rereading the scene that the masterful diplomatic plan fails, however, regardless of Claudius's optimism and the favorable report returned by the ambassadors in 2.2.

Claudius's agenda also projects control through a careful sense of priority in the items of business he takes up. First he recaps the question of Denmark's sovereignty (1-16). That settled, he proceeds to external threats (17-41). Next he moves to the concern of the son of the king's chief counselor (42-63). Finally he turns to personal business of his own—his chiefest courtier, kinsman, and son.

Hamlet's black costume and usually his stage position put him at the center of visual attention, but Claudius has been avoiding him until this moment. This care, though right policy in showing what should be the king's priorities, also may *appear* to be from Claudius's distaste for the coming interview with Hamlet; such a reading is inconsistent with the Claudius who is in full control and savoring not only power but the ability to rub others' noses in what they must dislike about his having power. But the drunken, unsure Claudius would certainly not relish this conversation with his nephew.

Claudius underlines the relationship:

But now, my cousin Hamlet, and my son— (64)

Claudius is gloating (Hamlet has gone from a rival potentially more powerful than the uncle to a son who was not even considered for the succession and who now is under the uncle-father's control) or he is offering (genuinely or out of policy) peace with the greeting that they are more than kin; the latter reading is what Hamlet picks up in the next line. Claudius then asks a question which denies what he himself has said about the "greenness" of his brother's death:

How is it that the clouds still hang on you? (66)

Hamlet's answer is his first piece of insolence, if we choose to have him read the line that way. This passage, until the king's exit, is as rich in possibilities for diverse readings as any in the play. The first exchange between the two men can be anything from cool to hot, and Gertrude's first speech either a continuation of Claudius's friendly urging or an attempt to bring the temperature down by getting a concession from Hamlet. Gertrude makes two mistakes in talking to her son here. Hamlet, like the clown in act 5, is being absolute—Gertrude has to speak by the card, or equivocation will undo her. She first says it is common for men to die—for all that lives must die. Hamlet's response might be spoken quietly enough:

Ay, madam, it is common. (74)

But it is more than likely that he emphasizes one of these words, and almost any one of them emphasized will have the same effect: the implication is that Gertrude should realize that death is common, and will occur to her as well, and the further implication is that she should be acting differently, considering that fact. The message is the same as that which Hamlet wants to send in 5.1 when he speaks to the skull of Yorick:

Now get you to my lady's chamber, and tell her, let her paint an inch thick, to this favor she must come. Make her laugh at that. (180-83)

His line may also suggest that she and Claudius are treating death as *common* in the sense of that which touches only the common and will not touch them (odd, since they are talking about the death of a king).

If Hamlet's reply is spoken kindly, Gertrude continues kindly:

If it be,
Why seems it so particular with thee? (74-75)

If his response is sharp, she answers in kind, with some impatience. And her answer is the second mistake in that she uses the word *seems*, which sets Hamlet off; it is as if he has been waiting for some word that denotes dissimulation so that he may unburden himself of what he is thinking about the scant mourning duties afforded his father by all but himself. Hamlet's "I know not seems" speech can certainly be read savagely, but can it be read any other way? Can it be seen as a dutiful response, and one which does not insult all those present, and especially Claudius and Gertrude? Later in the scene Hamlet says he is holding his tongue (159), and he does not in fact say explicitly here that the others are seeming—performing actions that a man might play and only pretending to mourn old Hamlet.

Claudius chooses to put the best construction on this and Hamlet's following speech—they are dutiful, filial sentiments. But Claudius's speech—one of his longest—has manifold playing possibilities as well. Is it avuncular advice of the kind offered to Margaret in Hopkins's poem and a genuine attempt to bring Hamlet to his side, have him look on Claudius as a father? The way Claudius concludes the scene points to that (121-24). But other things make possible a different reading. Before he pleads with Hamlet to think of him as of a father, he has suggested that the way sons should think of fathers is as of any trivial sign of mortality in the world. Genuine mourning, he says, is absurd, peevish, impious, naive, simple and unmanly. Having said this about how relations between fathers and sons ought to be, he makes the rather equivocal comment, again couched in his negative way:

> with no less nobility of love
> Than that which dearest father bears his son
> Do I impart toward you. (110-12)

Finally he repeats the sentiment that seems to gall Hamlet so, that the younger man is both cousin and son to him.

When Gertrude begs that his *mother* not be allowed to lose her prayers, is she merely furthering what she takes to be Claudius's good advice? Or is she saying, in effect, pay no attention to the insulting speech you've just heard from your uncle-father, but listen to my reasonable request?

When Hamlet responds, his answer depends partly on the way Gertrude has just spoken to him; the possible variations in this single line are as great as in any other line of the play, though we will look at only four.

I shall in all my *best* obey you, madam. [I am not about to obey you in what you seem to be counseling, which is anything but good.]

I shall in all my best obey *you*, madam. [I am certainly not going to obey Claudius.]

I shall in all my best *obey* you, madam. [But my obedience does not reflect what is in my mind. See line 159, where he says his heart is breaking but he must hold his tongue.]

I shall in all my best obey you, *madam*. [What you ask of me is hardly filial, or the asking maternal. I will not call you *mother*. You have made yourself something less than either kin or kind.]

There is a neutral reading, which Claudius chooses to hear, and in it the *you* may be addressed to either Gertrude or to both her and Claudius. Even this hardly seems a loving reply, even if it is a fair one.

Claudius leaves, as he entered, with a flourish, promising that his cannons and the heavens themselves will announce every time he drinks today. Again there is the intentional doubling of Denmark in his remarks: "Be as ourself in Denmark"—with its irony, since Hamlet has been preempted in any possibility of *being* Denmark, and thus really like Claudius; and "No jocund health that Denmark drinks today"—meaning, "That *I* drink today." Denmark is a thing or place—Hamlet's prison, Claudius's plaything. It is also the king himself. Hamlet cannot be as Claudius in Denmark, cannot be Denmark, cannot escape Claudius in Denmark because Claudius *is* Denmark.

Hamlet, left alone, speaks his first soliloquy. The speech is one of the most distinctive marks in defining the character for audience or reader, and its ambiguities define the range of interpretation for the character, at least in the play's beginning. This qualification—at least in the play's beginning—is necessary because although we have most possible Hamlets in this speech, the Hamlet of action is missing and does not emerge until Horatio has entered and told his tale. Hamlet begins with self-pity and goes toward anger, madness and despair, or prissiness, depending on the reading. The movement toward anger will stress those things that Hamlet will finally bring to his mother in a resolution of his anger in 3.4. The reason has failed to govern the heyday in the blood; the beast is in control. Old Hamlet, excellent king and excellent husband, has been replaced by a man who is neither. It is both an aesthetic and a moral failure, making Hamlet angry and puzzled. The speech concludes with angry condemnation of unrighteous tears, wicked speed, incestuous acts.

But this speech is the first textual evidence for readings which see Hamlet's madness as something more than the deliberate antic disposition he puts on after his talk with the ghost. Here the stress will be on Hamlet's contemplation of suicide, his extension of his mother's perceived grossness to the whole world, the memories of old Hamlet and Gertrude that he cannot get from his mind:

> Heaven and earth,
> Must I remember? (142-43)

Here also is stressed that mounting hysteria in which Hamlet compresses time so that the two months (if that is indeed the interval, and it seems short enough for impropriety) between his father's death and Gertrude's marriage becomes first a month, then less than a month. And here we must look forward to that point where Hamlet compresses the time to its frightful shortest:

> For look you how cheerfully my mother looks,
> and my father died within's two hours. (3.2.120-21)

The line has the force to jog even the most confirmed believers in Hamlet's calculated madness to a momentary doubt.

For prissiness the speech has much to underwrite the sort of interpretation Olivier gave to Hamlet in his film version. Hamlet wishes to separate himself from the foulness of the world. He comes close to imaging Gertrude and Claudius as rutting dogs in 150-51. He fills his condemnatory phrases with hissing sibilants: "unrighteous tears," "the flushing in her galled eyes," "most wicked speed, to post / With such dexterity to incestuous sheets!"

III

Each scene of *Hamlet* may be looked at as a kind of complete performance, with rising, sustained, and falling rhythms—as a whole and finished play—but the mood and atmosphere surrounding the protagonist are those of a rehearsal. Gielgud seized on this aspect of the play when staging his 1963-64 "rehearsal" *Hamlet* with Richard Burton in the lead; this quality of the play is also what gives it its familiar resemblance to the sometimes dreadful improvisations of real life. Hamlet frequently seems to be rehearsing for a possible play while the rest of the ensemble are acting in quite another, real one. The easiest way for them to deal with this lack of synchrony is to call it madness. If madness is an unwillingness to choose one arbitrary reality and exclude the rest, then Hamlet is indeed thoroughly mad, but it is the madness of his audience as well. Hazlitt said, "It is *we* who are Hamlet" (232). The prince may be forgiven some indecision in having to take on all of our indecisions.

This is of course not the traditional humanist approach to the question of madness in the play. That approach would first define madness (something which I have assiduously avoided doing) and next sketch out hypotheses as a series of answers to questions that contextualize *Hamlet*: Does Shakespeare suggest in the tragedies that sanity is so delicate a balance and so language-bound that dwelling on a series of chaotic images is enough to upset it? Are the romances and comedies about the restoration of this balance? Is the question of madness unique in *Hamlet* because not thematic as it is in *King Lear*, for example?

The urgency of the mind's theater is ignored in the humanist approach, whatever leisurely rewards are offered by it. The play is always going on, must go on now as we read. One consequence of the fact that we are Hamlet is that all of the critical problems of the play become our problems. What have traditionally been seen as problems of the play or of the protagonist become the reader's problems. Is Hamlet mad? For the reader, the issue of Hamlet's madness is no academic question, but an immediate one that must be decided again and again as the play is produced in the mind's eye. No scholarly argument or elaborate justification of absolute convictions is useful here; the play is waiting to go on. How can Hamlet's madness be played? This is the question the scholarly problem translates to—how will Hamlet read this speech if he is mad? How will his mother react when he reads it thus? Why will Claudius refuse to accept Hamlet's madness as real? What ironies are possible when Claudius, refusing to see Hamlet's real madness as other than madness in craft, yet says "Alas, alas" (4.3.26) to his speeches, implying to those assembled that Hamlet *is* really mad?

I know that reading *Hamlet* in this way begs certain questions about intention in literary works and outrages certain assumptions about intention in dramatic works. I know also that it is more than a little like juggling to hold these various interpretations in mind at once. But I do not know of another way to read such a text that does justice to its recognized multivalence, or what else would we mean by the "pluralism" of the play if not that there is more than one Hamlet in Hamlet's lines.[2] In fact there are many Hamlets, some mad and some sane, as *Hamlet* is played on the stages of the mind's eye.

Notes

[1] The debate about Hamlet's madness was first set out in formal terms in *The Hamlet Controversy. Was Hamlet Mad? or, The Lucubrations of Messrs. Smith, Brown, Jones and Robinson* (Melbourne: H.T. Dwight, 1867), purporting to be the correspondence of four gentlemen responding to a production of *Hamlet* with particular reference to whether the prince is mad or not. Smith says yes; Brown and Jones say no and that his own remark that he pretends madness to accomplish his purpose (1.5.172) is enough to explain away whole speeches of malapropos remarks or even gibberish. Robinson, the last correspondent, says maybe Hamlet is mad— sometimes (Sacks and Whan 82-94). Very little has been added to the debate since. Lily Bess Campbell insisted that Hamlet suffered from a

condition of excessive grief called "melancholy adust" (Campbell 110). For Ernest Jones the problem was an Oedipal psychoneurosis (Jones 77). Maynard Mack decided that the prince's mental state was accurately represented by his clothes: mourning (but sane) at the beginning; seriously disturbed during the middle three acts; saner, wiser, and readier in the last (Mack 511-12). There is no real agreement about what might constitute madness (sanity may be the more problematic concept in the dramatic world of Elsinore), let alone whether Hamlet suffers from it.

²Whether or not Hamlet's plural sides and contradictions can exist at the same time within the character—in one stage interpretation—is a critical question still current. See, for example, Donald Hedrick's article which argues that the satiric and heroic aspects of Hamlet's character are not incompatible.

Works Cited

Booth, Stephen. "On the Value of *Hamlet.*" *Reinterpretations of Elizabethan Drama*. Ed. Norman Rabkin. New York and London: Columbia UP, 1969.

Bradley, A.C. *Shakespearean Tragedy*. 1904. New York: Fawcett, 1965.

Campbell, Lily Bess. *Shakespeare's Tragic Heroes: Slaves of Passion*. 1930. New York: Barnes and Noble, 1963.

Coleridge, Samuel Taylor. *Coleridge's Shakespearean Criticism*. Ed. Thomas M. Raysor. Cambridge: Harvard UP, 1930.

Eliot, T.S. "Hamlet and His Problems." *Selected Essays: 1917-1932*. New York: Harcourt, 1932.

Gottschalk, Paul. *The Meanings of Hamlet: Modes of Literary Interpretation Since Bradley*. Albuquerque: U of New Mexico P, 1972.

Harbage, Alfred. *As They Liked It: A Study of Shakespeare's Moral Artistry*. 1947. New York: Harper, 1961.

Hazlitt, William. *Characters of Shakespear's Plays*. 1817. *The Complete Works of William Hazlitt*. Vol. 4. 1930. Ed. P.P. Howe. New York: AMS P, 1967.

Hedrick, Donald K. "'It Is No Novelty for a Prince to be a Prince': An Enantiomorphous Hamlet." *Shakespeare Quarterly* 35 (1984): 62-76.

Jones, Ernest. *Hamlet and Oedipus*. New York: W.W. Norton, 1949.

Knight, G. Wilson. *The Imperial Theme*. 3rd ed. London: Methuen, 1951.

____. *The Wheel of Fire*. London: Oxford UP, 1930.

Knights, L.C. *Explorations: Essays in Criticism Mainly on the Literature of the Seventeenth Century*. 1947. New York UP, 1964.

Lewis, C.S. "Hamlet: The Prince or the Poem?" British Academy Annual Shakespeare Lecture, 1942. *Proceedings of the British Academy* 38. London: Oxford UP, 1942.

Mack, Maynard. "The World of Hamlet." *The Yale Review* 41 (1952): 502-23.

Robertson, J.M. *"Hamlet" Once More.* London: Richard Cobden-Sanderson, 1923.

Sacks, Claire, and Edgar Whan, eds. *Hamlet: Enter Critic.* New York: Appleton-Century-Crofts, 1960.

Schlegel, August Wilhelm von. *A Course of Lectures on Dramatic Art and Literature.* Trans. John Black. Reviewed by A.J.W. Morrison. London: Henry G. Bohn, 1861.

Shakespeare, William. *Hamlet.* Ed. Willard Farnham. The Pelican Shakespeare. Baltimore: Penguin Books, 1957.

Stoll, Elmer Edgar. *Art and Artifice in Shakespeare.* Cambridge: Cambridge UP, 1933.

___. *"Hamlet": An Historical and Comparative Study.* Minneapolis: U of Minnesota P, 1919.

Traversi, Derek. *An Approach to Shakespeare.* Vol. 2. 3rd ed. New York: Anchor Books, 1969.

Walker, Roy. *The Time Is Out of Joint.* London: Andrew Dakers, 1948.

Wilson, J. Dover. *What Happens in Hamlet.* Cambridge: Cambridge UP, 1935.

Vision, Madness, Myth
and William Blake

Paul Youngquist

To an artist's reputation, the taint of madness is the touch of death. Far better to be called a drunkard, a criminal or a letch; to be branded mad is simply lethal. And once so disposed of, a reputation is difficult to resurrect. For madness serves as a boundary beyond which all meanings fall silent, all art proves mere parody of more reasonable designs. An artist who crosses it in truth or in rumor becomes a kind of ghost to his culture and forces his critics to do some crafty conjuring. William Blake provides a case in point. During his lifetime and for years after, Blake was all but invisible as an artist, in no small part because word circulated that he might be mad. Then began the effort to revive him, which meant ridding his reputation of the taint of madness. Criticism for the last century and a quarter has diligently pursued that end, so effectively in fact that Blake stands before us as the sanest of men, his poetry the smartest of verse. We now know Blake as his contemporaries never could— as an exemplary artist and human being. But I wonder if we know Blake the better for this rehabilitation. Have we purged with the taint of madness some essential quality of his art? To ponder his achievement even briefly is to realize with some chagrin that, in his poetry at least, Blake finds madness a rich subject, one he returns to time and again. From his early lyrics to his late myth Blake writes disturbingly about it, which is not to say that he was himself mad, only that he took the subject more seriously than have his recent critics. In what follows I want to put the madness question once again to Blake's achievement. By doing so we will discover that the myth Blake evolves is an uncannily astute description of madness.

In 1809, tired of being shunned by the Royal Academy, Blake held an exhibition of his paintings at his brother's house on Broad Street. The show was a flop (not a single painting sold), but it did

Adapted from *Madness and Blake's Myth*, Paul Youngquist. Pennsylvania State University Press, 1989. Reprinted with permission.

113

attract the attention of Robert Hunt, who published its only known review in *The Examiner*. Irritated by the obvious eccentricity of what he saw, Hunt dismissed Blake as "a lunatic, whose personal inoffensiveness secures him from confinement" (qtd. in Bentley 216).[1] Hunt was not the first to call Blake a madman and certainly not the last. Blake's notebook contains bitter jabs at friends and philistines who harbored similar convictions. There Blake strikes a defiant pose: "Madman I have been called Fool they Call thee / I wonder which they Envy Thee or Me" (507). But beneath the bravado of these lines sounds a note of real concern, for the charge of madness posed a mortal threat to Blake's existence as an artist— and he knew it.

It has grown conventional to assume that such a charge was utterly without warrant. But this assumption suppresses all awareness of Blake's strange experience of our world. For Blake was a visionary and took his visions literally as an experience like any other. When as a child he saw a tree whose boughs were spangled with angels, home he ran to tell his parents, much to the displeasure, we are told, of his pragmatic father. When choosing a profession, he received visionary counsel: "The spirit said to him 'Blake be an artist & nothing else. In this there is felicity.'"[2] Such visions were for Blake an essential fact of his experience. If reports of his conversation are to be trusted, he had a host of familiars, among them the Virgin Mary, the Spiritual Sun, the Angel Gabriel— even Milton and Shakespeare![3] Nor was visionary experience without its effect upon Blake's art. In his *Descriptive Catalogue*, a document in part responsible for Hunt's withering review, Blake writes of "having been taken in vision into the ancient republics, monarchies, and patriarchies of Asia," of having "seen those wonderful originals called in the Sacred Scriptures the Cherubim" and of having in his own works "endeavored to emulate the grandeur of those seen in his visions, and to apply it to modern Heroes, on a smaller scale" (531). As visionary, Blake's experience gave a touch of strangeness to his life and work, distinguishing both from the common lot, stamping both as somehow different.

Thus it was vision that in large part marked Blake a madman in his own day. If it is now routine to assert that anyone who knew Blake well knew him to be utterly sane, that is only because the issue of vision has long since ceased to concern his critics. But like all blanket disclaimers, this one merits some scrutiny.[4] The sculptor Flaxman, who for a long time was very close to Blake, observed in a letter to William Hayley that "Blake's irritability as well as the association and arrangement of his ideas do not seem likely to be soothed or more advantageously disposed by any power inferior to that by which man is originally endowed with his faculties" (qtd. in Keynes 74). More succinctly, Henry Fuseli, whom Blake always held in high esteem, is said to have remarked that "Blake has something of madness about him" (Bentley, *Blake Records* 52). Comments such as these prove nothing about Blake's mental health, but they do provide a context in which to situate similar pronouncements.

Indeed, a kernel of truth may lie hidden in the judgment of Wordsworth, who reacted to *Songs of Innocence and of Experience* with a mixture of sympathy and censure for its author: "There is no doubt this poor man was mad, but there is something in the madness of this man which interests me more than the sanity of Lord Byron and Walter Scott!" (qtd. in Bentley, *William Blake* 30).[5] Wordsworth's remark differs more in degree than in kind from those made by Flaxman and Fuseli and attests to a growing conviction that Blake might be mad. Blake's early biographers strengthened this conviction by savoring the many tales of his visionary eccentricities. J.T. Smith, Alan Cunningham, and Frederick Tatham all wrote biographical sketches of Blake within five years of his death, though only the first two were published (Bentley, *Blake Records* 455-533). These accounts are largely appreciative and do their best to popularize an obscure artist, but by rehearsing Blake's eccentricities they tend to call his sanity into question. The reminiscences of Henry Crabb Robinson have the same effect since, whether in earnest or in jest, Blake treated Robinson to some of his zaniest ideas and speculations, as for instance that wives should be held in common or that he had once been Socrates and a kind of brother to Jesus (Bentley, *Blake* 536-49). After his death, Blake's reputation had become so clouded by suspicions of madness that it was possible for an essay in the *Revue Britannique* (Paris, 1833) to describe Blake, "surnommé le *Voyant*," as one of the two most famous inmates of Bedlam.[6] A garbled and unscrupulous translation of two biographical sketches that had appeared earlier in the *Monthly Magazine*, the essay shows only how intimately madness had become associated with the career of William Blake. Posterity finally bestowed what life itself had denied: residence in Bedlam.

When interest in Blake's poetry developed later in the nineteenth century (thanks in large part to the effort of Dante Gabriel Rossetti), serious criticism labored to discredit the common conviction that Blake was mad. Alexander Gilchrist, whose *Life of*

William Blake: Pictor Ignotus remains the best of many biographies, devoted a chapter to this end entitled "Mad or Not Mad?" (536-49). Gilchrist believed that in an earlier age Blake's visionary eccentricities would have been proof not of lunacy but of prophetic illumination. The visionary artist in the nineteenth century, he argued, may indeed be prone to mental stress and anguish, but does not therefore deserve the label "mad." Such anguish is in fact evidence of the intensity and sincerity of his message. When Swinburne, five years later, wrote the first full-length critical study of Blake's poetry, he paid little heed to the charge of madness, except to say that "on his own ground no man was more sane or more reverent" (5). Such a claim, however, is less vindicating than patronizing. Belief in "the mad Blake" refused to die. It was in part to refute it that Yeats and Ellis, when they published the first complete edition of Blake's poetry with commentary, made him a mystic, emphasizing the systematic coherence of his thought. Blake's symbolic system, they argued, was the signature of his genius and "the guarantee of his sanity" (Ellis and Yeats vii). By interpreting that system as a modern contribution to the tradition of Western mysticism, they tried to legitimize Blake's eccentricity and once and for all squash the persistent conviction that he was mad.

Had they succeeded, twentieth-century criticism would not have worked so doggedly to defend Blake's character. With the publication in 1925 of a scholarly edition of Blake's complete writings, it became possible for critics to judge the poems, short and long, on their own merits. But this opportunity did not put to rest the question of Blake's madness. As readers discovered the strangeness of the prophetic writings, their opacity to under-standing, rumors continued to circulate, enough to warrant Mona Wilson's efforts to dispel them in a new biography (1927). The issue of madness runs like a leitmotif through her narrative of Blake's life, and although she does her best to dismiss it, her very efforts arouse suspicion. Why this preoccupation, one is forced to ask, if Blake were so manifestly sane and madness bore no relevance for his poems? With the appearance in 1947 of Northrop Frye's landmark study of Blake's myth, *Fearful Symmetry*, the question seemed answered, or at least rendered meaningless. Frye minimized the eccentricity of Blake's art and mind by locating both within "a permanent structure of ideas" (14). Because this structure ultimately embraces the whole of English literature, it ensures the legitimacy of Blake's poetry. And because it is a mental construct, its very existence guarantees the balance of Blake's mind. Frye brought a new coherence to Blake's art and moved it from the fringe to the center of the literary. It was left for his followers, most notably Harold Bloom in *Blake's Apocalypse,* to investigate and explicate those passages left unilluminated by Frye's sweeping archetypal method. The old question of madness sank finally into disrepute and became a matter of bad taste.[7]

Blake criticism since Frye has begun to chip away at the fearful symmetry of his own approach. David V. Erdman has shown in marvelous detail how thoroughly alive Blake was to the political issues of his age. Leopold Damrosch has sounded the contradictions at the heart of Blake's mythmaking. And Jerome McGann has begun to interrogate the activity of Blake's art in the social field of human experience.[8] But criticism yet awaits a reassessment of the old conviction that Blake was mad. I want to begin that project by trying to understand why the specter of madness haunts Blake's reputation and what it might reveal about the meaning of Blake's myth.

Blake reached maturity in the latter days of what has been described as an Age of Reason. In matters of conviction and taste the world was an orderly place. Newton's third law and Pope's heroic couplet ensured, in their respective spheres, a well-tempered and balanced creation. It therefore comes as something of a shock to realize that, in literature at least, this Age of Reason gave birth to an Age of Madness.[9] In the years after Pope's death, a startling number of poets suffered mentally, and some went mad. A partial explanation of this phenomenon can be found in the way the Age of Reason defined madness and treated the madman. Blake's visionary eccentricities made him susceptible to these assumptions and to a certain extent he became their victim.

In *Madness and Civilization* Michel Foucault argues that the opposition of reason and madness is one of the defining features of Western culture (Foucault ix-xii). According to Foucault, social power establishes its validity by means of a privileged language of reason and various structures of exclusion that support the crystal walls of reason's castle. These structures confine the unruly and silence the unreasonable, and become visible in the great institutions of confinement that were first established in the Age of Reason: the poorhouse, where an ethic of work makes poverty socially beneficial, and the madhouse, where a metaphysics of reason strips certain men and women of humanity. Both institutions silence elements of society that contradict the order of things. And in one way or another, both menaced Blake. Poverty dogged him most of his life; only the devoted support of friends like Thomas Butts and John Linnell allowed him to die debt-free. Penury like Blake's substantiated the charge of madness that the mind of reason brought against the visionary. As Foucault explains it, the relationship between poverty and madness in the Age of Reason grew out of the social ethic of labor that replaced the old religious ethic of faith: "madness was perceived through a condemnation of idleness and in a social immanence guaranteed by the community of labor" (58). This community segregated forms of social uselessness, creating a world apart where the poor and the mad acquired a meaning. Those inhabiting this world bore responsibility for being there, since poverty and madness signified a fall from social grace.

In the Age of Reason, then, the madman, like the poor man, divorced himself from the immanent authority of social order. In Foucault's terms, "he crosses the frontiers of bourgeois order of his own accord, and alienates himself outside the sacred limits of its ethic" (58). Once beyond these limits, the individual lost the social identity that united him with others. He stepped into the no-man's land Pope describes in the *Dunciad*, a place "where Folly holds her throne," and, "concealed from vulgar eye," there is a cell that holds the quack wordsmith and the enthusiast alike, "The Cave of Poverty and Poetry" (Pope 308, 11.29, 34-35). Blake knew poverty well enough to understand its political and moral causes:

> Pity would be no more,
> If we did not make somebody Poor:
> And Mercy no more could be,
> If all were as happy as we. (27)

The virtues of pity and mercy are weapons in the arsenal of social order. By attacking this order, Blake alienates himself from it and enters that other world peopled by the economically disinherited: the impoverished and the mad.[10]

The implications of this alienation are nothing short of metaphysical. Foucault maintains that during the Age of Reason the madhouse gave a special kind of visibility to the metaphysics of social power. Leprosy having disappeared from its exclusive position of the margins of Western culture, another affliction—madness—moved in to take its place. The madhouse became the Enlightenment avatar of the lazar-house because madness, like leprosy, validated the order of things by negating it. Where the leper confirmed the coherence of Christian civilization by being unable to participate in it, the madman proclaimed the authority of reason by embodying its denial. But the difference between what the leper and the madman signified was a profound one. A kind of anti-church, the lazar-house signified the same redeeming transcendence—the Almighty God—that medieval culture stood for as a whole. The madhouse in the Age of Reason lacked this transcendental reference. It signified what reason is not; in other words, it signified nothing. In the Age of Reason,

Madness...ceased to be the sign of another world;...it became the paradoxical manifestation of non-being.... Confinement corresponds most exactly to negativity of reason; by confinement, madness is acknowledged to be nothing. (Foucault 115-16)

The madhouse became the domain, not of aberration, but of absence, and the madman, the meaningless parody of all that is human.

This, then, is the historical context in which we must situate the question of Blake's madness. To the eye of his age, his poetry and painting appear meaningless because they embody nothing, just the empty negativity that Foucault calls unreason. In such an age poetry must be the oracle of the obvious. To express any but reason's truth is to disturb a universe, as Hunt's attack on Blake illustrates pointedly. Hunt deplores the seduction of sober minds by the meaningless sports of lunacy: "That men of taste, in their sober senses, should mistake its unmeaning and distracted conceptions for the flashes of genius is indeed a phenomenon" (Bentley, *Blake Records* 67). To the man of taste, the line that divides meaning from unmeaning is absolute. To cross it is madness, a proud assertion of self, the secular equivalent of impiety. Hunt writes at a time that has begun to witness a rehabilitation of the irrational undertaken by writers like Rousseau, Wordsworth, Coleridge and others. Even so, he sees in Blake's work only a naive emptiness, and reduces it to silence by labeling it mad. Blake's artistic fate thus becomes a benign kind of confinement, and it is little wonder that a story eventually circulated of his residence in Bedlam. Blake's solitude and social disenfranchisement mark his work as meaningless, placing him in the curious position of announcing a prophecy in a language that nobody could—or would— understand.

Blake was not, however, the only poet to be labeled mad in the late eighteenth century. If the difference between madness and sanity is in part an institutional one, then those possessing the keys to Bedlam have the power to determine its population. In Blake's day, the rationalist played the warden while the enthusiast often played the prisoner. "There are states," Blake writes on the Laocoön engraving, "in which all Visionary Men are accounted Mad men" (274). The poet Christopher Smart fell into such a state when his religious fervor delivered him up to the madhouse.[11] No lesser authority than Samuel Johnson endorsed the sincerity of Smart's enthusiasm with his famous observation, "he insisted on people praying with him; and I'd lief as pray with Kit Smart as any one else" (Hill 1: 397). But in society's judgment, Smart's religious enthusiasm signified madness, even if it did make the impression of a close proximity to the deity. This association of madness with the poet, a notion going back to Plato's Ion, for the first time takes on personal urgency as the Age of Reason draws to a close.[12] No era in the history of literature displays so much mental suffering among its poets as the one Frye calls "the Age of Sensibility."[13] Gray's melancholy and Collin's depression, Smart's monomaniacal enthusiasm and Cowper's obsessive guilt, are all symptoms of chaos at a time when order has not bowed to originality as the standard of value in verse.

Blake's closest literary cousins, these poets share an intensity of vision new to eighteenth-century literature. A reckless animism afflicts their poems, as if the world and the things in it passed through the furnace of the poet's consciousness on their way to a brighter vitality in verse.[14] But with this vision of vitality comes a heightened sense of separation from others. Collins, Cowper, Smart, and to a lesser extent Blake, all labored under the conviction that vision was somehow hostile, alienating them from the common lot. And indeed, the first three were, at various times, considered mad by their contemporaries; Cowper and Smart even saw confinement.[15] Although all announced in their poems a vision of vitality, what distinguishes the others from Blake is their inability to interpret it by any other standard than religious orthodoxy. Collins and Cowper pine as isolated individuals, guiltily aware of a vitality that is not finally human but divine. Smart soars beyond individuality to embrace that vitality, but at the cost of all human relationships. In both cases a religious transcendence legitimizes vision but alienates the visionary.

The madness of the Sensibility bards is thus a measure of their originality; by devoting themselves to vision they become victims of social exclusion. Blake shares their vision of vitality and like them becomes susceptible to the charge of madness leveled by an ideology of reason. But the conditions that breed real mental suffering in the Sensibility bards bring Blake metaphors for poetry. By making madness a central subject of his myth, Blake undertakes a therapeutic enterprise of cultural proportions. The project of the Romantic poets generally is to create a poetry of healing, an art that expresses a vision of vitality while promoting the health of the human spirit. Hence the conservatism of a poet like Wordsworth, who works devotedly to avoid the intensities of the Sensibility bards, diffusing such a vision over genial landscapes and childhood memories. The Age of Sensibility awakens to a psychology that it lacks the conceptual equipment to sustain and provokes the next generation of poets, with Blake at their forefront, to forge an art equal to the task of life. Blake's myth is about madness because, like the Sensibility bards, he felt its challenge—to himself and to his culture.

Blake's early poetry shows him keenly aware of the dilemma of the Sensibility bards.[16] If he knows the same vitality ("Every thing that lives is holy"), he knows too the anguish of the alienation it inflicts. In the unsettling lyric "Mad Song," he both dramatizes and parodies the pained monomania of a Collins or a Cowper, though probably without having either specifically in mind. The speaker of this poem is in love with darkness and the nightly oblivion of sleep. He seeks to escape therein the burden of himself, which acquires pathological proportions in the light of day. But Blake uncovers the narcissism at the heart of this anxiety. The speaker inhabits a world animated by his own neurosis, ruled by a sadistic God he has created to punish himself:

Lo! to the vault
 Of paved heaven,
With sorrows fraught
 My notes are driven:
They strike the ear of night,
 Make weep the eyes of day;
They make mad the roaring winds,
And with tempests play. (415)

Note the irony of the fourth line: the speaker acts in the passive voice. Blake shows a mind utterly dependent upon the very forces that persecute it. The madness of Collins and Cowper, or anyone else so besieged, boils down to a religiously sanctioned self-love, the passion of the sinner for the sins that give him some distinction, however ignoble, in the face of the Almighty.

But how to avoid the fate of the Sensibility bards, balanced precariously on the brink of madness? Blake solves this problem by shaping their metaphysical dualism into a psychological dialectic. His strategy for doing so appears even in as early a poem as "Mad Song," for he introduces into his lyrics a dramatic element that diffuses the strength of feeling. The speaker of "Mad Song" is not Blake, but a persona created to voice certain convictions.[17] A similar dramatic displacement characterizes his nascent myth and allows such conviction to take the form of psychologically objective symbols.[18] As Blake's artistic confidence grows, he elaborates dialectical relations between these symbols (which come to be called Urizen, Los, Urthona, etc.), organizing them ultimately into a comprehensive myth, a myth that dramatizes the dissociation of a unified mind into constituent personae. Blake thus shapes the metaphysical dualism of the Sensibility bards into a dialectical psychology of dissociation and recovery that renders inappropriate anxieties about the alienating effects of vision. The psychological drama of Blake's myth, then, places madness thematically at its center.[19]

The Book of Urizen demonstrates the large role that madness plays in Blake's myth. The poem is usually interpreted as an intellectual satire of traditional accounts of creation.[20] A more psychological reading, however, reveals *The Book of Urizen* to be more than sardonic midrash. Blake wrote the poem to dramatize the madness of the archetypal tyrant, Urizen, who separates himself from an eternal brotherhood, the better to serve his own designs. After his withdrawal from eternity, Urizen labors to escape its scorching passions "In howlings, pangs, and fierce madness" (6: 24). Like Collins and Cowper, he reacts to the vitality around him by retreating into his embattled ego.

But the madness that Blake dramatizes here goes beyond the isolated anguish of the Sensibility bards. It embraces all humanity, for *The Book of Urizen* stages the dissociation of a universal sensibility. This psychodrama, which constitutes the poem's main action, recapitulates in mythological terms a mental dynamic typical of madness. For the universal sensibility Blake represents as eternity dissociates in two ways: an ego divides from the vitality around it, and thought separates from feeling.[21] The first of these divisions involves the fabrication of an inner reality that acquires greater value than the outer, a process dramatized by the autistic withdrawal of Urizen from eternity. The second involves the splitting up of idea and emotion, a fission depicted in the "wrenching apart" of Urizen and Los. Although we usually think of madness as an individual problem, Blake's myth gives it collective significance. The universal sensibility that dissociates when Urizen retreats into himself includes all men and women as potential victims of a maniacal self-love.

Urizen comes into being through the division of an originally unified and homogenous consciousness that Blake describes only obliquely in phrases like "forms of Energy" and "Flames of eternal fury."[22] Leslie Tannenbaum accounts for this division by suggesting that Blake noticed the self-divided character of the Biblical creator (whose personality seems split between his Elohim and Yahweh aspects) and transferred this division to his own myth, Elohim becoming Urizen and Yahweh becoming Los (Tannenbaum 204). But like most purely intertextual interpretations, this one misses Blake's psychological point. If the Bible's creator is self-divided, then man, his real father, must be too, since for Blake all deities reside in the human breast. The act of creation in *The Book of Urizen* represents not so much the *fall* of God as his *birth*, which Blake presents as a species of madness, the dissociation of a unified psyche. In the original division that separates Urizen from eternity, a mentality is born whose individual avatar is self-consciousness and whose collective representation is the jealous god of antiquity. The unsettling implication of this theogony is that such a god comes into being through a pathological division in the mind.

Blake traces this division to its logical conclusion in madness. In the initial phase of the universal mind's dissociation, consciousness contracts into itself. As the poem opens, the only thing known about Urizen is that he is unknowable; his existence begins in negation.

Lo, a shadow of horror is risen
In Eternity! Unknown, unprolific!
Self-closed, all-repelling: what Demon
Hath form'd this abominable void
This soul-shudd'ring vacuum?—some said
"It is Urizen," But unknown, abstracted
Brooding secret, the dark power hid. (3: 1-7)

Urizen initiates the withdrawal of consciousness into self, and as a result reason dissociates from the energy that sustains and directs its primordial function.[23] Blake describes the "dark separation" of Urizen as an "abominable void" to suggest that self-consciousness ends logically in solipsism. Unknown to eternity, the self knows only itself, which is why Blake never endorses the traditional wisdom of the temple at Delphi.

For in his view eternity is a strenuous place, full of change and opposition. Self-consciousness turns pathological when unequal to the task of this existence. Urizen's withdrawal from this reality is an attempt to flee its fires and ends ultimately in autism, the last resort of a mind besieged by life. Valuing its own fantasies over life's pressures and demands, the autistic mind withdraws into itself and creates a surrogate reality where it can be the center of significance. Eventually the outer world comes to figure for the inner world, and all that exists refers somehow to the private workings of the solitary mind.[24] Urizen retreats in this way into a world of his own devising. Life in eternity is too much for him. He has nothing to hold on to, no stability in his existence:

> I have sought for a joy without pain,
> For a solid without fluctuation
> Why will you die O Eternals?
> Why live in unquenchable burnings? (4: 9-12)

The sad irony of this complaint is that Urizen himself is its cause. Self-consciousness separates joy and pain, and allows him to believe that only joy is acceptable and good. So he retreats from the pain of life into the autistic shell of himself.

A world arises that is the objective correlative of this dissociated sensibility. When Urizen withdraws from eternity, he creates not only himself, but also the natural world of suffering and death. As consciousness contracts into self, the barren object-world of nature appears. This is the world of Newton and Locke, a "forsaken wilderness" of "dark deserts" inhabited by "fragments of life," and its creation is contemporaneous with Urizen's acquisition of self-consciousness:

> First I fought with the fire; consum'd
> Inwards, into a deep world within:
> A void immense, wide dark and deep,
> Where nothing was; Nature's wide womb. (4: 14-17)

These lines are startling, for they locate Nature's womb *within* the autistic fantasy of Urizen. If reality is a mental construct, then a fragmented mind will create a fragmented world. The most concrete evidence of Urizen's madness is the broken world he inhabits, the brainchild of his autism.

By implication, Urizen's historical identity is merely a self-inspired fantasy. Urizen is alone among the eternals in having a personal history. As Paul Cantor suggests, he literally makes a name for himself, and in the process creates the conditions of an historical existence (38). Inventing himself, he invents the idea of experience and the authority that arises from the facts of natural life:

> And self-balanc'd, stretch'd o'er the void
> I alone, even I! the winds merciless
> Bound; but condensing in torrents
> They fall & fall; strong I repell'd
> The vast waves, & arose on the waters
> A wide world of solid obstruction. (4: 18-23)

Urizen uses his new concept of experience to build a narrative that will subject others to his designs. He codifies his past into a system of law, a song of himself with leaves of brass. But Urizen's attempted tyranny is just more proof of his madness, for he once again labors to assert part of the mind over the whole, this time in the arena of history. His madness reduces consciousness to self and self to the natural world.

Los advances this dynamic in the second phase of Blake's myth, which dramatizes the dissociation of thought and feeling in the universal mind. Los embodies that part of the mind which both creates and completes the self through the affections. If Urizen represents this self, then Los represents a higher identity revealed in time through impassioned activity. The dissociation of Urizen and Los therefore advances the autism begun by the withdrawal of the former from eternity.

> Los wept howling around the dark Demon:
> And cursing his lot; for in anguish,
> Urizen was rent from his side;
> And a fathomless void for his feet;
> And intense fires for his dwelling. (6: 2-6)

Blake's point here is crucial to his myth: divided from thought, feeling becomes subordinate, and identity, which reveals itself by force of the affections, remains paralyzed by self-consciousness. The eternals enjoin Los to contain Urizen's contraction, so Los builds a bodily identity around an empty name. But since all thought belongs to Urizen, Los has no mind of his own, and his whole labor goes into shaping a partial being. Originally they worked together, every impulse fully known, every idea fully felt, but no longer; their dissociation consolidates Urizen's autistic fantasy.

Under such circumstance, feeling labors strenuously to maintain the image of the self that confronts the real world. Los hammers out a living form for the empty name that inhabits the world of natural history. Many critics have noticed how badly Los's creation turns out, and attribute its failure to Blake's satire (Tannenbaum 204; Cantor 45; Bloom 170). We must look, however, to what motivates this creation to appreciate fully why it fails. Los creates as defensively as Urizen contracts, and under a similar inspiration. Where Urizen fears the activity of life, Los fears the stasis of death:

> ...Los rouz'd his fires, affrighted
> At the formless unmeasurable death
> ....
> And the surging sulphureous
> Perturbed Immortal mad raging. (7: 8-9, 8: 3-4)

Los's fear of finality complements Urizen's fear of futurity, but in laboring against death he ironically substantiates it. The body he builds calcifies Urizen's debilitating changes, giving madness a bodily form. As creator, Los is entirely derivative, and his creation is a pure, petrified mimesis.

> He watch'd in shuddering fear
> The dark changes & bound every change
> With rivets of iron & brass. (8: 10-12)

Urizen's body becomes the organic equivalent of his laws: confining, absolute, and deadly. Los's fear of death inspires a doomed creation that perpetuates the end it would evade.

The striking thing about Urizen's body is its disembodied character. With hallucinatory intensity, Blake numbers the stages of its fossilization, which appear before us with the force of a dream. Cantor reminds us that Los creates not so much a body as a way of perceiving it (46). The disembodied quality of his creation attests to the dissociation of thought and feeling in the universal mind. Blake is describing the genesis of the mentality that appears so often in modern literature, pure self-consciousness stripped of feeling and reduced to an automatic bodily response. Urizen prefigures Kafka's K., Camus's Meursault, Sartre's Roquetin, Borges's Funes and a host of other disembodied moderns. By fabricating Urizen's bodily existence, Los defends himself against the death he fears. Death now belongs to a body that is the unique possession—and perception—of the self. But this creation is ultimately a botch because it makes final Los's own separation from eternity. Such a defense is an existential fiction, and subordinates a higher identity to bodily appearance.

Los unwittingly completes the separation of the inner world from the outer that begins in Urizen's withdrawal. R.D. Laing describes a similar situation in *The Divided Self*, his existentialist analysis of schizophrenia. Seeking protection from the dangers of existence the self withdraws and creates a public fiction that confronts the world in its place (Laing 94-105). Urizen withdraws to escape the fires of eternity, fabricating a world of death in the process. Then Los forges an image of Urizen to defend against the trials of the natural world. A primordial unity becomes constitutionally divided between thought and feeling, the inner world and the outer. Los reacts in horror to his creation, fading away from eternity into a circumscribed, private existence:

> Los suffer'd his fires to decay
> Then he look'd back with anxious desire
> But the space undivided by existence
> Struck horror into his soul. (14: 44-47)

Los cannot bear the abyss of nature. He too contracts into an autistic existence that remakes the world in the image of his own fantasy. Eternity dwindles into time as the universal mind divides against itself.

It should be clear by now that Blake's myth is very much about madness. Even though *The Book of Urizen* offers no program for recovery from the madness it depicts, it diagnoses that condition with impressive psychological acumen. The effort to reunite the divided mind must wait until *The Four Zoas*, Blake's sublime allegory of psychic dissociation, which culminates in a potentially therapeutic apocalypse. A large and ominous question looms ahead, however, one that critics have not begun to ask with much sophistication: what is the relation between madness as literary subject and biographical fact? It was not necessary for Blake to be mad for him to write authentically about madness. But much in his biography points to mental anguish and eccentricity. Blake's visionary experience was enough to taint—almost mortally—his reputation as an artist. Perhaps the old saw about Blake's madness reveals something decisive about his art. A reading of Blake's poems fully informed by the psychological facts would show, I believe, that Blake used his myth to defend against the very affliction it dramatizes. The dramatic displacement characteristic of his myth gives a therapeutic form to mental suffering, saving Blake from the fate of the Sensibility bards. By making madness into myth, Blake works sickness into health. Such at least might be the conclusion of a criticism that restored an historical and psychological context to his myth.[25] Blake has much to teach us about madness. We must resurrect an interest in his eccentricity.

Notes

[1] For details of Blake's exhibition, see Bentley, 215-20.

[2] So reports Henry Crabb Robinson. See *Blake Records*, 311. And see page 7 for the previous anecdote.

[3] These tales were all told by people who knew Blake personally: Henry Fuseli, Crabb Robinson, and Thomas Phillips. See *Blake Records*.

[4] Alexander Gilchrist put the first seal of approval on Blake's mind in his *Life of William Blake: Pictor Ignotus* (1863; New York: Phaeton Press, 1965). On the point of Blake's sanity, Gilchrist declares that "all are unanimous." Blake criticism since has acquiesced.

[5] Wordsworth was not alone in his opinion. Southey met Blake at his exhibition and had this reaction: "You could not have delighted in him—his madness was too evident. It gave his eyes an expression such as you would expect to see in one who was possessed" (41). Lamb never met Blake, but took an interest in his work, dubbing him "the mad Wordsworth" (246). Landor also sensed Blake's affinity with Wordsworth: "he protested that Blake had been Wordsworth's prototype, and wished they could have divided his madness between them; for that some accession of it in the one case, and something of a diminution of it in the other, would greatly have improved both" (48).

[6] For a full transcription of this strange piece, see Mona Wilson, *The Life of William Blake*, ed. Geoffrey Keynes, 2nd ed. (1927; London: Oxford University Press, 1971: 384-85).

[7]Frye and Bloom have all but prevailed in dispelling the cloud of madness that has hung over Blake's reputation. Frye asserts that "The complaints that Blake was 'mad' are no longer of any importance, not because anybody has proved him sane, but because critical theory has realized that madness, like obscenity, is a word with no critical meaning." See "The Keys to the Gates," in *Romanticism and Consciousness*, ed. Harold Bloom (New York: Norton, 1970: 233). Bloom is even more vehement: "The legends of Blake's madness never seem to cease, despite all scholarly rebuttal...The people who still think Blake to have been mad are merely defending themselves from the keenest diagnostician of their own maladies." See *Blake's Apocalypse*, (1963; Ithaca: Cornell University Press, 1975: 442). Such comments create clouds of their own around Blake's reputation.

[8]See David V. Erdman, *Prophet Against Empire*, rev. ed., (Princeton University Press, 1977); Leopold Damrosch, *Symbol and Truth in Blake's Myth* (Princeton University Press, 1980); Jerome J. McGann, *Social Values and Poetic Acts* (Cambridge: Harvard University Press, 1988) and *Towards a Literature of Knowledge* (University of Chicago Press, 1989). Of related interest are the following critical studies: John Middleton Murry, *William Blake* (1933; New York: McGraw-Hill, 1964); Mark Schorer, *The Politics of Vision* (New York: Henry Holt. 1946); E.D. Hirsch, Jr., *Innocence and Experience* (University of Chicago Press, 1964); Morton Paley, *Energy and the Imagination* (Oxford: Clarendon, 1970).

[9]On the issue of mental illness and its literary implications during the latter part of the Age of Reason, see W.B.C. Watkins, *Perilous Balance: the Tragic Genius of Swift, Johnson, and Stern* (Princeton University Press, 1939), and Max Byrd, *Visits to Bedlam: Madness and Literature in the Eighteenth Century* (University of South Carolina Press, 1974).

[10]The insidiousness of this social piety appears openly in a letter Blake's patron Hayley wrote to Lady Hesketh concerning the artist: "I...shall ever be glad to do Him all the little good in my power, & for extraordinary reasons, *(that may make you smile) because* he is *very apt to fail in his art*—a species of failing peculiarly entitled to pity in *Him*, since it arises from nervous irritation, & a *too vehement desire to excel*,—I have also wished to befriend him from a *motive*, that, I know, our angel Cowper *would approve*, because this poor man with an admirable quickness of apprehension & with uncommon powers of mind, has often appeared to me *on the verge of Insanity*" (Keynes, Letters, 118, Hayley's emphasis). In a single breath, Hayley links Blake's social failure and madness!

[11]It is interesting to note that Smart came to inhabit both of the Enlightenment's institutions of exclusion. After release from confinement in

the madhouse he became more and more destitute, until he was arrested for debt and put in prison, where he died. G.B. Hill, ed. *Boswell's Life of Johnson*. 6 vols. Reviewed by L.F. Power (Oxford University Press, 1934-50: 1.397).

[12]For a sense of this tradition, see Plato's "Phaedrus," in *Phaedrus and Letters VII and VIII*, trans. Walter Hamilton (Middlesex: Penguin, 1973), esp. "Socrates' Second Speech: Types of Divine Madness," 46-49. For a sweeping survey of madness as a literary theme, see Lillian Feder, *Madness and Literature* (Princeton University Press, 1980).

[13]Frye coined this term in his article, "Toward Defining and Age of Sensibility," *ELH* 22 (1955): 144-52.

[14]Frye emphasizes the "imaginative animism" of the Age of Sensibility, which is characterized by "treating everything in nature as though it had human feelings and qualities" and a "curiously intense awareness of the animal world." See "Toward Defining an Age of Sensibility," 150.

[15]For an account of Smart's confinement, see the introduction to *The Poetical Works of Christopher Smart*, ed. Katrina Williamson, 2 vols. (Oxford: Clarendon, 1980); for an account of Cowper's, see *Visits to Bedlam*, 150.

[16]For a study of Blake's juvenilia that ponders its relationship to the poetry of the Sensibility bards, see Robert F. Gleckner, *Blake's Prelude* (Baltimore: Johns Hopkins Press, 1982).

[17]The best discussion of the importance of perspective in Blake's lyrics remains Gleckner's essay, "Point of View and Context in Blake's Songs," *Bulletin of the New York Public Library*, 11 (1957: 531-38).

[18]Blake's technique of "dramatic displacement" anticipates Browning and other practitioners of the dramatic monologue. The most complete discussion of the relation between dramatic and lyric elements in post-enlightenment poetry is *The Poetry of Experience* by Robert Langbaum (New York: Norton, 1957), especially Chapter 6 and the conclusion, 182-235. See also David Wagenknecht's discussion of the poem "Spring" in *Blake's Night: William Blake and the Idea of Pastoral* (Cambridge: Harvard University Press, 1973: 24-25). Wagenknecht points out the emergence of a dramatic quality from the poem's lyrical opening.

[19]Brian Wilkie and Mary Lynn Johnson argue similarly in a different context. Discussing *The Four Zoas*, they suggest that "the entire poem reflects the universal, less strictly clinical, psychosis of mankind." See *Blake's Four Zoas: The Design of a Dream* (Cambridge: Harvard University Press, 1978: 76).

[20]As Bloom suggests in his commentary, 906 in Erdman's edition. Illuminating readings of *The Book of Urizen* abound. See Frye, 254-59; Bloom, 164-75; Schorer, 232-35; Paul A. Cantor, *Creature and Creator*

(Cambridge University Press, 1983: 29-54); Clark Emery, "Introduction," *The Book of Urizen,* ed. Clark Emery (University of Miami Press, 1966: 1-47).

[21]This dynamic is typical of major mental illness, in particular schizophrenia. For a full description, see Kayla Bernheim and Richard Lewine, *Schizophrenia: Symptoms, Causes, Treatments* (New York: Norton, 1979), and Eugene Bleuler, *Dementia Praecox, or the Group of Schizophrenia,* trans. Joseph Zinkin (New York: International University Press, 1950), esp. 63-68.

[22]Morton Paley interprets *The Book of Urizen* as a history of the individual mind, the *principium individuationis* that supersedes the infant's oceanic consciousness. See *Energy and the Imagination,* 67.

[23]For an intelligent description of this process, see Hazard Adams, "Blake, *Jerusalem,* and Symbolic Form," *Blake Studies* 2 (1975: 143-65). Adams was the first to describe the dynamic of Blake's myth as a "dissociation of sensibility." As he points out, this dissociation is identical with the Fall.

[24]As Bleuler remarks, "The reality of the autistic world may...seem more valid than that of reality itself; the patients hold their fantasy world for the real, reality for an illusion (66).

[25]I develop these issues at much greater length in *Madness and Blake's Myth* (University Park: Penn State Press, 1989).

Works Cited

Bentley, G.E. Jr., ed., *Blake Records.* Oxford: Clarendon, 1969.

_____. *William Blake: the Critical Heritage.* London: Routledge and Kegan Paul, 1975.

Bloom, Harold. *Blake's Apocalypse.* 1963. Ithaca: Cornell UP, 1975.

Cantor, Paul. *Creature and Creator.* Cambridge: Cambridge UP, 1983.

Ellis, E.J., and W.B. Yeats, eds. *The Works of William Blake, Poetic, Symbolic, and Critical.* London: Bernard Quaritch, 1893.

Foucault, Michel. *Madness and Civilization.* Trans. Richard Howard. New York: Random House, 1965.

Frye, Northrop. *Fearful Symmetry.* Princeton: Princeton UP, 1947.

Gilchrist, Alexander. *Life of William Blake: Pictor Ignotus* 1863.

Keynes, Geoffrey, ed. *The Letters of William Blake.* 3rd ed. Oxford, Clarendon: 1980.

Laing, R.D. *The Divided Self.* Middlesex: Penguin, 1965.

Pope, Alexander. *Selected Poetry of Alexander Pope.* Ed. Aubrey Williams. Boston: Houghton Mifflin, 1969.

Swinburne, Algernon Charles. *William Blake*. 1868. New York: Benjamin Blom, 1967.

Tannenbaum, Leslie. *Biblical Tradition in Blake's Early Prophecies*. Princeton: Princeton UP, 1982.

Postmortem Diagnoses
of Virginia Woolf's "Madness":
The Precarious Quest for Truth

Nancy Topping Bazin

The reputation of British writer Virginia Woolf (1882-1941) is now well established. Her brilliance as a writer is seldom contested, and her place in the literary canon is assured. Whether interested in literary traditions, textual studies, applied feminism, or postmodern theory, most scholars and critics admire what she had to say and how she said it. The variety, volume, and quality of her writings are impressive; her skill as a writer is seen not only in her eight novels but also in her essays, diaries, letters, short stories, biographies and nonfictional works *A Room of One's Own* and *Three Guineas*. A principal area of scholarly discussion and controversy in recent years has centered, however, on what she and her husband, Leonard Woolf, referred to as her periods of "madness." These scholarly discussions have been characterized by imprecise use of language, difficulties stemming from the lack of real knowledge (as opposed to guesswork) that prevails still in psychology, psychiatry, and psychoanalysis, and a desire to say the cause of her mental illness was predominantly this or that when it could have been any number of causes. Since no accurate diagnosis was made while she was alive due to the ignorance and/or biases of the doctors who attended her, the truth has probably slipped away. Therefore, it is important not to oversimplify and to admit that we can only speculate upon the various factors that caused her breakdowns, her suicide attempts, and finally her death. The causes overlapped and intertwined until it is probably impossible to isolate, to any meaningful extent, one from another. Furthermore, although the trauma of incest or bereavement may well have caused her mental illness, the bipolarity prominent in her aesthetic vision and philosophy could as easily have come from genetic factors. Certainly, bipolarity, characteristic of the manic-depressive experience and the larger category of bipolar disorders, does match with her perceptions of her parents' personalities (described in her autobiographical novel *To the Lighthouse*) and with her own ways of conceptualizing both life and art.

Roger Poole stated that his purpose in writing *The Unknown Virginia Woolf* was "to show that the words 'mad,' 'insane,' 'lunacy' must be withdrawn, since Virginia's behaviour throughout her life is...explicable in terms of cause and effect" (3). He prefers the terms "nervous collapse" or "a temporary lack of control, or some kind of breakdown" (22). In *All That Summer She Was Mad*, Stephen Trombley insists "the image of Virginia as a bedridden lunatic is one that ought to be dispelled"; instead he says she had "breakdowns," all explicable in terms of the traumatic events and pressures that preceded them (9). The preference of both Poole and Trombley for the word "breakdown" seemingly has more to do with connotations than denotations, for Evelyn Stone's *American Psychiatric Glossary* defines "nervous breakdown" as "a nonmedical, nonspecific euphemism for a *mental disorder*." In a quote featured on the dust jacket of Louise DeSalvo's fascinating book *Virginia Woolf: The Impact of Childhood Sexual Abuse on Her Life and Work*, May Sarton claims that after reading DeSalvo's book "no one will ever again believe that [Virginia Woolf] was mad."

These rejections of "madness" as the proper word to describe Woolf's "breakdowns" are put forth without defining "madness" or acknowledging that "madness" is a general, lay word similar to the slightly more precise term "psychosis." A psychosis is "any mental disorder in which the personality is very seriously disorganized." There are two kinds of psychoses: "(a) functional (characterized by lack of apparent organic cause, and principally of a schizophrenic or manic-depressive type), and (b) organic (characterized by a pathological organic condition, such as general paresis, brain tumor, alcoholism, etc.)." "Madness" and "insanity" are frequently used interchangeably. The general definition of "insanity" includes "mental illness or derangement" (*Webster's*). In light of these definitions, was Virginia Woolf at times "mad," "psychotic" or "insane"? And if scholars can show specific causes for her breakdowns, does that mean, as Trombley concludes, that she was none of these? Or if the primary cause of her periods of mental illness was incest, as DeSalvo says, or her inability to grieve, as Spilka says in *Virginia Woolf's Quarrel with Grieving*, does that mean she was not periodically "mad"? And if Woolf was sometimes psychotic or, in that sense, "mad" (for at times she required full-time nursing care or confinement to a rest home), what kind of "madness" was it?

The general label of "neurasthenia" applied by Woolf's doctors has been universally dismissed. Was it then a manic-depressive illness as her husband, Leonard Woolf, initially claimed in his autobiography and then later denied in correspondence (Kenney 162fn)? Did she have a "narcissistic personality disorder" as claimed in 1979 by Ernest and Ina Wolf? Could it be labeled "post-traumatic stress disorder"? Or was it, whatever the cause or causes, an undetermined form of bipolarity, within which one possible diagnosis might be manic-depressive psychosis? Is psychoanalyst Alma Halbert Bond accurate in describing Woolf's illness as "an example of the most severe form" of "manic depression" (21-22)? Was there a single primary cause or, as I contend, multiple causes, probably including genetic factors?

A postmortem diagnosis is risky, and all of the cited scholars have been somewhat reductive in their efforts to find a label and a primary explanation for Virginia Woolf's breakdowns and suicide attempts. Nevertheless, each developed and clarified, more than their predecessors, one or more of several possible causes of Virginia Woolf's instability; furthermore, Trombley, in particular, documented the lack of knowledge and sensitivity of the doctors treating her. Yet, whatever new information has been uncovered, the bipolar nature of her experiences remains evident in her diaries, letters, essays, and fiction. Whatever the specific causes of her instability, her vision of life and her views on fiction show such a keen sensitivity to bipolarity that it is difficult to believe that it can be totally disassociated from what her husband in the final volumes of his autobiography described as her periods of "despair" and "excitement" (Kenney 162).

For example, bipolarity permeates *Mrs. Dalloway*, the novel in which Woolf deals most directly (through the character of Septimus Smith) with her periods of "madness." Clarissa Dalloway and Septimus Smith were originally one character; then Woolf split them, making Clarissa predominantly manic and Septimus predominantly depressed in nature. Although only Septimus goes "mad," both show symptoms of mania and depression. For Clarissa, as for Septimus who has killed himself, the moments of rapture are frequently not strong enough to ward off a sense of terror. At such times, Clarissa, too, felt suicidal. Therefore, she admires rather than pities Septimus: "She felt somehow very like him—the young man who had killed himself. She felt glad that he had done it; thrown it away" (283). Woolf emphasizes the bipolar experience in Clarissa at the very end of the novel. When she enters the room, Peter Walsh thinks: "What is this terror? what is this ecstasy?"

Based upon experiences during her periods of both real or threatened "madness," Virginia Woolf was familiar with both terror and ecstasy. She had at least four major breakdowns (1895, 1904, 1912-15, and 1941), made two suicide attempts (1904 and 1913), and committed suicide in 1941. Contributing causes for Virginia Woolf's psychological problems are numerous. Given the traumatic nature of each of these causes, it is surprising she functioned as well as she did for most of her life.

Sexual abuse is known to be a possible cause of long-lasting mental health problems and of sexual dysfunction (Bryer 1426, Burnam 843, Romans-Clarkson 41, Shearer 169, Walker 75). If Roger Poole is correct in his estimate that Virginia Woolf was abused from approximately age 6 to age 22 by her stepbrothers George and Gerald (29), that situation may have provoked her sexual dysfunction with Leonard and possibly the times when she felt she was approaching "madness and that end of a drainpipe with a gibbering old man" (*Letters* 4: 2336). A similar image of a damp "tunnel" with a "little deformed man who squatted on the floor gibbering" appears in her first novel *The Voyage Out* (86), and its protagonist, Rachel, conveniently dies before she has to face marriage. By dying, Rachel successfully escapes her fiance's desire for intimacy and domination and protects both her virginity and her privacy. In both *The Voyage Out* (1915) and *The Years* (1937) Woolf refers to the story of Antigone who is imprisoned in a rock vault because she defied Creon whose son she was to have married; the "grave" was made her "bridal chamber." Not surprisingly, one of Virginia's periods of mental illness began after her honeymoon and recurred after a visit "a year and ten days" later to the site of her honeymoon (Trombley 58).

Obviously, Virginia Woolf was extremely disturbed by her decision to marry Leonard, having admitted quite bluntly that she did not feel sexually attracted to him (*Letters* I: 615). But whether her history of sexual abuse was the source of her indifference is complicated by indications of lesbianism in her relationship with her sister Vanessa as well as with Madge Vaughan, Violet Dickinson, Vita Sackville-West, and Ethel Symth. Passionate physical contact with some of these women is suggested by a number of Virginia's letters (Cook 727-28). Given her history and her inclinations, Virginia was fortunate to find a husband who was willing to forego a sexual relationship as an expected aspect of their marriage and who was content not only to assume the role of her caretaker but also to tolerate her love for a number of women.

Even so, Virginia's serious breakdowns and suicide attempt during the 1912-15 period were clearly related to her attempt to adopt the heterosexual way of life expected of her. Her attempt to conform to society's norms set up conflicts for her that threatened her life.

But before the 1912-15 period of mental turmoil, Virginia Woolf had had two earlier breakdowns provoked by the deaths of her parents. Indeed, the impact on Virginia Woolf's life of sexual abuse and repressed lesbianism cannot be disentangled from the impact of her mother's death in 1895. Julia Stephen's death left her not only with a troubling phantom (to whom she spoke when "mad") but also with an insatiable need for maternal protection. Quentin Bell cites Virginia's observation that her lover Vita Sackville-West lavished upon her "the maternal protection which, for some reason, is what I had always most wished from everyone" (2: 118). Her husband and her sister Vanessa likewise had had to help make up for the enormous loss she experienced when her mother died and "everything had come to an end" (*Moments* 84).

Worse yet, within an 11-year period, Virginia was traumatized by the death not just of her mother but also of her stepsister, her father, and her older brother. Just two years after her mother died, in 1897, her newly married stepsister Stella died while pregnant. Virginia identified with the feelings of Stella's husband, even seemingly with his sexual feelings. Woolf wrote: "Subconsciously I knew that he meant that his sexual desires tore him asunder, together with his anguish at her loss. Both were torturing him. And the [leafless] tree, outside in the dark garden, was to me the emblem, the symbol, of the skeleton agony to which her death had reduced him; and us; everything" (*Moments* 121). From Stella's death in 1897 until Leslie Stephen's death in 1904 were what Woolf referred to as "the seven unhappy years" (*Moments* 117). Leslie Stephen's prolonged illness and death provoked her second major breakdown in 1904. Just two years after that in 1906, Virginia was traumatized once again by the sudden death from typhoid of her brother Thoby.

The manner in which both her mother and her father had responded to death themselves set poor examples for their children. Julia Stephen had grieved so for her first husband that when she died, Virginia had a vision of a man sitting on the bed with her mother's corpse. Mark Spilka suggests that the hallucinated man was Herbert Duckworth to whom Virginia imagined her mother returning "after eight years of widowhood and seventeen years of marriage to Virginia's father" (6). Spilka speculates that this vision provoked Woolf's inappropriate response to the death scene (laughter rather than tears) for which she remained years later plagued with guilt. He claims that "her mother's seeming desertion of the family for this long-lost ghost—the source in life of her private sorrows and of her continuing widowhood even through her second marriage—was the secret cause of Virginia's scornful laughter" (6-7). Virginia's vision emphasizes the extent to which she had been affected by the ever present melancholy that lay just beneath the gaiety of her mother's social self. Julia's failure to resolve her grief or to protect her children from her lasting sorrow over Herbert Duckworth's death made her a poor model for the resolution of their own griefs.

Virginia's father was likewise a poor model for coping with death. As Louise DeSalvo points out, Leslie Stephen had neglected his first daughter, Laura, leaving her care to a German nursemaid for two years after her mother's death (28-29). Later he behaved in the same selfish way after Julia died, both towards her children and his own. He had never assumed a fatherly role with the Duckworth children (which may explain some of George and Gerald's problems) (Love 170-71); yet when Julia died, he expected everyone to wear black, mourn, and minister to him (Moments 56, 93-94). His failure to assume adult responsibility for the children and his demand that they should instead mother him was recklessly egotistical. Moreover, Leslie Stephen's self-pity, his rages over household expenses, his groans and silences made life unbearable. He even expected his stepdaughter Stella to console him with more physical contact than was proper (Love 172). The price paid by Virginia Woolf for Leslie Stephen's childish behavior was very great; for when her mother died, she lost, in a sense, not one parent but two. Since only mothers, not fathers, were to care for children, Leslie assumed no parental role to fill the gap (DeSalvo 29).

Virginia must have suffered, too, from the consequences of Leslie Stephen's neglect of Laura. By the time he remarried, Laura's behavior was rebellious and, as DeSalvo points out, there was probably no room in a Victorian family for a rebellious, emotionally damaged child whose will could not be broken (27-29). Despite rather precocious reading skills at an earlier age, she was, in addition, stumbling over her reading (26). Leslie and Julia Stephen found her impossible and eventually isolated her in a different section of the house (23). Laura having been banished, the consequences of not reading well, misbehaving, or behaving insanely were evident to the younger Stephen children.

Hence, there existed a network of possible causes for Virginia Woolf's mental instability—sexual abuse, repressed lesbianism, a series of traumatic deaths in the family, Julia and Leslie's defects as parents due to their own inability to overcome grief, and the ever present threat of being treated like Laura. Underlying all of this is the possibility that Virginia's mental illness may have been genetic. Manic-depressive psychosis, for instance, usually is. Certainly, there was an amazing record of mental illness in the family. Louise DeSalvo points out that Leslie himself had breakdowns and was sometimes suicidal (35, 114). His brother (James Fitzpatrick Stephen) and his brother's son (J.K. Stephen) both had mental problems. Indeed, according to psychoanalyst Alma Bond, the nephew, "floridly psychotic manic-depressive," died in an asylum as did Virginia's stepsister Laura, whom she labels schizophrenic (24). Virginia's younger brother Adrian was subject to a "lifelong depression" (DeSalvo 257), and her older brother Thoby had made a suicide attempt (35-36). Her sister Vanessa also had a history of depression, was "virtually incapacitated" by depression for two years after her marriage, and suffered a severe breakdown after her son Julian was killed in Spain (DeSalvo 83). Therefore, Virginia Woolf's "madness" may not have been stress-related but genetic in origin. Or it may have been both stress-related and genetic.

Certain facets of the tragedies Virginia Woolf experienced served to enrich her art. For example, when Thoby died in 1906, Virginia's vision of life was clearly affected. She wrote: "I would see (after Thoby's death) two great grindstones...and myself between them. I would typify a contest between myself and 'them'—some invisible giant." It was these visions of the grindstones that made her aware of what she called "Reality" (*Moments* 118)—that underlying, eternal essence she sought to capture in her fiction. She reports a similar increase in the intensity of her perceptions after her mother died—"as if a burning glass had been laid over what was shaded and dormant." Virginia had her vision then of the glass dome at Paddington Station which parallels her description of what, in *To the Lighthouse*, Lily Briscoe tried to obtain in her painting: "It was glowing yellow and red and the iron girders made a pattern across it" (*Moments* 93). In Lily's vision of how she wanted her paintings to be (and Woolf her novels), "she saw the colour burning on a framework of steel; the light of a butterfly's wing lying upon the arches of a cathedral" (75).

Virginia Woolf felt that her writing was also enriched by her periods of "madness." In her diary on September 16, 1929, she wrote: "these curious intervals in life—I've had many—are the most fruitful artistically—one becomes fertilised—think of my madness at Hogarth—& all the little illnesses—that before I wrote To The Lighthouse for instance. Six weeks in bed now would make a masterpiece of Moths [*The Waves*]." Given this belief, it is not surprising that both she and Leonard Woolf rejected psychoanalysis as a possible treatment for her mental illness because it might threaten her talents as a novelist (Goldstein 446-51). However, psychoanalysis (preferably accompanied by a feminist analysis) might have offered her more help than the methods of the doctors Leonard selected. Although psychoanalysis was still a new field, Virginia and Leonard, of all people, as the publishers of the Standard Edition of Freud, should have been more open to exploring its possibilities for Virginia (Goldstein). Instead, as Stephen Trombley has made so clear, Leonard chose doctors who assumed her "madness" was pathological in its origin. They assumed she had weak nerves; to strengthen them, she had to gain weight, rest, and do no intellectual work (Goldstein 445-47; Trombley 139). At one point she was forced to almost double her weight (Spater and Parsons 69); this "deliberate overfeeding" was thought to "stabilize the irregular brain cells supposedly responsible for the illness" (Goldstein 445). The doctors ignored the possible psychiatric consequences of traumas like those Virginia experienced, such as the incest and the series of family deaths. Moreover, they seem to have discussed her condition more with Leonard than with her, and Leonard often went to see them without her.

Worst of all perhaps was the way in which Leonard Woolf consulted behind her back three doctors and Jean Thomas, "who kept a nursing home," about whether it was wise for Virginia to bear children (Bell 2: 8). When Virginia's regular doctor said children "would do her a world of good," Leonard disliked that prescription and quickly consulted with the others. Although Quentin Bell reports that the opinions of the others "differed," "Leonard decided and persuaded Virginia to agree that, although they both wanted children, it would be too dangerous for her to have them." This decision not to have children was "a permanent source of grief to her" (2: 8). Considering this and similar incidents, it is not surprising that she felt there was a conspiracy against her. Too often Leonard assumed a parental role, relegating hers to that of the child, and the doctors listened to him rather than to her (L. Woolf, *Beginning* 156).

Virginia seemingly recorded in *Mrs. Dalloway* (1925) her own experiences in 1913 (Poole 138-47). As in the case of Septimus Smith, a visit with one of the doctors led her, in 1913, to attempt suicide. Like Septimus, she was tormented by guilt over her "lack of feeling" after a death; moreover, it was probably her preference for a homosexual relationship that made her, like Septimus, unresponsive to a spouse (Bazin, *VWAV* 109-10). Post-traumatic stress disorder, commonly experienced by soldiers, may have been an aspect of her problem too; for so Septimus' "shell-shock" would probably be labeled today. Through her fiction she skillfully analyzed the factors that provoked her own suicide attempt. She evidently thought she understood her case better than her doctors, for she scoffed at the doctor in the novel who offered only "a sense of proportion": "To his patients he gave three-quarters of an hour; and if in this exacting science which has to do with what, after all, we know nothing about—the nervous system, the human brain—a doctor loses his sense of proportion, as a doctor he fails" (149).

When Virginia Woolf succeeded in committing suicide in 1941, the oncoming war was undoubtedly an additional factor. In *Jacob's Room*, she associated how she felt about Thoby's death with how mothers must have felt about losing their sons in war. Is it any wonder that both World War I and World War II would be upsetting to someone who knew so well what those losses meant to the families (Bazin and Lauter 15). Added to her deeper psychological problems, the fear in 1941 that Hitler would invade England, her plans with her Jewish husband to commit suicide should that happen, and the presence of bombers overhead provoked in her a sense that she was "going mad" again and that this time she might not recover (Bell 2: 226); therefore, she ended her life in the Ouse River.

Virginia Woolf had every reason to be "mad"—a history of sexual abuse, lesbian yearnings frustrated by her marriage, the trauma of the deaths of four close family members within a period of 11 years, parents who displayed before the children their inability to overcome grief, the haunting presence of Laura banished from the family circle, a family history of mental disturbances, doctors who had no understanding of the causes of her psychological stress, and the strain of two world wars. Another piece of the puzzle is Leonard Woolf who, however well-meaning and devoted, may have overmanaged Virginia, encouraging her to behave as an adult child.

Surprisingly few questions have been asked about the psychology and sexuality of Leonard Woolf, a man who stayed married to a woman from whom he could not expect much sexually and who, before his marriage, was an ultra-efficient, ruthless ruler for the British empire in Ceylon. In "Old Bloomsbury" Virginia reported to their friends that one night Leonard "dreamt he was throttling a man and he dreamt with such violence that when he woke up he had pulled his own thumb out of joint" (*Moments* 166). Leonard claimed he spent three days hitting Arabs with a walking stick because they "treated [him] as a fellow human being." He explained: "It was this attitude of human equality which accounted for the fact, oddly enough, that I hit them" (*Growing* 94-95). In *The Journey Not the Arrival Matters* (20-21), he told how surprised he was to discover what would have been obvious to most people—that it was a terrible experience to drown a day-old puppy. Trombley has assembled other stories of Leonard Woolf's arrogance, insensitivity, and exactitude (269-70; 298-99). Bond notes that Leonard compulsively kept many detailed records, including one of how many words he wrote each day (71). As Poole has pointed out, Virginia was living with a man whose mind was very different from her own (39). Poole suggests that this fact and Leonard's controlling ways may even have contributed to her mental instability and ultimately her death. He sees Leonard's brutality and extreme rationalism in Virginia's portrait of Bart in her final novel *Between the Acts*. Yet, as Virginia once wrote, "nothing was simply one thing" (*Lighthouse* 286). Leonard Woolf's devotion still seems commendable. His management of Virginia Woolf's life kept her alive and well enough most of the time to continue her writing (Bond 97).

But causes aside, what was the nature of her mental illness? During her intermittent periods of "madness," she had many of the symptoms listed in the American Psychiatric Association's *Diagnostic and Statistical Manual of Mental Disorders, III-R* under bipolar disorders, major depressive episode: depressed mood daily, "significant weight loss," persistent "feelings of worthlessness or excessive or inappropriate guilt (which may be delusional)," insomnia, "diminished ability to think or concentrate," possible delusions or hallucinations, "recurrent thoughts of death" and suicide and/or "a specific plan for committing suicide" (222-23). In manic episodes, there can be "decreased need for sleep," greater talkativeness, a feeling that "thoughts are racing," "mood disturbance sufficiently severe to cause marked impairment in occupational functioning or in usual social activities or relationships with others, or to necessitate hospitalization to prevent harm to self or others" (217). Psychiatrist Sherman C. Feinstein was convinced by evidence in Woolf's letters and diaries that she had a "classical case of manic-depressive illness which fulfills every criterion" (339). Parallels between Virginia Woolf's periods of "madness" and the characteristics of manic-depressives are spelled out by Thomas C. Caramagno in "Manic-Depressive Psychosis and Critical Approaches to Virginia Woolf." Leonard Woolf describes one of her manic periods: "she talked almost without stopping for two or three days, paying no attention to anyone in the room or anything said to her. For about a day what she said was coherent; the sentences meant something, though it was nearly all wildly insane. Then gradually it became completely incoherent, a mere jumble of dissociated words" (*Beginning* 172-73). Virginia herself reports "hearing the voices of the dead" and being "exquisitely happy" (*Diary* 2: 283). On another occasion Virginia "became violently excited, thought her mother was in the room, and began talking to her" (L. Woolf, *Journey* 79-80). Manic-depressive disorders are usually genetic and frequently passed from father to daughter (Caramagno 13). Today it would be controlled by prescribing lithium (Jamison 110-12).

The duality or bipolarity inherent in Virginia Woolf's illness meshes with the bipolar personalities of her parents which, in turn, are reinforced by their gender roles. In Woolf's best-known novel, *To the Lighthouse* (1927), the portraits of Mr. and Mrs. Ramsay are based upon her parents. Mrs. Ramsay's personality embodies not only her female roles as nurturer and unifier but also elements of the manic experience, and Mr. Ramsay's personality embodies not only the male role of risk-taker and dauntless leader but also elements of the depressive mode. Their visions of life parallel those of the manic and depressive experiences (cf. Bazin, *VWAV* 17-19). This may be demonstrated by John Custance's descriptions of his experiences as a manic-depressive recorded in his book *Wisdom, Madness and Folly*.

Considering differences in personalities and the limited information we have about Virginia Woolf's experience while ill, we cannot say that her bipolar or manic-depressive experiences were exactly like John Custance's. Yet there are basic similarities in the ways their minds worked: he envisioned the world in terms of the masculine and the feminine; he associated the masculine with depression and the feminine with mania, and he felt that individuals and societies should be androgynous; they had gone wrong because

they were not feminine enough (cf. *Three Guineas*). His descriptions
of depression and mania (31-81) offer parallels to her portraits of the
personalities of Mr. and Mrs. Ramsay respectively.

In depression, Custance was in a universe of horror, feeling
miserable and ill. In mania, he was in a universe of bliss. In
depression, he, like Mr. Ramsay, did not notice visual detail; in
mania he had, like Mrs. Ramsay, an artist's eye. Woolf shows the
difference between Mr. and Mrs. Ramsay's ways of seeing in this
passage: "And looking up, she saw above the thin trees the first
pulse of the full-throbbing star, and wanted to make her husband
look at it; for the sight gave her such keen pleasure. But she stopped
herself. He never looked at things. If he did, all he would say would
be, Poor little world, with one of his sighs" (112). In one state,
Custance withdrew like Mr. Ramsay into his own ego and felt
isolated from others and from God just as Ramsay, in the boat,
looked "as if he were saying, 'There is no God'" (318). In the other
state, Custance felt, as Mrs. Ramsay sometimes did, a "mystic sense
of unity with the All" (*Wisdom* 37; cf. *Lighthouse* 100). In one
mood, he felt repulsion for the outside world and for himself; in the
opposite mood, he felt what Mrs. Ramsay often felt—a protective,
indiscriminate love for all people and a sense of godlike power over
their lives (19, 131). While depressed he felt guilty and, like Mr.
Ramsay, inadequate and dissatisfied; whereas in mania he felt, as
Mrs. Ramsay often did, proud and elated (163). Finally, when a
victim of depression, he was, like Mr. Ramsay, cut off from the
secret of the universe; metaphorically speaking, he could not reach
"Z." But as a manic, he seemed to have "some clue, some Open-
Sesame to creation" (52); so too the artist in *To the Lighthouse*, Lily
Briscoe, depicted Mrs. Ramsay's heart and mind as containing
"tablets bearing sacred inscriptions, which if one could spell them
out would teach one everything" (82). These striking similarities
help to suggest what Leonard Woolf meant when he wrote in
Beginning Again: "the connection between her madness and her
writing was close and complicated" (81).

Despite the ways in which Virginia's episodes of "madness"
enriched her writing, she still dreaded, of course, the suffering she
often endured in these states. Hence, with Leonard's help, she
wanted to maintain her equilibrium, to avoid the swings towards
one pole or the other. Custance envisioned the problem of
equilibrium in these terms: "Normal life and consciousness of
'reality' appear to me rather like a motion along a narrow strip of
table-land at the top of a Great Divide separating two distinct

universes from each other"; and he added, "In the condition of manic-depression, this table-land is so narrow that it is exceedingly difficult to keep on it" (29). Virginia Woolf knew that to slip off it, into mania or depression, meant that she could no longer write or take care of herself. Like her fictional self Lily Briscoe, she was in danger of stepping "off her strip of board into the waters of annihilation" (278). Furthermore, lurking behind the fear of attacks of her manic-depressive illness or, to use the more general term, her bipolar disorder, was the greater fear of prolonged insanity (Bazin, "VWQE" 318).

Virginia Woolf's mental illness fascinates her readers precisely because it is so closely intertwined with her approach to life and her aesthetics. The intertwined genetic and social factors that undoubtedly caused Virginia Woolf's "madness" (or "breakdowns" or "bipolar disorder") and her continuous struggle against instability intensified her metaphysical sensitivities and evoked the experimental forms she invented to express her vision. As she said in her essay "Phases of Fiction," to be "spherical," meaning "comprehensive," a writer's vision must be "double." The novelist must see the evanescent details, which exist in time, and intuit the invisible underlying whole, which is timeless. Virginia Woolf associated a sensitivity to the evanescence of life with depression and her father's vision of life, and she associated a sensitivity to the timeless or eternal with her mother and the "one-making" of mania. She conceived of each of her novels as a little "globe" of life which holds in equilibrium life's two opposite qualities, the "shifting" and the "solid" (*Diary* 3: 218). Attaining wholeness in her art was as important as maintaining a sense of wholeness in her life. Although the bipolarity of her vision could not be eliminated, it could be encircled.

Works Cited

American Psychiatric Association: Diagnostic and Statistical Manual of Mental Disorders. 3rd ed. Rev. Washington, DC: American Psychiatric P, 1987. See Mood Disorders 213-25, Narcissistic Personality Disorder 351, Post-Traumatic Stress Disorder 247-50, Schizophrenia 194-95.

Bazin, Nancy Topping. *Virginia Woolf and the Androgynous Vision*. New Brunswick, NJ: Rutgers UP, 1973. Cited as *VWAV*.

___. "Virginia Woolf's Quest for Equilibrium." *Modern Language Quarterly* 32.3 (Sept. 1971): 305-19. Cited as "VWQE."

Bazin, Nancy Topping, and Jane Hamovit Lauter. "Virginia Woolf's Keen Sensitivity to War: Its Roots and Its Impact on Her Novels." *Virginia Woolf and War: Fiction, Reality, and Myth.* Ed. Mark Hussey. Syracuse: Syracuse UP, 1991. 14-39.

Bell, Quentin. *Virginia Woolf: A Biography.* 2 vols. London: Hogarth, 1972.

Bond, Alma Halbert. *Who Killed Virginia Woolf? A Psychobiography.* New York: Human Services, 1989.

Bryer, Jeffrey B., et al. "Childhood Sexual and Physical Abuse as Factors in Adult Psychiatric Illness." *American Journal of Psychiatry* 144.11 (Nov. 1987): 1426-30.

Burnam, M. Audrey, et al. "Sexual Assault and Mental Disorders in a Community Population." *Journal of Consulting and Clinical Psychology* 56.6 (1988): 843-50.

Caramagno, Thomas C. "Manic-Depressive Psychosis and Critical Approaches to Virginia Woolf's Life and Work." *PMLA: Publications of the Modern Language Association of America* 103.1 (Jan. 1988): 10-23.

Cook, Blanche Wiesen. "'Women Alone Stir My Imagination': Lesbianism and the Cultural Tradition." *Signs: Journal of Women in Culture and Society* 4.4 (Summer 1979): 718-39.

Custance, John. *Wisdom, Madness and Folly: The Philosophy of a Lunatic.* London: Victor Gollancz, 1951.

DeSalvo, Louise. *Virginia Woolf: The Impact of Childhood Sexual Abuse on Her Life and Work.* Boston: Beacon, 1989.

Feinstein, Sherman C. "Why They Were Afraid of Virginia Woolf: Perspectives on Juvenile Manic-Depressive Illness." *Adolescent Psychiatry: Developmental and Clinical Studies.* Annals of the American Society for Adolescent Psychiatry 8. Chicago: U of Chicago P, 1980. 332-43.

Goldstein, Jan Ellen. "The Woolfs' Response to Freud: Waterspiders, Singing Canaries, and the Second Apple." *The Psychoanalytic Quarterly* 43.3 (1974): 438-76.

Goodwin, Jean, et al. "Letter: Reporting by Adult Psychiatric Patients of Childhood Sexual Abuse." *The American Journal of Psychiatry* 145.9 (Sept. 1988): 183.

Jamison, Kay Redfield. "Psychotherapeutic Issues and Suicide Prevention in the Treatment of Bipolar Disorders." *Psychiatry Update: American Psychiatric Association Annual Review* 6 (1987): 108-24.

Kenney, Susan M., and Edwin J. Kenney, Jr. "Virginia Woolf and the Art of Madness." *Massachusetts Review* 23.1 (Spring 1982): 161-85.

Love, Jean O. *Virginia Woolf: Sources of Madness and Art.* Berkeley: U of California P, 1977.

Poole, Roger. *The Unknown Virginia Woolf*. Cambridge: Cambridge UP, 1978.

Romans-Clarkson, Sarah, et al. "Letter: Long-Term Psychiatric Sequelae of Physical and Sexual Abuse of Females." *The Lancet* 2.8601 (2 July 1988): 40-41.

Shearer, Steven L., and Carol A. Herbert. "Long-Term Effects of Unresolved Sexual Trauma." *American Family Physician* 36.4 (Oct. 1987): 169-75.

Spater, George, and Ian Parsons. *A Marriage of True Minds: An Intimate Portrait of Leonard and Virginia Woolf*. New York: Harvest-Harcourt, 1977.

Spilka, Mark. *Virginia Woolf's Quarrel with Grieving*. Lincoln: U of Nebraska P, 1980.

Stone, Evelyn M. *American Psychiatric Glossary*. Washington, DC: American Psychiatric P, 1988.

Trombley, Stephen. *All That Summer She Was Mad. Virginia Woolf: Female Victim of Male Medicine*. New York: Continuum, 1982.

Walker, Edward, et al. "Relationship of Chronic Pelvic Pain to Psychiatric Diagnoses and Childhood Sexual Abuse." *American Journal of Psychiatry* 145.1 (Jan. 1988): 75-79.

Webster's New Twentieth Century Dictionary of the English Language. Unabridged. Eds. Jean L. McKechnie, et al. San Francisco: William Collins, 1979.

Wolf, Ernest S., and Ina Wolf. "We Perished, Each Alone. A Psychoanalytic Commentary on Virginia Woolf's *To the Lighthouse*." *International Review of Psycho-Analysis* 6 (1979): 37-47.

Woolf, Leonard. *Beginning Again: An Autobiography of the Years 1911 to 1918*. New York: Harcourt, 1964.

____. *Downhill All the Way: Autobiography of the Years 1919 to 1939*. New York: Harcourt, 1967.

____. *The Journey Not the Arrival Matters: An Autobiography of the Years 1939 to 1969*. New York: Harcourt, 1969.

Woolf, Virginia. *The Diary of Virginia Woolf*. 5 vols. Ed. Anne Olivier Bell. New York: Harvest-Harcourt, 1977-84.

____. *The Letters of Virginia Woolf*. 6 vols. Eds. Nigel Nicolson and Joanne Trautmann. New York: Harcourt, 1975-80.

____. *Moments of Being. Virginia Woolf: Unpublished Autobiographical Writings*. Ed. Jeanne Schulkind. New York: Harcourt, 1976.

____. *Mrs. Dalloway*. New York: Harvest-Harcourt, 1925.

____. *To the Lighthouse*. New York: Hogarth, 1927.

____. *The Voyage Out*. London: Hogarth, 1915.

Herman Melville
and "The Sane Madness of Vital Truth"

Alisa von Brentano

In "Hawthorne and His Mosses," Herman Melville's review of Nathaniel Hawthorne's *Mosses from an Old Manse*, he formulated a phrase which illuminates his own works more than those of Hawthorne. In comparing Hawthorne to Shakespeare he says that Shakespeare through his "dark characters," such as Hamlet, Lear and Iago, manages "craftily" to express, directly or by insinuation, "those deep far-away things...those occasional flashings forth of the intuitive Truth...those short quick probings at the very axis of reality" which we perceive "to be so terrifically true, that it were all but madness for any good man, in his own proper character, to write, or even hint of them." As an example he cites King Lear who, "tormented into desperation...tears off the mask and speaks the sane madness of vital truth." It was a pervading "blackness, ten times black," which so fascinated him in Hawthorne, the blackness of some unspeakable truth so awesome as to be "maddening" and, when uttered, to be called "madness," for, according to Melville, "The great art of Telling the Truth" is so unorthodox, if not dangerous, as to have to be told "covertly and by snatches."[1]

It is crucial to bear in mind that this notion of "madness" is one of the central themes in all of Melville's major works and without question the only one which unites an otherwise somewhat bewildering diversity of literary approaches and subject matters. The development of this notion, from the society- and heaven-defying "madness" of the main characters in *Moby Dick* and also in *Pierre* to the doubly ironic use of it in *Billy Budd*, therefore best exemplifies and defines Melville's tragic vision. Like many great writers, he varies his perspectives but not the central object viewed from them, and tracing this central concern enables the "eagle-eyed reader" (*The Piazza Tales* 251) (the only kind Melville really cared about) to arrive at a consistent interpretation of his canon.

For Melville the idea of "sane madness" was not only artistic perception but personal experience.[2] His family, frightened by his

149

father's delirium preceding his death, was constantly concerned about Melville's mental state, especially during and after his work on *Moby Dick*. Herman's "condition" was at one point thought to be so serious that one or more physicians were called in to examine him—an event which prompted Melville's whimsical defense of his sanity in the sketch "I and My Chimney."[3]

Not that he had *ever* been considered quite "normal." Even his father had talked about him as being a "slow" boy. His first book, *Typee*, had dealt with his desertion from the whaler *Acushnet*, his subsequent stay amongst a cannibal tribe and his dramatic escape to "civilization." Though the work was enormously popular, his insistence that the cannibals were more "civilized" than his own society and his relentless attack on the powerful Christian missionary system in the Pacific islands made his friends uneasy and his critics hostile. Aware of his reputation, he gleefully wrote to Hawthorne: "What 'reputation' H.M. has is horrible. Think of it! To go down to posterity is bad enough, any way; but to go down as a 'man who lived among the cannibals!'" (*The Letters of Herman Melville* 130).

The matter of his "reputation" was far from amusing, however, for even with *Typee* the clouds of alleged "madness" began to gather. Nineteenth century Christianity was not openly to be assailed; its representatives were influential and relentless. One critic, for instance, found *Typee* suitable only for a "morally inferior" readership in England and added that he was sorry "that such a volume should have been allowed a place in the [Wiley and Putnam] Library of American Books." Another found *Typee's* author "actuated either by a perverse spirit [or]...utterly incapable, from moral obtuseness, of an accurate statement" (Hetherington 47, 49). Thus Melville's best instincts and most humanitarian concerns were destined to clash with the pious pretentiousness of the established order. His outrage at the fact that in Honolulu, for instance, "the small remnants of the natives had been civilized into draught horses and evangelized into beasts of burden" by "devoted self-exiled heralds of the cross" (*Typee* 196, 198) was described as moral insensitivity or manifestation of a "perverse" mind.

In such experiences, which were to increase in hostility on both sides, lay the seeds for Melville's lifelong preoccupation, if not to say obsession, with a social system whose values he found hypocritical and indeed, as he had pointed out in *Typee*, inverted. But far from merely becoming its personal adversary, he would draw from his polar opposition to this system the dramatic configuration for his future works. The strict Calvinistic background of his childhood did nothing to alleviate his increasingly anti-Calvinistic views. To his pious family and acquaintances, of course, this was "madness," and even close friends who liked him in general took issue with this particular aspect of his character. So wrote Mrs. Sarah Morewood, a neighbor and close friend of the Melville family, regarding her husband's view on Melville: "he dislikes many of Mr. Herman's opinions and religious views—It is a pity that Mr. Melville so often in conversation uses irreverent language—he will not be popular in society here on that account—but this will not trouble him—I think he cares very little as to what others may think of him or his books" (Metcalf 251).

It was true that Melville did not write for the "superficial skimmer of pages" (*The Piazza Tales* 251); those "eagle-eyed," like himself, could, he hoped, decipher the hidden levels of meaning in his work. Therefore the obscureness of his deepest thoughts called for a systematic inversion, an opposition of plot and theme, as it were, which, born of necessity, at the same time demanded astonishing artistic imagination, ingenuity and control. By the time he wrote *Moby Dick*, he was a master of subterfuge (of what Thompson has called "Melville's triple-talk") (*Melville's Quarrel with God* 8-9, *passim*). Only to Hawthorne, with whom he shared or at least imagined to share a secret kinship of spirit, did he attempt to bare his innermost soul, and although we do not know exactly what was privately discussed between the two men, Melville's letters to Hawthorne give a deep enough insight into his own state of mind.[4] From them we learn about Melville's bitter frustration in attempting to write for conventional public taste: "What I feel most moved to write, that is banned,—it will not pay. Yet, altogether, write the *other* way I cannot," he explained. "So the product is a final hash, and all my books are botches."

But Melville never really lost faith in his work—only in the judgment of the public: "Try to get a living by the Truth—and go to the Soup Societies.... Truth is ridiculous to men." Caught in this dilemma he could on one hand exclaim "Dollars damn me" and on the other proudly confess: "I have written a wicked book, and feel spotless as the lamb" (*Letters* 127, 128, 142). Ahab's "mad" blasphemous words during his unholy baptism of the harpoons, "Ego non baptizo te in nomine patris, sed in nomine diaboli" (*Moby Dick* 489), he confides in Hawthorne, are "the Book's motto (the secret one)" (*Letters* 133).

Given the essentially autobiographical nature of Melville's writing, the elements of obscureness and subterfuge should not surprise. What surprises is the degree of artistic control with which he managed to employ this strategy—to the extent that all structural and thematic devices become subservient to them. Inversion, thus, far more than a means, became the central and most profound concern in most of his writing. It constitutes a relentless attack on society's most cherished conventions and is therefore "madness"[5] in the eyes of the world.

Moby Dick, Melville's greatest work, also contains his most extensive exploration of this kind of "madness." Ahab's "insanity" is in constant juxtaposition to Starbuck's "sanity" or "right reason," which signifies nothing more than a conventional Christian attitude and adherence to a "truth" which, for Melville, is based on deception and "the incompetence of mere unaided virtue or right-mindedness" (126). This definition of Starbuck's "right reason" must be born in mind as a clue to the somewhat puzzling note Melville made on the flyleaf of a volume of his copy of Shakespeare: "Madness is undefinable—It & right reason extremes of one" (Olson 54, 55).

For Starbuck, of course, it is "madness" that his captain "be enraged with a dumb thing" (164), and Ahab is well aware of his first mate's opinion. "They think me mad—Starbuck does; but I am madness maddened. That wild-madness that's only calm to comprehend itself" (168). By use of the term "madness maddened," Melville actually negates the conventional meaning of the word—as he does in some subtle manner almost every time he uses terms referring to sanity and madness.

In Ahab's (and Melville's) eyes conventional Christian belief, as expressed by Starbuck, is *real* madness; in Melville's ambiguous language (where *white*, not *black*, signifies evil) Ahab's "madness" stands for ultimate sanity. Yet it is a "wild" and "maddening" sanity because Ahab has recognized what he perceives to be the inherent malevolence of God toward man, and it is therefore "madness" caused by a painfully gained "wisdom that is woe" (425). But yet Ahab's "madness" is deliberate and in essence logically motivated. Relentless and irrevocable (like God's "malevolence") it is "only calm to comprehend itself" (168). Indeed "in that broad madness not one jot of his great natural intellect had perished" (185). What Melville presents, in fact, is Ahab's rational madness compared to Starbuck's irrational "sanity."

Clearly, then, "right reason" is in diametrical opposition to "great natural intellect," one standing for the unconditional acceptance of orthodox doctrine and values, the other for the assertion of a superior and independent mind. Like God, Ahab never swerves from his "predestined" course and is in that sense "monomaniacal." If God is ultimately unjust to man, then Ahab, "maddened" by the "woe" of this knowledge, will strike back at the only tangible target "be the white whale agent, or be the white whale principal" (164). As such

The White Whale swam before him as the monomaniac incarnation of all those malicious agencies which some deep men feel eating in them.... That intangible malignity which has been from the beginning.... All that most maddens and torments...all evil, to crazy Ahab, were visibly personified, and made practically assailable in Moby Dick. (184)

As usual, Melville's language is ambiguous here; it is not clear, for instance, whether the whale is Ahab's or God's "monomaniac incarnation." But, as noted earlier, Melville deliberately blurs our senses. Whenever he describes Ahab's "madness" he suggests something other than what he *apparently* says. Another sentence may be considered to exemplify this: "If such a furious trope may stand, [Ahab's] special lunacy stormed his special sanity and...turned all his concentrated cannon upon its own mad mark" (185). Having had numerous hints about the true nature of "madness," the careful reader can only smile—with Melville.

Yet, like Hamlet, Ahab must keep his secret, at least for a while. He knows that to everyone around him "he did long dissemble" and has been able to conceal his "mad secret," the "audacious, immitigable, and supernatural revenge" which has been his dark purpose long before the *Pequod* sets sail. "All my means are sane, my motive and object are mad" (186), he admits, again calmly ascribing "madness" to himself. Since much could be made of a strictly clinical analysis of the precise nature of Ahab's "madness"[6]—an attempt which, though on the surface quite profitable, could only lead to an ultimate misinterpretation of the work at large—it should be remembered that genuinely insane individuals are never capable of discussing and analyzing their "madness" the way Ahab does.

Thus, far from being insane, Ahab is in the true context of the work a "mighty pageant creature, formed for noble tragedies," and his very presence aboard the *Pequod* conveys a palpable sense of grandeur which does not elude even the most prosaic or simple-minded crew members. Long used to think "untraditionally and independently" (73), he is not only the unquestioned master of his ship but becomes the champion of a very special group of men with a special, "predestined"—if not consciously perceived—mission. As such, "now federated along one keel," they constitute an "Anacharsis Clootz deputation from...all the ends of the earth, accompanying old Ahab in the *Pequod* to lay the world's grievances before the bar from which not many of them ever come back" (121).

So strong is Melville's conception of the universal tragedy to be acted out on the *Pequod* that he alludes to the "tragic graces" which are befitting even the "meanest mariners" in this epic struggle (117). Even Starbuck cannot ultimately withstand Ahab—whom earlier he almost tried to kill—his soul, he concedes, being "overmanned; and by a madman!" (169). The rest of the crew, of course, easily succumbs to its captain's hypnotic volition: his "special lunacy." As a harpooner himself, Ahab forges an even closer bond with his harpooners in the "mad" and blasphemous "baptism" of their weapons "in nomine diaboli."

The crew also provides structural balance for the work in that, like a subplot in Elizabethan drama (which strongly influenced Melville), it closely echoes the main events and theme. From the beginning of the journey, for instance, the sailors' "merry" madness (175) parallels the "wild" and "woeful" madness of their captain. Their references to him as "crazy" or "daft," furthermore, are consistent with the general ambiguity of this notion and never detract from their respect and awe of Ahab's "unholy" presence.

But nowhere is the relationship between plot and subplot more important than in the story of Pip, the little black boy who, innocent and cheerful "but at the bottom very bright" (411), is the victim of a set of cruel circumstances which causes him three times to jump in terror off a whaling boat during the attack on a whale, each time nearly to be lost at sea. The first time he gets entangled in the whale line and is carried off by the whale's fierce run. Everyone being "in the hands of the gods" (413), Pip jumps again, despite the warnings of other crew members, is left in the ocean and only "by the merest chance" rescued again. This experience leaves the boy permanently changed: "an idiot; such, at least, they said he was" (414).

Pip jumps yet a third time, much to the wrath of his more experienced companions. When one of them calls the boy a "crazy loon," Ahab mutters to himself, "The greater idiot ever scolds the lesser" (522). Regarding Pip with utmost tenderness and compassion, he takes his hand and escorts him to his own cabin which he will henceforth share with the unfortunate boy.

In this episode Ahab not only reveals his own great and "ponderous" heart (73) but also the original cause of his own "madness." The "luckless" child, abandoned by the "frozen heavens," moves his "inmost centre" and is tied to him by "cords woven of my heart-string." Guiding the boy to his cabin, he exclaims: "Lo! ye believers in gods [sic] all goodness, and in man all ill, lo you! see the omniscient gods oblivious of suffering man; and man, though idiotic, and knowing not what he does, yet full of the sweet things of love and gratitude" (522).

Pip's fate parallels Ahab's in that, like Ahab, he has repeatedly been the victim of a senseless and cruel fate. Alone in the fathomless sea, he has caught a glimpse of the ultimate "Truth," and it has made him "mad." Unlike Ahab, however, he is unable to fight back with courage and defiance: he is simply a poor, unfortunate child who, though completely innocent, has suffered a fate much like Ahab's. In this sense Pip's fate is also prophetic, for he has been abandoned in the ocean three times during an attack on a whale and has been caught in the whale line which nearly killed him. Ahab will be thrown overboard three times during his final battle with Moby Dick and will become enmeshed by the line in the same manner. Like Ahab, Pip in his suffering "saw God's foot upon the treadle of the loom, and spoke it; and therefore this shipmates called him mad." And so ("reasons" Melville) "man's insanity is heaven's sense; and wandering from all mortal reason, man comes at last to that celestial thought, which, to reason, is absurd and frantic" (414). Watching Ahab lead Pip away, an old sailor comments: "There go two daft ones...One daft with strength, the other daft with weakness" (522).

The similarity of this incident to the one in *King Lear* is obvious. Like Lear's fool on the storm-whipped heath, Pip, stripped of all "human sense" talks the insanity of "heaven's sense." Melville's ambiguous language, like Shakespeare's, casts doubts on the actual sanity of heaven. Both, therefore, repeatedly use a somewhat vague reference to "the gods." Ahab, himself "mad," like Lear, not only understands the poor frightened boy but feels his heart moved in a very special way by him and shares with him what scanty shelter there is. Both Ahab and Lear, furthermore, recognize and comment on the ultimate state of man's condition in the universe—a condition which forges in them a profound feeling of pity for and comradeship with the least of their fellow men. In both cases the experience involves a recognition of a higher truth: "wisdom...that is a woe that is madness."

But right before Ahab's final battle with Moby Dick, Pip's unconditional devotion to him and his own compassion and pity for the little black boy threaten to sway Ahab from his ultimate purpose (while on the other hand, of course, they serve to strengthen his resolve). Ever sensitive to loyalty and love, yet he describes them at this point in his life to be "too curing to my malady" and this "malady" to be "for this hunt my...desired health" (534). His hatred of the "spirit" whom he sees personified in Moby Dick is such that no mortal ties can bind him in acting out what he sees as his "predestined" role. Addressing himself to the "spirit," he had observed: "I now know that thy right worship is defiance. To neither love nor reverence wilt thou be kind; and e'en for hate thou canst but kill; and all are killed" (507).

Ahab is well aware of the enormity of his deed. Addressing the all-governing spirit, he declares: "No fearless fool now fronts thee. I own thy speechless, placeless power." Yet, were it really a benign spirit, he would relent: "Come in thy lowest form of love, and I will kneel and kiss thee." To the seemingly merciless and "malignant" nature of this spirit, however, he will not bow "though thou launchest navies of full-freighted worlds" (507). Insisting on his God-like nature he reserves for himself, as a representative of mankind, the right or even the duty to rebel: "of thy fire thou madest me, and like a true child of fire, I breathe it back to thee" (507).

"In this matter of the whale," then, one could easily declare Ahab legitimately mad—and thereby perhaps inadvertently prove Melville's main point in the use of this term. But however much could be said of such an analysis, it would lead to a serious misinterpretation and underestimation of the work, for its central hero is an epic figure, Promethean, Faustian and magnificent in his conception. *Moby Dick*, therefore, stands alone in American literature, comparable only to Elizabethan tragedy in its global perception and to classical literature in the configuration of its hero.[7]

The meticulous artistic control exercised by Melville in *Moby Dick* has often been underestimated, especially in regard to Ishmael's rational and essentially agnostic philosophy as compared to Ahab's "mad" defiance of a prevailing universal dictum. In comparison to Ahab's presence, structurally and thematically, Ishmael, despite his far more detached and sophisticated view, does indeed tend to fade into the background. Both characters being extensions of Melville's own consciousness, their roles in the ensuing events are noticeably disproportionate, and there can be little doubt that Melville was well aware of the inherently more fruitful dramatic potential in Ahab's *Weltanschauung* as compared to Ishmael's. The narrator, therefore, though capable of much interesting observation and speculation, is ultimately destined to resign himself to the "coffins of his existence" (to coin a phrase). Trying to escape them by going to sea he actually floats back in one to be "saved." Not so Ahab! His grave is the fathomless sea, and with his inevitable defeat he nevertheless takes what measure of triumph mortal man can possibly snatch from heaven.

The completion of *Moby Dick* (or *The Whale*, as it was titled in its first, English edition) in an almost unbelievably short period of time had brought Melville on one hand the immense euphoria accompanying the knowledge that he had created a great work of art, on the other the physical and mental exhaustion which must inevitably follow such nearly superhuman accomplishment. However, the most important cause for his emotional turmoil was the fact that the general reaction to the book was devastating. His reviewers took issue with everything: its "disunity," its "strange" and "wild" language, its "worse than heathenish attitudes" and its "thrusts against revealed religion." Worse than that, most of them took the opportunity to insult its author as well. William Harrison Ainsworth's attack in the *New Monthly Magazine* of July 1843 is typical. The style, he wrote, "is maniacal—mad as a March hare— mowing, gibbering, screaming, like an incurable Bedlamite, reckless of keeper or strait waistcoat." The author, according to Ainsworth, was "maundering, drivelling, subject to paroxisms, cramps and total eclipse."

There can be no doubt that the obtuseness which marked the reception of *Moby Dick* had deep and irreversible effects on its author. Lewis Mumford sees this rejection as the centrally decisive factor in Melville's development as an artist. The "flat stupidity" of his critics, he writes, can affect an artist to the point that he

begins to doubt the possibility of literature in a world that so flagrantly misunderstands or ignores its higher manifestations. Faced with such contemporaries, the artist may retire within himself, as Ryder or Cezanne did; but it will only be a miracle that will keep him from taking into his retirement a deep contempt for the people around him. That contempt is worse than isolation; it brings isolation without hope.... There was nothing in the reception of *Moby Dick* that would have lessened Melville's scorn, or helped him to fortify himself against his own weaknesses. Quite the contrary. Like Pierre himself, he was to learn "and very bitterly learn, that though the world worship mediocrity and commonplace, yet hath it fire and sword for contemporary grandeur." (136)

This passage is not only perceptively descriptive of Melville's particular state of mind at the time he wrote *Pierre*, it also sheds valuable light on an otherwise problematic work. Thus while it may seem baffling that Melville could create *Pierre* so shortly after *Moby Dick*, yet Pierre and Ahab are essentially alike in that they challenge both societal and divine law and are therefore "mad." Acting according to his best and most noble instincts, Pierre incurs the wrath of a "system"—on earth as in heaven—which has no sympathy or even tolerance for his cause.

It is interesting that Pierre, as a character, seems to strike a somewhat uneasy balance between Ahab and Hamlet, in that, like Hamlet, he feels a moral obligation to rectify a wrong done by one of his parents (to give "respectability" to the alleged illegitimate daughter of his father, his half-sister Isabel). In doing so, however, he must, like Hamlet, "dissemble," especially to his mother, in order to obscure his true motive. Hamlet-like, he also becomes enmeshed in what he sees as one of the play's darkest and deepest dilemmas: that of incestuous relationships. Caught between the nobility of his purpose and the inevitable moral complications of its execution, Pierre, like Hamlet, is overcome by "nameless melancholy" which eventually turns into despair and climaxes as he reads from *Hamlet*:

> The time is out of joint;—Oh cursed spite,
> That ever I was born to set it right! (168)

Shortly after that, and again parallel to a scene in which Hamlet takes leave of Ophelia, Pierre, seemingly mad, takes leave of his fiancée, Lucy, with the untrue statement that he has married Isabel.

In Pierre's relentless struggle to be true to himself and to what he conceives to be his duty he incurs the wrath of society and finally attempts to break out of the narrow constriction of his condition by declaring himself free from convention; and as his "madness mounted" (183), he exhibits the "reckless, sky-assaulting mood" which characterizes Ahab, rather than Hamlet. Seeing himself as on one side "grandson of the sky" (147), he equates himself with the Titan Enceladus, both son and grandson of an incestuous union. Yet in *Pierre* Melville was neither able to create another epic hero such as Ahab nor indeed evoke the image of an American Hamlet. Thus while Pierre, like Hamlet, ultimately incurs the moral guilt of murder, he is more victim than victor, in however limited a sense.

The reviews of *Pierre* were even more hostile than those of *Moby Dick* and contained even more charges that it and its author were "mad." Typical of them is the one in the Boston *Post*, which said that it was "perhaps, the craziest fiction extant," which "might be supposed to emanate from a lunatic asylum," and that in *The Southern Quarterly Review*, which declared: "That Herman Melville has gone 'clean daft' is very much to be feared; certainly he has given us a very mad book.... The sooner this author is put in ward the better" (Hetherington 235).

The extreme limitations of *Pierre*'s setting, alone, had made it nearly impossible for Melville to project against it a hero of cosmic dimensions, and although the book has been seen as an early study in depth psychology (Murray "Introduction," *Pierre*), artistically it is not satisfactory. But on the other hand *Pierre* illustrates, first, Melville's continuous concentration on the inverse relationship of madness and sanity and, second, his shifting view concerning the balance between the two. In effect the book is most important in that it indicates a transition from the author's already ambiguous concept of sane "madness," in *Moby Dick*, to the even more sinister mad "sanity" in *Billy Budd*.

This distinction, which may appear to be a minor one, actually made it possible for Melville's artistry once again to come into full bloom, for it allowed him to portray that "blackness, ten times black" which had almost obsessively preoccupied him throughout his career as a writer. This much-revised last work, *Billy Budd*, far from constituting any "acceptance" (Watson)—as has often been held—is in fact his darkest vision and indictment of what he saw to be all-pervasive divine malevolence. In such a world there can be no human assertion, no effective defiance (as there had been in *Moby Dick* and to some extent in *Pierre*). Man, however good, noble and potentially heroic, never gets a chance; like the protagonist, Billy Budd, he inevitably must get "nipped in the vice of fate" (*Billy Budd* 118)—*nipped in the bud*, as it were—by the dominant forces of evil whose depravity is pictured as *truly* demented and mad.

For the utterance of such "unspeakable truths," however, Melville's considerable talent for revealing and at the same time obscuring his thought was challenged more than ever. The fact that *Billy Budd* is still commonly misread and that critics have not yet come to any consensus about its true meaning attests to its author's masterful treatment of the subject matter. For anyone familiar with Melville's consistent bent of mind, however, *Billy Budd*, though subtle and complex in its conception, should not pose any serious problems of interpretation.

The action takes place on the sea "which is inviolate Nature primeval" (110) and always Melville's artistically most fruitful domain. Billy Budd, a young sailor of great innocence, "masculine beauty" (52), and inherent nobility of heart and mind, has been impressed by an officer of the British warship *Bellipotent*, from the merchant vessel *Rights-of-Man* (named by her captain after Thomas Paine's book). Billy becomes almost immediately the unsuspecting target of an evil master-at-arms, Claggart, who eventually falsely accuses Billy of having attempted to start a mutiny. Confronted in the presence of his captain ("Starry" Vere) with Claggart's abominable lie, Billy, who at times of great emotional agitation tends to be afflicted with a stutter, strikes Claggart in an almost unconscious reflex to his treachery. Claggart is killed by the blow, and Vere sees to it that Billy is sentenced by a drumhead court and hanged the next morning.

Within this plot, partially derived from the notorious *"Somers affair,"* in which in 1842 Melville's cousin, Guert Gansevoort, presided over a similar military court that decreed the hanging of three mutinous sailors (one the son of an admiral), Melville meticulously sets up a system of allegorical values which, though deliberately obscured by a "naive" narrator, unequivocally establishes the real meaning of the work. Billy clearly represents prelapsarian man—Adam-like in his innocence—Claggart a dark and mysterious agent of the "underground," and Captain Vere absolute or divine authority, be it "agent" or "principal." The Articles of War are the immutable and inhumane laws which govern life on a man-of-war on which, according to Melville, man must ever sail: under "martial Law" and "with sealed orders" (*White-Jacket* 398).

It is interesting that in his darkest work Melville uses Shakespeare's Iago as a model for Claggart, his case study for human depravity which to him is actual madness. Like Iago, for instance, Claggart is intelligent, seemingly reasonable and possessed of many other attributes which are normally admirable. Also like Iago, he hides his dark purpose under the cloak of his "honesty"—

and hides it so well that his victim never suspects his animosity though repeatedly warned by an old experienced sailor, the Dankser, that: "*Jemmy Legs* [Claggart] is *down* on you." Claggart's depravity, like Iago's, stems partially from a perverse sense of pride. Always quick to take offense, he seems almost anxious to do so and, having persuaded himself that he has been wronged, "action is taken upon surmise as upon certainty" (67, 71, 80). This is a verbal parallel to Iago's words:

> I know not if't be true,
> But I for mere suspicion in that kind,
> Will do as if for surety. (I, iii, 380-83)

Needless to say, in Iago's as in Claggart's case, "the retaliation is apt to be in monstrous disproportion to the supposed offense" (80).

Possible "motives" for Iago's and Claggart's boundless yet selective hatred have often been discussed, though to little avail. Since Billy is extremely handsome, envy seems to be the most plausible reason for Claggart's malice toward him, especially in view of the fact that he tends to refer in a sarcastic manner to Billy's handsomeness, even calling him "Beauty" in front of the crew. But Claggart himself, like Iago, is by no means physically so disadvantaged that he should hate anyone for looks alone. He does, of course, attempt to justify his hatred for the young sailor (as does Iago regarding Othello) by imagining that he has "reasons" for offense; but this is self-defensive behavior and part of his general depravity. He does, after all, have an unusually sensitive perception of Billy's true nature in that, the captain excepted, he "was perhaps the only man in the ship intellectually capable of adequately appreciating the moral phenomenon presented in Billy Budd" (78). In this, too, he is exactly like Iago, who, though incapable of any moral rectitude yet is acutely aware of it in others. Talking about his hatred of Cassio, Iago says: "He hath a daily beauty in his life that makes me ugly" (V, i, 19). This seems to be the key to the mystery. Iago, like Claggart, is evil and instinctively hates that which is good, being quite able to discern the manifestation of moral goodness as "beauty."

Whereas Shakespeare does not further explain the nature of evil—or attempt to permit evil to explain itself—Melville does and for the first time uses the words *madness* and *sanity* in a straightforward manner—which is not to say in a conventional context. Of individuals such as Claggart he writes:

These men are madmen, and of the most dangerous sort, for their lunacy is not continuous, but occasional, evoked by some special object; it is protectively secret...so that when...most active it is to the average mind not distinguishable from sanity.... the aim is never declared—the method and the outward proceeding are always perfectly rational. (*Billy Budd*)

But Claggart, who is afflicted with the "mania of an evil nature," has not come by it through "vicious training or corrupting books or licentious living." This is a madness "born with him and innate, in short 'a depravity according to nature.'" Having said this much, the narrator is quick to caution that some readers might interpret what has been said as "Dark sayings" because they might be reminded somehow of "Holy Writ in its phrase 'mystery of iniquity,'" which was "far enough from being intended [!], for little will it commend these pages to many a reader of today" (76). (This is vintage Melville, especially in view of the fact that this same phrase will later be used by Captain Vere as he persuades his officers that they must sentence Billy Budd to death!)

The narrator's assurance notwithstanding, Claggart's condition, which, incidentally, is described within the space of a few lines as "insanity," "madness," "lunacy," and "mania," is promptly linked to a higher, all-pervasive madness. This "depravity according to nature" is, in Melville's language, preordained and reflective of a greater, universal depravity, or madness. "Apprehending the good, but powerless to be it; a nature like Claggart's, supercharged with energy as such natures almost invariably are," has no other choice "but to recoil upon itself and, like the scorpion for which the Creator alone is responsible, act out to the end the part allotted it" (78). Thus preordained, Claggart is ultimately no more capable of being good (or sane) than Billy is of being eloquent in times of emotional turmoil, and both become tools as well as victims in the unfolding drama. In this sense Melville's vision of evil varies from Shakespeare's, where human evil is always to some measure a matter of self-determination. Following Melville's allegorical structure, the "ultimate authority," Captain Vere, must bear the responsibility and the burden of guilt thus allotted him.

There can be no doubt that by indicting Billy Budd, Vere indicts himself. But whereas Melville is unambiguous in the portrayal of Claggart's and Billy's emblematic status, he is far more circumspect when it comes to Captain Vere. The evidence against Billy, in fact, is largely *circumstantial*, and the narrator (as one might imagine) cannot be relied upon in this matter. It is this fact which still causes much confusion about the real nature of "Starry" Vere and of which a very brief summary will be given here.

Vere certainly is as insightful about Billy's exceptional qualities and as sure of his innocence as the accuser himself. He is equally cognizant of the essential corruptness of his master-at-arms, and it is therefore somewhat strange that he sets up a confrontation between the two men in his own quarters, with himself as the only witness and with Billy in a very uncomfortable if not to say dangerous situation. Claggart, who in effect risks incurring a death sentence for bearing false witness, repeats his accusation to Billy while fixing him with the "mesmeristic glance" of a "serpent." The young sailor, momentarily paralyzed by the enormity of the charge and the "horror of the accuser's eyes," is repeatedly told by Vere to "speak" but can react only with inarticulate sounds and an agony "which was as a crucifixion to behold" (98-99). When he recovers his faculties, he strikes out, instinctively and by reflex—as one would in defense against an attacking snake. Claggart falls to the ground and dies instantly.

Vere, after whispering, "Fated boy...what have you done," and asking Billy to help him raise Claggart's body, which "was like handling a dead snake," covers his eyes for a moment and after that is completely transformed. No longer the benevolent fatherly figure of a moment ago, he is now, and will remain throughout Billy's "trial," every inch the "military disciplinarian" (Martial Law, one must remember, for Melville being equal to Divine Law). Vere calls for the surgeon to verify Claggart's death and excitedly refers to it as "divine judgment." He knows that the death was accidental and the blow the result of almost irresistible provocation. The surgeon, an experienced and level-headed man, is taken aback by hearing the captain exclaim: "Struck dead by an angel of God! Yet the angel must hang!" A few moments thereafter he announces his intention immediately to call a drumhead court, leaving the surgeon to wonder whether his captain is "unhinged" (99-102).

The surgeon continues to wonder "professionally and privately" whether Vere has become "the sudden victim of any degree of aberration," but, concludes Melville, that is something "every one must determine for himself by such light as this narrative may afford." With the same ambiguity he speculates:

Who in the rainbow can draw the line where the violet tint ends and the orange tint begins? Distinctly we see the difference of the colors, but where exactly does the one first blendingly enter into the other? So with sanity and insanity. (102)

Having predetermined, if not to say *planned*, Billy's death, Vere loses no time in convening the court, acting as its sole witness. As such he precisely relates Claggart's accusation but mentions neither his own disbelief regarding it nor any alleviating circumstances. Unreceptive to the implied inclination of his officers to keep the unfortunate incident quiet, to defer judgment or to mitigate the sentence, he urges Billy's speedy death by hanging, overruling even the presiding officer of the court and thus making himself both judge and jury—all this under the "appealing glance" of the doomed sailor, who still looks to him as "his best helper and friend" (107). The officers, having been told that nothing can be considered except the deed itself, grow increasingly uncomfortable about their captain's relentlessness: "Couched in it seemed to them a meaning unanticipated, involving a prejudgment on the speaker's part. It served to augment a mental disturbance previously evident enough" (108).

After Vere has effected Billy Budd's death sentence he nevertheless visits him for a last and very private conversation. The narrator, not being omniscient, only speculates as to what might have transpired on that occasion: the captain probably having discussed the sentence and his own part in it in a very blunt fashion but Billy having accepted it—and with a certain sense of pride and joy besides! In any case, he concludes: "holy oblivion, the sequel to each diviner magnanimity, providentially covers all at last" (115). The young sailor is now abandoned to die, his only visitor being the ship's chaplain, who has "the good sense" to realize that Billy, who listens "less out of awe or reverence...than from a certain natural politeness," has no need for him. It is the chaplain, in fact, who seems in awe: "Stooping over, he kissed on the fair cheek his fellow man, a felon in martial law, one whom though on the confines of death he felt he could never convert to a dogma; nor for all that did not fear for his future" (121).

Lest there be any doubt about Melville's general method and purpose, the following passage should make both clear:

Marvel not that having been made acquainted with the young sailor's essential innocence the worthy man lifted not a finger to avert the doom of such a martyr to martial discipline. So to do would not only have been an audacious transgression of the bounds of his function, one as exactly prescribed to him by military law as that of the boatswain or any other naval officer. Bluntly put, a chaplain is the minister of the Prince of Peace serving in the host of the God of War—Mars. As such, he is as incongruous as a musket would be on the altar at Christmas. Why, then, is he there? Because he indirectly subserves the purpose attested by the cannon; because too he lends the sanction of the religion of the meek to that which practically is the abrogation of everything but brute force. (121-22)

Billy dies at dawn, hanged on a yardarm. His last words are "God bless Captain Vere!" (123). Soon thereafter an "authorized" navy chronicle, though "for the most part written in good faith," publishes a completely distorted version of the incident on the *Bellipotent*, charging that "one William Budd" had "vindictively stabbed to the heart" the "respectable" and "patriotic" master-at-arms, Claggart, while he was in the process of reporting "some sort of plot" (130) of which Budd was the ringleader. To the sailors on the *Bellipotent*, however, who "instinctively felt that Billy was a sort of man as incapable of mutiny as of willful murder," he becomes a Christlike hero, and chips of the yardarm became "as a piece of the Cross" (131). All is well on the *Bellipotent* until she engages in hostilities with a French warship, the *Athée*, or the *Atheist*. Trying to board her, Captain Vere is hit by a musket ball and eventually dies from this wound.

It is important that, as the above-mentioned series of events unfolds, no further reference is made to any kind of madness. Instead the action itself signifies constant, unmitigated madness against which any momentary intrusion of logic, prudence or plain sanity seems futile if not downright "crazy." The whole order of things is now so consistently inverse and insane that it constitutes a norm and therefore poses—almost convincingly—as sanity. Melville has come full circle from Ahab's sane "madness" to Vere's mad "sanity." This does not, of course, make Vere a hero of any kind; he merely represents the system, such as it is. In Melville's final vision there could hardly be a hero. Billy Budd, who does possess some heroic qualities, is by no means equipped to fight against the forces which combine to entrap man. As for such heroes as Ahab: they can hardly be invoked more than once in a lifetime and assuredly not on a man-of-war.

Interestingly enough, *Billy Budd* does evoke an echo of Ahab. The old Dankser (a Dane, like Hamlet), who keeps warning Billy about Claggart, seems to recognize "the Truth," as Melville saw it. Marked by the same kind of ghastly white scar which marred Ahab's face—a scar which seemingly caused by lightening also *is* "enlightening"—he also resembles Lear in that he has the "mad" wisdom born of some woe. Yet the Dankser does not get involved in the action. Aware of all that happens around him, he confines himself to a few oracular comments and otherwise stays on the side lines, observing—a grim smile sometimes flickering across his face as he rubs his god-given scar.

If *Billy Budd* is Melville's testament of acceptance it is certainly as dark and grim as the Dankser's smile. In *Moby Dick* Melville had written: "All men live enveloped in whale-lines. All are born with halters round their necks" (281). In this Ahab and Billy Budd are indeed alike even though Billy is much closer to the innocence and pathos of Pip than to the heaven-challenging "mania" of Ahab. It is significant that nearly 40 years after Melville had written *Moby Dick* he ended his literary career with a view essentially unchanged and chose to use yet another life-strangling rope to seal the fate of man.

Notes

[1]Though the madness of Ahab and Pip in *Moby Dick* has often been pointed out by critics, the only consideration of madness as a major theme in Melville's works is that of Lawrance Thompson in *Melville's Quarrel with God*.

[2]The chief facts about Melville's life come from Leon Howard, *Herman Melville*, and Jay Leyda, *The Melville Log*.

[3]Merton M. Sealts, Jr., "Herman Melville's 'I and My Chimney,'" discusses this episode and suggests that Oliver Wendell Holmes was one of the physicians.

[4]Hawthorne's letters to Melville have not been preserved.

[5]Quotation marks are placed around the words "mad," "madness" and the like when not occurring in the texts to indicate they are ironically used.

[6]Henry Nash Smith, "The Madness of Ahab," makes a generally clinical analysis.

[7]Only Marlowe's *Dr. Faustus* is consistently comparable to *Moby Dick*. For a comparison of Ahab and Faustus, see my forthcoming *Melville and Marlowe: A Biographical and Critical Comparison*.

Works Cited

Hetherington, Hugh W. *Melville's Reviewers. British and American. 1846-1891*. Chapel Hill: U of North Carolina P, 1961.

Howard, Leon. *Herman Melville: A Biography*. Berkeley: U of California P, 1951.

Leyda, Jay. *The Melville Log: A Documentary Life of Herman Melville. 1819-1891*. 1951. 2 vols. With a New Supplementary Chapter. New York: Gordian P, 1969.

Melville, Herman. *Billy Budd, Sailor: An Inside Narrative*. Eds. Harrison Hayford and Merton M. Sealts, Jr. Chicago: U of Chicago P, 1962.

____. *The Letters of Herman Melville*. Eds. Merrell R. Davis and William H. Gilman. New Haven: Yale UP, 1960.

____. *Moby Dick. An Authoritative Text, Reviews and Letters by Melville, Analogues and Sources, Criticism*. Eds. Harrison Hayford and Hershel Parker. New York: W.W. Norton, 1967.

____. *The Writings of Herman Melville*. Eds. Harrison Hayford, Hershel Parker, and G. Thomas Tanselle. Evanston and Chicago: Northwestern UP and the Newberry Library. I, *Typee: A Peep at Polynesian Life* (1968); V, *White-Jacket: or The World in a Man-of-War* (1970); VI, *Moby Dick or the Whale* (1988); VII, *Pierre or the Ambiguities* (1971); IX, *The Piazza Tales and Other Prose Pieces, 1839-1860* (1987).

Metcalf, Eleanor Melville. *Herman Melville: Cycle and Epicycle*. Cambridge: Harvard UP, 1953.

Mumford, Lewis. *Herman Melville*. 1929. *A Study of His Life and Vision*. Rev. ed. New York and Burlingame: Harcourt, 1962.

Murray Henry A. Introduction. *Pierre*. Herman Melville. New York: Hendricks House, 1949.

Olson, Charles. *Call Me Ishmael*. New York: Reynal and Hitchcock, 1947.

Sealts, Merton M., Jr. "Herman Melville's 'I and My Chimney.'" *American Literature* 13 (Nov. 1941).

Shakespeare, William. *Hamlet, Prince of Denmark*. Ed. Harold Jenkins. London: Methuen, 1979.

____. *Othello, the Moor of Venice*. Ed. Norman Sanders. Cambridge: Cambridge UP, 1984.

Smith, Henry Nash. "The Madness of Ahab." *The Yale Review* 66 (Oct. 1976): 14-32.

Thompson, Lawrance. *Melville's Quarrel with God*. Princeton: Princeton UP, 1952.

Watson, E.L. Grant. "Melville's Testament of Acceptance." *New England Quarterly* 6 (June 1933): 319-27.

Inmates Running the Asylum:
The Institution in Contemporary American Fiction

Barbara Tepa Lupack

Numerous critics—from Ortega y Gassett to T. S. Eliot, Louis Rubin and Leslie Fiedler to Susan Sontag and Norman Podhoretz—have taken up the cry of the curious death of the novel.[1] But the novel is not dead; the postwar experimental novel in particular is alive, well (though largely misunderstood)—and in search not so much of an audience but of the critical acclaim it rightly deserves.

Different from conventional novels, different even from the modernist novels of Joyce, Kakfa and Faulkner, postwar experimental fiction searches for ways to deal with the violence, brevity and rigidity of life and carries to great extremes the themes of combativeness, fragmentariness, coolness and meaninglessness that are the marks of much modern fiction. It may originate, as Josephine Hendin suggests in her excellent essay on "Experimental Fiction," "in the modernist sense of life as problematic, but unlike the great experimental fiction of the 1920s, it does not lament the brokenness of experience as a sign of the decline of Western civilization. Instead it offers an acceptance of dislocation as a major part of life and perhaps a hope that the displacement of traditional ideals might permit new ways of dealing with the human situation" (Hendin 240).

The modernist hero was shaped by the humanist ethos—political, religious, anthropological and psychoanalytic; the experimental hero of the postwar period is shaped by the concern with the functioning and behavior that spawned and accelerated the growth of ego psychology in the late 1940s, 1950s and 1960s, and is characteristic of an age of increasing technical sophistication (Hendin 240). That hero searches for meaning—adaptation, to use Ihab Hassan's term[2]—which will change his condition; yet his sense of self is shattered and his personality is fragmented. The stabilizing forces of memory and attachment are supplanted by a sense of personal crisis that may be unique to a culture in which consolidation of economic power and estrangement from political process throw the individual back upon himself. As Hendin writes, "The drama of power and vulnerability, once played out in our literature on a social and economic stage, [now] fills the arena of personal relations" (Hendin 243).

From a sociohistorical perspective, the changes which modern man has witnessed in the last few decades have been both innumerable and incredible. From the atrocities of the concentration camps and the bombings of Japanese cities in the 1940s to the Korean conflict in the 1950s, from the Bay of Pigs invasion in the early 1960s to the Vietnam War and the Watergate scandal of the 1970s, from the CIA involvement in Latin America and the Iranscam scandal of the 1980s to the Gulf War in the early 1990s, national and international crises have abounded to haunt the collective American conscience. The rate of cultural change and the spate of massive social dislocations have been formidable: they include assassinations and attempted assassinations of U.S. Presidents, political leaders and idealists, rock stars and a Pope; peaceful and violent racial agitation; ghetto insurrections and white repression; the profound alienation of the young from even sympathetic members of older generations; the seeming inability of political, educational and social institutions to recognize, much less repair, tears in the social fabric; widespread government inefficiency and corruption (Hicks 5); the escalating arms race and the growing fear of nuclear annihilation (which continues still, with the nuclear capability of a surprising host of smaller countries); depression, repression and record unemployment. The insensitivity of a Republican administration which, in the face of increasing hunger among the poor, declared ketchup an "eligible vegetable" for the federally funded school lunch program; the evidence that the Bulgarian national who shot the Polish Pope in Vatican Square was supported by the KGB; the discussion on national television of the presidential "Star Wars" nuclear policy, in which the superpower Soviet Union was referred to as "the Evil Empire"; the mere pose of an Ayatollah Khomeini or a Moammar Khadafy or a Saddam Hussein—all these seem the stuff of absurdist drama or black humor fiction.

Yet they are real, as real as the year 1984 which passed all too unceremoniously, since big brothers like J. Edgar Hoover and Richard M. Nixon had been watching and taping for decades. Science fiction has become science fact. Men and women have traveled to outer space; their journeys are the right stuff for the movie and television industries. Until the Challenger tragedy, the launch of the space shuttle seemed almost as commonplace as American Airlines' take-offs from O'Hare; and hijackings are once again terrorist chic. The political stage has gone from the sublime to the ridiculous to the ridiculously sublime. Kennedy's exhortation to "ask not what your country can do for you" is now as much a part of memory as the original Peace Corps; 1960s idealists were replaced by MBAs who marched to the beats of their personal computers and took bytes out of Wall Street. The bejeaned hippie was relegated to comic book caricature status when conservative college students turned to the Reagan right and the unemployed were urged to read the want ads and then to "vote with their feet."

Little wonder, then, as Raymond Olderman observed in *Beyond the Waste Land*, that in our time, "fact and fiction constantly blur" (2-3). This "fine fading line between fantasy and reality," to borrow Bruce Jay Friedman's phrase, presents a peculiar dilemma for the contemporary writer. It challenges him to shape the shapeless, define the undefinable, legitimize the bizarre and reconcile the paradoxical. As Philip Roth noted in "Writing American Fiction," the twentieth-century American writer, particularly the contemporary novelist

has his hands full in trying to understand, and then describe, and then make *credible*, much of the American reality. It stupefies, it sickens, it infuriates, and finally it is even a kind of embarrassment to one's own meager imagination. The actuality is continually outdoing our talents and the culture tosses up figures almost daily that are the envy of any novelist. (224)

How indeed could contemporary fiction compete with modern fact? It is a problem which writers have faced for years, but one which became particularly acute for the contemporary author. As long ago as 1923, in his famous essay on *Ulysses*, T.S. Eliot observed that the modern writer must give a "shape and significance" to the panorama of futility and anarchy. Eliot himself did just that, in brilliant and innovative works like "The Waste Land" and "The Love Song of J. Alfred Prufrock." But in the intervening years, the shock of Eliot's futuristic vision wore off. Although he debated how to wear his hair and whether to eat a peach, the benumbed Prufrock at least had some options; the contemporary Everyman, even more etherized, had fewer. Eliot's worst fears were confirmed. In a society where the middle class underwrites corporate greed and the tax shelters of the affluent,

April *is* the cruelest month; where James Watt and Anne Burford Gorsuch could staff high environmental posts, there is little wonder "the dead tree gives no shade" or "the dry stone no sound of water" ("The Waste Land," lines 23-24). "I will show you fear in a handful of dust," warned Eliot in 1922, and 23 years later the dust became a mushroom of nuclear proportions. All things considered, life in the wasteland, a "rat's alley where the dead men lost their bones" (l. 115), looks better than half-life in a contemporary Mexico City barrio or a South Bronx slum.

How then can the postwar novelist, whose sense of futility is more panoramic than Eliot's—or Hemingway's or Kakfa's—achieve his task? Heir to the disillusionment not only of the First World War but of the depression and the Second World War, his innocence has been thrice violated. While muteness is one response, fiction is another, and the new experimental novel becomes the vehicle for protest of the absurd circumstances and for the exploration of the shattered self. Born of "Freud, Einstein, jazz, and science," that "swift new novel," according to Anais Nin, can—and must—match "our modern life in speed, rhythms, condensation, abstraction, miniaturization, X rays of our secrets, [and become] a subjective gauge of external events" (Nin 19). In short, it must hold up a mirror to the current sociopolitical madness and allow the contemporary hero (and his reader), by confronting it, to begin to conquer it.

Years ago novels used to end in institutions—marriage (if it was a happy novel), an insane asylum (if it was touched by despair); but contemporary novels *begin* in the institution and aspire to go beyond. "It is," writes Raymond Olderman, "as if Holden Caulfield's quest in *Catcher in the Rye*, ending in an insane asylum, signaled the end of American quests for the pure Utopia" (22). The contemporary novel starts where Holden left off, often right in the actual asylum, which becomes an apt symbol for the organized madness of modern life, particularly for those absurd forces which attempt to deprive the hero of his identity and individuality— ironically, at one time the very measures of his sanity and worth. Madness is both a result of the startling reality and a way of commenting on it. Only one who is out of step with the absurd world, as Roth and other contemporary novelists have defined it, is truly sane—though, since he is at odds with most of society, he is considered insane. And by being out of step, that protagonist is often relegated to the institution, which takes many forms, from the actual hospital ward in *One Flew Over the Cuckoo's Nest*, *Slaughterhouse-Five*, and *God Bless You, Mr. Rosewater*, the hospital prison cell of *Lancelot*, and the military hospital of *Catch-22* to the computerized educational network in *Giles Goat-Boy* and the television collective in *Being There*.

The Tin Drum, though written by German Günter Grass, had a tremendous impact on both European and American literature. A modern parable of Germany, *The Tin Drum* opens in 1953. Oskar Matzerath, a mental patient convicted of a murder he did not commit, sits on his hospital bed writing and drumming on a tin drum the story of his life. Unwilling to settle into the bourgeois shopkeeper's existence which his parents led, Oskar decided at the age of three not to grow anymore and thus to evade his parents' desire to put him behind their grocery counter. His mother, wearied by Oskar's perpetual childhood, gorges herself on fish and dies. Uncertain of his paternity, Oskar eventually kills both his father and his mother's lover, begets a child (who ironically inherits a shopkeeper's instincts) by his father's second wife, apprentices himself to a tombstone cutter, grows to be four feet tall and hump-backed, buys his mistress a delicatessen, takes up drumming again, and becomes a famous musician. Yet he is haunted by guilty memories of all his past misdeeds. His conscience appears in the form of a Black Witch (linked in his mind with a children's game), who contrasts with the motherly women and white-clad nurses to whom he has been drawn throughout his 30 years. Finally he allows himself to be prosecuted for the murder of a nurse he had loved at a distance and thereby gains the antiseptic safety of the mental institution in which he writes his story. In Oskar's willful stunting of his growth, in his erotic infatuations, in his rejection of his fathers, in his postwar successes and in his intermittent remorse, Grass dramatizes Germany's (and by implication the twentieth-century world's) turning from traditional frugal and serious ways to chase after exotic and profane lures (Schulz 140-41). And only in the institution can Oskar reflect on and make some sense out of the loss of values in our age. (It is not until Grass's *The Rat* that Oskar's voice is restored: now a sixtyish, balding video producer, Oskar "creates the future" with his new mythologies.)

In some of the most significant contemporary American novels, as in Grass's novel, the asylum becomes the place in which the protagonist defines his relationship to the cruelly absurd reality of the "sane" world. Published in the same year as *The Tin Drum* was Ken Kesey's *One Flew Over the Cuckoo's Nest*. The hero Randle Patrick McMurphy (whose initials R.P.M. suggest his power) enters the asylum at full throttle but soon collides with the mechanical (and, as her name implies, the ball-cutting) Nurse Ratched (Olderman 36). Big Nurse rules her ward with an iron hand and a mind to match; her patients are all "Vegetables" or "Chronics," though as McMurphy points out, they don't seem "any crazier than the average asshole on the street" (Kesey, *Cuckoo's Nest* 61). Big Nurse, however, does not work alone; she is the agent of the Combine, which rules all things, including time and the heart of man. McMurphy dares to challenge Ratched's authority, and the contest between them becomes intense. As Olderman convincingly demonstrates, McMurphy becomes the modern Grail Knight in the wasteland of the asylum (which in turn is the wasteland of modern society). He gives life to the injured Fisher King, the giant Indian Bromden, and even pierces the institution's silent void by restoring the Chief's voice, while Big Nurse, the Madame Sososstris, is deprived of hers in the last moments of the book. Similarly, he restores manhood to the wastelanders. First he takes the Chief and his other 11 disciples on a fishing trip (despite the fact that the Chief fears death by water: "Afraid I'd step in over my head and drown, be sucked off down the drain and clean out to sea"); later he revives them spiritually as well (Olderman 35-36).

McMurphy soon realizes that if he is to defeat Ratched and all she represents, he must pass his strength on to the others. And so he does; he even helps to initiate the virginal Billy Bibbitt into physical manhood—but his victory is a mixed one. While the inmates increase in mental health, McMurphy is given shock treatments, a chance to capitulate, and—when he refuses—a lobotomy. Nevertheless, his lifeblood strengthens Chief Bromden, who smothers the lobotomized messiah, lifts Big Nurse's control panel, throws it out the window and escapes the asylum. Other inmates follow, by checking themselves out of the ward. Madness here is antiorder, and so a sign of health (Olderman 46); it takes a brain-damaged redeemer like the lobotomized McMurphy to show the way.

Though McMurphy provides much of the action, it is Bromden, who is both the main character and the narrator, who provides the deep and poetic resonances of the novel. Kesey's own experiences on the psychiatric wards allowed him to render accurately the hallucinatory and haunting quality of Bromden's narrative.

While attending graduate school at Stanford University on a creative writing fellowship in the late 1950s, Kesey volunteered to be a paid subject for "psychomimetic" drug experiments at the Veteran's Hospital in Menlo Park. The drugs he took—"long as it's for the U S of A" (Kesey, *Garage Sale 7*)—included Ditran, LSD and other hallucinogens, like mescaline and peyote. After the experiments ended, Kesey remained among the inmates by taking a job as a night attendant on the psychiatric ward. (According to Barry Leeds in *Kesey*, it was this confluence of stimuli—the drugs and the hospital environment—which led him to begin his first novel, still his best-known work [7].) Working the midnight shift, during which he "had nothing to do but a little mopping and buffing, check the wards every forty-five minutes with a flashlight, be coherent to the night nurse stopping by on her hourly rounds, write my novel, and talk to the sleepless nuts," he would help himself to various drugs. During one of these sessions, after choking down "eight of the little [peyote] cactus plants" (Kesey, *Garage Sale 7*, 14), Kesey got the inspiration for Bromden and wrote the first pages of the manuscript which remained virtually unchanged throughout the various revisions. To lend further veracity to Chief's vision of the asylum, Kesey even arranged to be given electroshock therapy. Himself as rebellious and irreverent as his characters Bromden and McMurphy, Kesey believed that authority is not always absolute, and *One Flew Over the Cuckoo's Nest* is his personal statement that the [mad]men who challenge it can triumph; so long as they attempt change (e.g., McMurphy's trying to lift the panel), even their failures are noble, precisely because they try.

The themes of the asylum as institution and madness as a kind of divine sense are also common in Kurt Vonnegut's novels. Combine-like asylums appear in Vonnegut's early works, particularly in the technological world of Ilium in *Player Piano* and the mechanical system of Titan in *The Sirens of Titan*. And the organized madness of government—Nazi as well as our own— drives Howard Campbell crazy in *Mother Night*; the novel takes place in a cell, where Campbell, who tried to remain patriotic to the U.S. while serving the Nazi enemy as a double agent, finally sees the insanity of his own actions and prepares to commit suicide. Campbell's situation dramatizes a negative artistic conversion in which he faces his crimes by interring the multiple pretender selves he abuses (Giannone 50). Madness recurs in more recent works, with the twin characters Wilbur Daffodil-11 Swain and Eliza Mellon Swain in *Slapstick*. Even the original ending of *Breakfast of Champions*, changed at the publisher's request, had both author Vonnegut and his protagonist Dwayne Hoover in an asylum.

Like Kesey's novel, Vonnegut's *God Bless You, Mr. Rosewater* is the story of another redeemer and another asylum. Eliot

Rosewater is the president of the Rosewater Foundation; guilty about his own enormous personal wealth and about accidentally causing the deaths of his mother and of three unarmed German firemen in the Second World War, he retires to Rosewater, Indiana, to save the souls of those who have been bilked or employed by (often one and the same) the Rosewater Foundation. He finds the needy in curious ways, such as pasting stickers which read "Don't Kill Yourself. Call the Rosewater Foundation" on phone booths and on the cars of volunteer firemen. His strange philanthropy causes his wife's nervous breakdown and ultimately his own amnesia and incarceration in a sanitarium. While Eliot is confined, cousin Fred— of the poor Rhode Island Rosewaters—learns that if Eliot dies or is declared insane without issue, Fred stands to inherit his fortune. Naturally, Fred brings a suit against Eliot, but he is not the only litigious one: over 50 paternity cases have also been filed. Fortunately, Eliot comes out of his stupor just in time to settle with Fred and to insure the continuation of his Foundation and its philanthropy by admitting the paternity of every child in Rosewater County alleged to be his. Vonnegut plays Eliot in Indiana off against Fred in Rhode Island: Eliot, crazy, doing what he wants and helping the needy; Fred, normal, immersed in a routine of waste, his spirit exhausted by a life he does not comprehend (Karl 345). Which cousin, then, is the mad one?

In this novel which indicts America's obsession with wealth, the nature of Eliot's good works is sometimes as ambiguous as Vonnegut's epigraph to the book. In that epigraph, Eliot describes himself crossing Times Square at high noon with a Purple Heart on; his self-sacrifice in war and in peace is, however, deflated by the pun on his sexuality which in turn is deflated by the awareness of his impotence (Schulz 46). The quirky Eliot, who works his miracles while sitting on a toilet in an abandoned dental office, is the man who loves best but who can't love at all. Yet very possibly, in Vonnegut's crazy world of technological superiority and obsolescent humanity, the mad Eliot is the sanest man around.

Similarly, Billy Pilgrim in Vonnegut's *Slaughterhouse-Five* is crazed by his wartime experiences. As a replacement in an infantry unit caught in the Battle of the Bulge, Billy was captured without ever having fired a shot—without even having been issued boots or a helmet. Sent to Dresden as a prisoner of war, he survived the 1945 firebombing (just as Vonnegut himself did) by spending the night in a meat locker below the ground. The experience is so intense and traumatic that Billy tries to bury it within himself and thus to escape its painful memory; instead, it causes him to become unstuck in time. On the night of his daughter's wedding in 1967, Billy is kidnapped by Tralfamadorians and taken back to their planet, where he is taught that time—as humans understand it—doesn't exist; everything is part of a continuum, so all past and future actions are part of an everlasting now. He learns to "remember" past and future by traveling backward and forward in his life. His pilgrimage consists of a series of flashbacks and flashforwards which take him to his boyhood; to his Second World War experiences; to his postwar family life in Ilium, New York; to a plane crash in 1968 which kills everyone on board except him and causes his wife's death; and to his own death, an assassination which occurs in 1976 while he is addressing a meeting on flying saucers and the true nature of time. Only the eccentric Kilgore Trout (like Billy, another of the personae Vonnegut assumes), whom Billy meets in the hospital, understands and appreciates his very special pilgrim's vision. It is, after all, precisely his craziness—his getting unstuck in time—which allows Billy to come to terms with the far greater lunacy of the war and of his own postwar society, the slaughterhouse of the modern world. Not simply does *Slaughterhouse-Five* indict contemporary obsession with destructive technologies (e.g., the firebombing of Dresden, a symbol of all that is best in Western culture); it provides Vonnegut the opportunity to comment on the insanity of war generally and, by comparing Americans to Nazis (as he had earlier done with Howard Campbell) and other butchers who operate in the slaughterhouse of contemporary society, the American insanity in Vietnam in particular.

Like Billy Pilgrim, the title character of Walker Percy's *Lancelot* is institutionalized. In fact, the novel is a dialogue which occurs in a prison hospital cell between Lancelot Andrewes Lamar, a Louisiana aristocrat and former football star and Rhodes scholar, and Percival, a psychiatrist-priest. Lancelot does almost all of the talking, with the exception of a few enigmatic "yes" and "no" responses Percival makes to questions posed to him at the end of the novel; but Percival's presence, real and symbolic, is necessary. After years of marriage, Lancelot has learned that his wife has been unfaithful to him. Out of disappointment—and, writes John Gardner, "out of his sophisticated modern sense that there are no evil acts, no good ones either, only acts of sickness on one hand, and acts flowing from unrecognized self-interest, on the other" (1)—he turns his wife's sexual betrayal into a central philosophical mystery: is good mere illusion? In his quest to understand the mystery of good he pursues evil, including voyeurism and murder. The climax to his quest occurs when he destroys the house of Lamar—and a number of people in it—on the night of a hurricane, while a crew is filming a fake hurricane on the premises. Whether the confession Lancelot makes to Percival is that of a madman or of the only sane man left in the world is up to the reader to decide (Simpson 183). Yet Frederick Karl concludes in *American Fiction: 1940-1980* that Lancelot "becomes the repository of moral wisdom about the modern world, the man seeking a pattern" and an illustration of Percy's belief, so consistent with the sixties and seventies, "that insanity is really sanity if the rest of the world is insane" (Karl 25).

In *Lancelot*, Percy says, he used silence to show the failure of communication and tried also to balance the normal and the pathological: "Who is worse off, the patient or the doctor, the inmates or the outside world?...Lancelot is not altogether unhappy in his cell at the prison hospital. He feels better than his doctors in the so-called world on the outside. And the girl in the next cell is mute. Lancelot tries to reach out to her" (Mitgang 1, 20). It is clearly in the asylum, here a retreat from the outside world, that Lancelot is able to define himself and to save, as did his heroic namesake, a damsel in distress. That damsel is Anna, the "new woman," violated back into innocence; buffeted by violence and silenced by its horror, she offers the real hope (if hope in fact exists) for Lancelot and the modern world. But her innocence—like McMurphy's triumph and Lancelot's own driving need to regain balance, sanity and individual worth—does not come cheap.

Percy's brilliant and perceptive portrait of the working of a troubled mind, while conveyed so masterfully in the novel, is not unique to *Lancelot*. All his protagonists grapple with the insanity and absurdity of modern life: the escapist Binx Bolling and his suicidal Kate in *The Moviegoer*; the distracted Will Barrett and the disturbed Dr. Sutter Vaught in *The Last Gentleman*; Dr. Thomas More in *Love in the Ruins* and *The Thanatos Syndrome*; the older Will Barrett and his new wife, escaped mental patient Allie, in *The Second Coming*. Not surprisingly, the psychiatrist figures prominently in each novel.

Percy himself trained as a doctor—interning at Bellevue in New York—though he never practiced medicine. Yet, as Robert Coles notes in his excellent study of Percy, he has written "with obvious understanding about psychiatry and psychoanalysis—to the point that he or those who publish his essays must upon occasion remind readers that he is not a psychiatrist. In fact, through both his articles and his novels he has contributed a good deal to a much needed but still incomplete social history of the feverish involvement between America's agnostic, secularist bourgeoisie and Freud's thinking" (xv). Each of his protagonists suffers from some sort of confusion or loss—in Percy's words, "the malaise"; all must confront their anxieties before they can escape the horrors of their surroundings, through which they pass as if across a lunar landscape (Coles 87). But they do escape, and so it appears that in Percy's view only the insane, who confront the forces which make them so, are sane.

A similar paradox occurs in Joseph Heller's *Catch-22*, which has become not simply a cult classic but also the catchphrase for the ruling philosophy in an absurd world. Caught in a Catch-22, the novel's main character Yossarian is no traditional hero—he is later pronounced clinically crazy by the army doctors and ends up in the base hospital—yet he is one of the few men to question, much less to confront, the military machine and its illogical logic. According to Catch-22, any flier who asks to be grounded is sane, since only insane men would want to fly to almost certain death in the war. But, to be grounded, a flier must demonstrate that he is not sane; however, by asking to be grounded, he demonstrates that he is sane—so he cannot be grounded. Yossarian's request to be grounded is denied because he asked in the first place, thereby proving himself sane and depriving himself of the only acceptable justification for not flying. An untouchable force that renders man powerless by usurping control over his own life and handing it over to an institution which manufactures fatal and incredible death traps, Catch-22 is thus an abstraction which can be—and is—evoked at any time (Olderman 99). "Catch-22 did not exist," claims Yossarian. "He was positive of that, but it made no difference. What did matter is that everyone thought it existed, and that was much worse, for there was no object or text to ridicule or refute, to accuse, criticize, attack, amend, hate, revile, spit at, rip to shreds, trample upon or burn up" (Heller 418).

Yossarian is not only fighting the Germans in a war which can be won: he is fighting the ultimate doublespeak which empowers the military's abuse of power and legitimates its lunacy. *Catch-22*, argues Olderman, does not really deal with the chaos of war, though that is its persistent backdrop; Heller's topic instead is "the one real terror that haunted the novel of the sixties—the organized institution which in the name of reason, patriotism, and righteousness has seized control over man's life" (Olderman 95). For Heller, then, only the crazy Yossarian sees and speaks the truth which the military machine, a collective nightmare and societal asylum far greater than the Combine in *One Flew Over the Cuckoo's Nest*, refuses to recognize.

Heller's novel is replete with half-mad characters. The base medical officer Doc Daneeka doesn't care about the ethics of war; he just wants the fighting to continue so he won't be transferred to the unhealthy climate of the Pacific. Commanding General Scheisskopf (the shithead in charge, as his name suggests) wants nothing but more and more parades: authority without substance. Major Major Major, involuntarily promoted to his current rank by a computer error and unwilling to make any decisions, is in to people only when he is out of the office; when he is in, his orderly must tell people he is out. (Caught by a surprise visitor, he crawls out his own window.) Dunbar doesn't care for any real action; he prefers that everything be boring so that his life will seem longer. And Milo Minderbinder, founder of M & M Enterprises, capitalizes on the war as he profits by everyone else's losses. For resale, he removes the morphine from the soldiers' first aid kits and strips their life jackets—and leaves instead for the dying and the drowning a note assuring them that what is good for private enterprise is good for the country. Excepting the dwarfish Orr, who appears briefly (and who, as his name suggests, provides the only alternative to the military hypocrisy), Yossarian is the sole character in the novel sane enough to appreciate the insanity around him and insane enough to keep trying to find a way out.

Characters like Yossarian, Billy, Lancelot, and McMurphy appear in other contemporary American novels as well, from Pynchon's *The Crying of Lot 49* to Kosinski's *Being There*, from Purdy's *Malcolm* to Styron's *Sophie's Choice*. Their comic angst and half-desperate delight in the illogical complications of life are the result of confronting contemporary institutional madness; that is perhaps why Bruce Jay Friedman, who first popularized the term "black humor," defined it as "one foot in the asylum kind of fiction" (Kiernan 38).

Friedman's description is appropriate, since in contemporary literature the asylum stands as a symbol for the many institutions which oppress man and attempt to deny him his individuality. Historically, as Michel Foucault noted in *Madness and Civilization*, the asylum was "not so much an effort to free the insane from the horrors of rat-infested cells as a drive to bring madness under the rigid and unbending control of reason.... Through the asylum the society would conquer madness by undermining it into conformity" (xvii). The real horror of the asylum in recent novels is that it becomes, in Robert Perrucci's phrase, the ultimate symbol of "the very normality of organized madness" (39).

In *Living By Fiction*, Annie Dillard asks: "Why is mathematics sane and numerology insane? Why is astronomy sane and astrology insane? Why is it sane to perform an autopsy and insane to read entrails?" (138). In the modern world, the distinction between sane and crazy is not always easy to make. Perhaps that is why the institution appears in so much of contemporary American literature—and why it seems that the inmates alone should be running the asylum.

Notes

[1]See Chester E. Eisinger, *Fiction of the Forties* (Chicago: Phoenix Books, 1963): 13; Louis Rubin, "The Curious Death of the Novel: Or, What to Do About Tired Literary Critics," in *The Curious Death of the Novel: Essays in American Literature* (Baton Rouge: Louisiana State University Press, 1967); Leslie Fiedler, "Cross the Border, Close the Gap," *Playboy*, 16 (Dec. 1969): 151; Susan Sontag, "Against Interpretation," in *Against Interpretation* (New York: Farrar, Straus, and Giroux, 1964) 3-14; Norman Podhoretz, *Doings and Undoings* (New York: Farrar, Straus, and Giroux, 1964). See also Jerome Klinkowitz, *Literary Disruptions: The Making of a Post-Contemporary American Fiction* (Urbana: University of Illinois Press, 1975).

[2]See Ihab Hassan, *Radical Innocence* (Princeton: Princeton University Press, 1961).

Works Cited

Coles, Robert. *Walker Percy: An American Search*. Boston: Little, Brown, 1978.

Dillard, Annie. *Living by Fiction*. New York: Harper Colophon Books, 1983.

Foucault, Michel. *Madness and Civilization. The Discovery of the Asylum: Social Order and Disorder in the New Republic*. David J. Rothman. Boston: Little, Brown, 1971.

Gardner, John. Rev. of *Lancelot*. *The New York Times Book Review* 20 Feb. 1977: 1, 16.

Giannone, Richard. *Vonnegut: A Preface to His Novels*. Port Washington, NY: Kennikat P, 1977.

Heller, Joseph. *Catch-22*. New York: Dell, 1969.

Hendin, Josephine. "Experimental Fiction." *Harvard Guide to Contemporary Writing*. Ed. Daniel Hoffman. Cambridge: The Belknap P, 1979.

Hicks, Jack. *In the Singer's Temple: Prose Fictions of Barthelme, Gaines, Brautigan, Piercy, Kesey, and Kosinski*. Chapel Hill: The U of North Carolina P, 1982.

Karl, Frederick K. *American Fictions: 1940-1980*. New York: Harper and Row/Colophon, 1985.

Kesey, Ken. *Kesey's Garage Sale*. New York: Viking, 1973.

____. *One Flew Over the Cuckoo's Nest*. New York: New American Library/Signet Book, 1962.

Kiernan, Robert F. *American Writing Since 1945: A Critical Survey*. New York: Frederick Ungar, 1983.

Leeds, Barry. *Ken Kesey*. New York: Frederick Ungar, 1981.

Mitgang, Herbert. "A Talk with Walker Percy." *The New York Times Book Review* 20 Feb. 1977: 1, 20.

Nin, Anais. *The Novel of the Future*. New York: Collier Books, 1972.

Olderman, Raymond M. *Beyond the Waste Land: A Study of the American Novel in the Nineteen Sixties*. New Haven: Yale UP, 1977.

Perrucci, Robert. *Circle of Madness: On Being Insane and Institutionalized in America*. Englewood Cliffs, NJ: Prentice-Hall, 1974.

Roth, Philip. "Writing American Fiction." *Commentary* 31 (Mar. 1961): 223-33.

Schulz, Max F. *Black Humor Fiction of the Sixties: A Pluralistic Definition of Man and His World*. Athens, OH: Ohio State UP, 1973.

Simpson, Lewis P. "Southern Fiction." *Harvard Guide to Contemporary Writing*. Ed. Daniel Hoffman. Cambridge: The Belknap P, 1979.

Faulkner and the Furies

Kenneth L. Golden

In many works, Faulkner—whether by design or inadvertently—seems to take a particularly Greek view of madness. To be insane or demoniacal is, for whatever reason, to disobey the Delphic admonition—"Nothing in excess." Again and again, major characters show something very close to what the Greeks called "hubris." A person puts an extreme emphasis on something—an idea, an ideal, or a part of himself—frequently in such a way that this emphasis causes a dangerous repression of a part of life or of his own psyche which is quite necessary for a healthy psychology. In the case of the character in which the problem is extreme, the Furies punish him, sometimes in the form of total disfunction (as in a despair leading to suicide), sometimes indirectly in what happens to him at the hands of others because of his imbalanced attitude. This definition of madness based on Greek myth is ignored in the criticism. It is never mentioned in the Joseph Blotner biography. Yet it has significant parallels in the work of twentieth-century psychologists C.G. Jung (1875-1961) and Rollo May (1909-).

Many of Faulkner's characters become so obsessed with some idea or attitude (frequently relating to Southern aristocratic ideals or to the past) that they become neurotic, and some become psychotic to the point of total disfunction because of their attachments to the past or to some ideal in one way or another. Gail Hightower in *Light in August*, has clearly crippled his social and psychological life by such a fixation. His fanatical volubility concerning the Civil War, especially his grandfather's part in it, has alienated him from the community and from his wife; indeed, it has perhaps been a factor in his wife's suicide. Hightower's problem, though a serious imbalance, must be termed a neurosis and not true insanity, since it does not drive him to a point of total and final disfunction. In fact, at the end of the novel, partly through the agency of his friend Byron Bunch, he has been so drawn back into the lives of others that his attitude becomes relatively objective and essentially healthy. Indeed, near the end of the novel, Hightower has something like a religious vision reconciling him to the dilemmas of his experience (465-67).

Yet Joanna Burden, another character in *Light in August,* has problems that fall in the more extreme category. Miss Burden, by the way, is not a Southerner, though she has lived in Mississippi much of her life. She comes from a family of New England abolitionists who instilled her with a fear of her own sexuality and with a missionary zeal to help the Negro as one would a class of people cursed by God (234 ff, 239-40). Her affair with Joe Christmas, a man clearly off balance himself and harried to the extreme by the question as to which race he belongs—represents a swing of the pendulum in the direction of her own femininity. Yet the compensatory swing has been too sudden, too extreme. The affair ends when the other side, the one for so long emphasized— the masculinized fundamentalism of her rearing—causes her to start praying over him (265). This motherly and religious attitude she develops toward him along with her own murderous-suicidal urges when she discovers she is pregnant goad her erstwhile lover into killing her (251-52, 263, 267-70).

Quentin Compson, in *The Sound and the Fury*, is obsessed to the point of extreme psychological imbalance by the ideal of past Southern nobility and respectability, especially as regards his own formerly aristocratic Compson family. This ideal is one of masculine control and, to some extent, of repression, certainly suppression. His final despair leading to suicide is brought on particularly by the realization of the sexual profligacy of his sister Candace as sign of the degeneration of the masculine-aristocratic, "Southern" ideal (97-98, 127-29 ff).

Thomas Sutpen, in *Absalom, Absalom!*, is clearly possessed to the point of madness by the masculine desire to carry out what he calls a "design" (263), a quest for an old style Southern dynasty characterized by wealth and social standing. Sutpen's case is perhaps the best example for illustrating the complexity and depth of the Greek pattern of psychological imbalance appearing typically in Faulkner characters. In the process of acting out his schemes, he becomes clearly excessive, like the Greek tragic hero in the grips of the masculine sin of hubris. In effect, he denies the feminine qualities of love, passive intuition, and relatedness. He rejects and represses these qualities both within himself and in others—in women, in particular—in the name of his willful "design." Thus, in a sense almost of destiny, as though it were the will of the gods,

women—and those with a close emotional bond to those women—
Sutpen has wronged take a heavy revenge on all of Sutpen's plans.
The ultimate disfunction of Sutpen is brought on by the deeds of
other people prompted by Sutpen's extreme hubris.

Sutpen's story is parallel to that of the mythological Orestes
punished by the Furies for his hubris and his sin against the feminine
involved in the murder of his mother. Indeed, Sutpen, in his
monomania, commits grievous wrongs against what psycho-
therapist Rollo May has termed the "daimonic."[1] The forces against
which Sutpen transgresses are the same as those symbolized in
Orestes' avenging Furies. Another aspect of his *inner being* Sutpen
has repressed is the feminine; indeed, it is what psychiatrist C.G.
Jung termed the "anima,"[2] the archetypally feminine side of man's
psyche, the compensations of which can come upon an excessively
masculine individual, like Sutpen, like retributory fate. Unlike
Orestes, whose punishment is lifted through his acquittal by the
court of the goddess Athena, Sutpen never makes peace with the
"anima," the feminine within himself, which he has so rejected as
to cause havoc in his relations with all the women in his life and
those related to them.

The criticism has tended to ignore both Sutpen's madness and
his Orestian nature.[3] Yet Richard P. Adams is correct in pointing out
that Faulkner repeatedly insisted that *Absalom, Absalom!* is Sutpen's
story (174, 183). Some critics, like Cleanth Brooks, recognize the
problem of Sutpen's extreme "passion," his being "totally
committed to the design" (299), without discussing the situation in
any depth as a psychological phenomenon. Olga Vickery makes
reference to Sutpen's "single-minded preoccupation with the
'design'" (93), without treating his masculine excess in any detail.
Though Sutpen has been compared to many literary figures—such
as Melville's Ahab (Swiggert 149) and Hawthorne characters like
Alymer and Rappaccini (Slabey 156)—his similarity to Orestes is
essentially ignored.[4] Very little emphasis is placed on the fact that,
psychologically, Sutpen suffers from an excess of masculinity
parallel to that of the Greek "hubris" (cf. Miller 38) and clearly
commits grievous sins against both the anima within himself and the
feminine in society. Also the commentators have ignored the
parallel between Sutpen's almost tribal compulsion to carry out his
"design" to right the wrong done him and all the dead ancestors
(*Absalom* 220) at the rich man's plantation house, on the one hand,
and, on the other, Orestes' actions to satisfy something like a tribal
justice in regard to the death of his father.

Despite the relative silence of the critics on the subject, a great deal of relevance and depth lies in a modern/classical Greek psychological perspective seeing Thomas Sutpen as the victim of masculine egomania denying for too long the daimonic principle (May) and the anima (Jung) and showing similarities to the situation of Orestes. Sutpen remains so hardened to the realities of life that he is ultimately unable to make the accommodations necessary for the on-going of sane social interaction. His fate catches up with him in the reactions of those individuals who embody the feminine and daimonic principles Sutpen has stifled in his own life. In Delphic terms, he has been "excessive."

Also valuable as a method for broadening the impact of the modern case of Sutpen and his madness is the use of the classical paradigm of the myth of Orestes, whose masculine hubris brings on the retribution of the Furies. In the Greek myth, Orestes witnesses the death of his father at the hands of his mother. He is compelled by moral law to take revenge on whoever causes the death of a blood relative, yet another moral law states that a child may not kill his parent. Thus Orestes is placed in a dilemma akin to that met by the modern individual when nothing is either/or, when whichever of two choices one makes, the outcome is still disastrous. But act the individual must, and Orestes also must act—tragically, as does his modern counterpart, Sutpen. Like Sutpen, Orestes acts by choosing the value nearer to his own ego—his persona,[5] or ego-mask, representing his ties with masculine social qualities such as will, legality, and rationality. Archetypally, the father symbolizes for a man the qualities of personal power, authority, and individual responsibility, as well as the order of things. Orestes' loss of his father symbolizes the individual's having his sense of the "father" aspect of his world within thrown seriously into question. In reacting to the trauma caused by the death of his father, Orestes kills his mother in revenge.

Thomas Sutpen's "design" in which he dreams of being a grandiose plantation owner is just such an over-compensation, in modern terms, and it causes him to kill the feminine within himself and to create havoc in the lives of those to whom he owes love. The blow to Sutpen's manhood occurs when he is yet a boy.

Sutpen undergoes a traumatic experience as a child which is the key factor in the unsettling of his self-confidence and in the birth of an ego-ideal by which he is eventually possessed. The insult that the young, poor, and innocent Thomas Sutpen suffers at the hands of the Tidewater Virginia plantation owner's "monkey nigger" is for

Faulkner and the Furies   187

him the incident paralleling the death of Orestes' father Agamemnon. This event is the palpable root of his hyper-masculine dream of dynastic splendor and social respectability—the fixed idea he calls the "design" (229-35).

Sutpen loses all footing, all grounding, psychologically speaking, because of the incident. Mr. Compson's reference to Sutpen as an innocent (220, 229) is probably quite accurate. He is indeed innocent in a pure sense of the word, especially at this point in his life (cf. Brooks 296-97). His childhood has been lived very close to nature, the world of the mountains, the woods, the animals, the plants—traditionally and archetypically, the world of the Mother. The snub he suffers somehow so affronts his sense of his own self-image that he is utterly traumatized, unable to continue in the same relation to those he deems responsible. He does not go around to the back door to deliver his message, as the slave has told him to do. According to Mr. Compson,

All of a sudden he found himself running.... He went into the woods. He said he did not even tell himself where to go: that his body, his feet, just went there...to a kind of cave.... Because he couldn't think straight yet...he was seeking among that little he had to call experience for something to measure it by, and he couldn't find anything. (232-33)

It is instinctively, then, by the processes of the unconscious and of the body, that Sutpen is driven to his cave-like hideout. In mythological terms, he has found refuge in the womb of Nature, the world of the Mother, has gone there for help and consolation. Yet, it is there that he makes a resolution that leads him henceforward to reject the feminine and all that is represented by the mother. Actually, it is not any representative of the mother world that has upset Sutpen's life. It is rather a hitherto unknown version of the father world that has caused his trauma. Young Sutpen's initiation into the realm of the father has been within the raw, individualistic domain of the American frontier in the mountains of West Virginia. There a man's measure was determined by his (usually narrowly defined) ability to ride a horse, shoot a rifle, or wrestle a bear or another man.

On the Tidewater plantation, however, the youth is faced with a highly evolved, complex social order which he neither comprehends nor can decipher. Further, he has no one to explain things to him. Being forced into the cave-womb, by the insult to his ego, he lacks any guide but his very inaccurate understanding of this example of the plantation world which he thinks has wronged him.

It is likely that archetypal compulsions go to work on the ego of young Sutpen in the cave episode. In his traumatized state, his fledgling ego has not the acumen to deal properly and critically with these forces from the depths of the unconscious. "All of a sudden" (according to Mr. Compson), Sutpen discovers

...not what he wanted to do but what he just had to do. Because if he did not do it he knew that he could never live with himself for the rest of his life, never live with what all the men and women that had died to make him had left inside of him to pass on, with all the dead ones waiting and watching to see if he was going to do it right, fix things right so that he would be able to look in the face not only the old dead ones but all the living ones that would come after him when he would be one of the dead. (220)

We can not be sure whether the above ideas come from Sutpen himself or whether they represent Compson's interpretation, his suggestion as to the young Sutpen's rationale. Whatever the case, this material does represent a part of the image of Sutpen established by the total impact of the novel. The attitude seems to represent the belief in a kind of tribal continuity and pride in one's place in the procession of generations. It contains the belief in some sort of immortality in which one eventually has to face the ancestors and learn their judgments concerning the way he has carried the standard for the clan during the period of his life. Interestingly, no reference is made to any aspects of the Christian cosmology. The impression is conveyed of an ethic which emphasizes the view that the individual shames his ancestors if he allows his own status as an individual and (in turn) their status, to be ignored or insulted. Nothing in the above passage indicates that the ancestors insist that in order to "fix things right" Sutpen is to reject his own blood descendants and family as he later does. Sutpen seems to go far beyond the charge of the ancestors. They would seem to be telling him not to allow his personhood to be taken away, not to forget who he is. In fact, he eventually engages in a quest for revenge which might heap shame on the ancestors. So, at 14, he begins to be seized by the monomaniacal ambition to become himself that which has injured him: "To combat them you have got to have what they have that made them do what the man did. You got to have land and niggers and a fine house" (238). His way of "fixing things right" is to adopt the tactics of the very one who has insulted him: it is as though he tells himself to "get what *he* has, so *you* can do the same to poor little boys like yourself."

One prototype for Sutpen's "design" is the nineteenth-century man of wealth and respectability, the kingly, egotistical individual who dominates nature, his social environment, even his own emotions with a ruthless willfulness. Yet the "design," or at least the state of mind it inspires, is also a modern embodiment of the sin of hubris, of overweening masculine pride and monomania suffered by Orestes and other tragic heroes.

Because of his possession by a compulsion arising from a misapprehension of the archetypes of time and eternity, the image of the individual's place between his ancestors and his descendants, Sutpen is stricken with what Jung calls psychic inflation.[6] Thinking the only way to revalidate his place between the past and the future is to usurp the position of the one who injured him, so that he can himself do the same things the injurer did, he adopts the persona or social mask of the wealthy plantation owner. Being innocent of any but a crude, simplistic sense of morality, Sutpen sets out to appropriate the ideals of the plantation owner's persona. Prompted by archetypal compulsions, he makes a kind of mad leap of faith in the cave, undergoing his own fateful metanoia, second birth, or conversion of character.

Sutpen's goal is to become just as powerful as the plantation owner, to own what he owns, so that he will be eternally revenged upon, and free from the danger of facing again, the insult he sustained at the planter's house. This ideal, however, *possesses* Sutpen. His entire ego is filled with, taken over by, his identification with a particular persona, to the exclusion and repression of other contents, particularly the anima and the daimonic element in the unconscious. This commitment involves a giving over of all his psychic energies, potentialities, and sensitivities to his concern with the "design." He seeks to identify himself totally with a single chosen persona, that of the plantation owner of property, family, and at least titular social standing. Yet Sutpen is forever innocent of any authentic meanings that such an ideal might hold. He merely grasps at the husk and trappings of the ideal with an indiscriminate monomania (cf. 262-64) and with a greed which ignores and represses the complementary opposites of masculinity and egotism represented in the feminine and the daimonic.

To achieve his goal, Sutpen singlemindedly follows as best he can the example of the wealthy and paternalistic planter, his injurer now become his ideal. He represses the feminine side of his own psyche and holds a negative attitude toward the feminine in regards to social relationships. From that afternoon during his 15th year when, in the "cave," he ponders his situation, Sutpen follows the ideal of his surrogate father, the plantation owner. Quentin Compson recalls what his father told him about Sutpen:

He went to the West Indies. That's how Sutpen said it: not...how he liked the sea, nor about the hardships of a sailor's life and it must have been hardship indeed for him, a boy of fourteen or fifteen who had never seen the ocean before, going to sea in 1823. He just said, "So I went to the West Indies." (239)

That is, nothing matters to Sutpen but the hard fact, in the form of a step in the direction of his power-oriented design. General Compson's words to Quentin make clear that the style of Sutpen's account indicated no concern with nor valuation of the emotionally charged details of such an enterprise as a journey to the West Indies undertaken at such an early age. With singleminded concentration on his goal, he ignores the rest of life—especially human emotions and, thus, the complementary feminine, feeling side of life. That is, he himself kills the mother, the feminine, both within himself and in his dealings with others.

Yet Sutpen undertakes heroic actions in the West Indies in the maintenance and protection of his and his partner's property—a sugar plantation. In time, he marries the partner's daughter. Later, when he discovers that his wife *may* have Negro blood—a possibility which, even if a mere suspicion, would not allow this woman to fit into the masculine oriented and authoritarian Southern design—he repudiates her and their child.[7] Here he oversteps the measures of human decency in deserting his wife and child and henceforth refusing to recognize them as his own. He represses the anima, his own internal feminine self, at the same time that he rejects the social demands of the woman and her child.

In casting out his wife and child, Sutpen places himself in a dangerous position as regards the force psychologist Rollo May calls the "daimonic." According to May, the daimonic encompasses the "urge in every being to affirm itself, assert itself, perpetuate and increase itself" (122). Thus, when Sutpen obeys the excessive and overbearing daimonic within himself—in the form of *his* desire to "fix things" and restore his standing with the ancestors—he denies and suppresses the expression of natural daimonic energies in others. Further, he denies the natural expression of the daimonic aspect of the feminine side of his own psyche, channeling those energies for use by his egoistic masculine ideals. "We can repress the daimonic," May warns, "but we cannot avoid the toll of apathy and tendency toward bitter explosion which such repression brings in its wake" (3).

Repressed feminine qualities can cluster and assume daimonic proportions in the form of explosive emotions in compensation for the stifling repression. Retribution of this sort can occur either in one's own psychic reactions or in the projected form of the reactions of others, who, consciously or unconsciously, seek revenge on the repressing agent. Sutpen's masculine willfulness—along with his apathy regarding the feminine—prevents his seeing the possibility of his rejected wife's plotting revenge.

Thus, when his true first-born Charles Bon appears, Sutpen is confused and dismayed. According to Mr. Compson, Sutpen "was not calling it retribution, no sins of the father come home to roost: not even calling it bad luck, but just a mistake" (276). To the heartless, masculine Sutpen logic, a wife—in a general sense, the feminine principle—is merely an instrument, a means to an end—that of the masculine order, the willful "design." Sutpen cannot conceive of a daimonic retribution from the rejected feminine element represented in the first Mrs. Sutpen and her son Charles.

Yet the unlived life of the anima and the daimonic *continues to come back* onto Sutpen through his children and, finally, through his childlike dependent, Wash Jones. The process is in keeping with a psychological principle elucidated by C.G. Jung:

Generally speaking, all the life which the parents could have lived, but of which they thwarted themselves for artificial motives, is passed on to the children in substitute form. That is to say, the children are driven unconsciously in a direction that is intended to compensate for everything that was left unfulfilled in the lives of their parents. (*Development* 191)

The appearance of the repudiated son Charles "Bon" is the beginning of the downfall of Sutpen's "design." Sutpen's Haitian wife moves with her son to New Orleans. Bearing the name Charles Bon, this son meets, at the University of Mississippi, his half-brother Henry Sutpen, son by Sutpen's "respectable" but inane wife, Ellen Coldfield. Ironically, it is now Charles Bon, Sutpen's own first-born son, who assumes the role Sutpen himself occupied at the age of 14. Rather than correcting the actions of his old enemy, the rich planter—in his madness, Sutpen emulates him. He rejects Bon and never acknowledges him as his son. As a person of mixed blood and a son by the wrong kind of woman, Bon is anathema to Sutpen's "design."

In an important sense, though sometimes in an exaggerated way, Bon represents the feminine side of life in a complex culture—something Sutpen has rejected and repressed in the name of a one-sided masculine ideal. Bon possesses many feminine qualities, such as passivity, intuition, and contemplative sensitivity. He is experienced in the cosmopolitan life of feminine sensuality in New Orleans and has about him an air of charm and mystery (93-96).

Charles Bon is the agent of his mother, Sutpen's Haitian wife, and of the daimonic feminine element. The first Mrs. Sutpen seems to have consciously plotted to contaminate Sutpen's ("pure") white, respectable family which forms such an important part of the "design." Mr. Compson, according to Quentin, speaks of Sutpen as "a man who could believe a scorned and angry woman could be bought off with formal logic" (269). Quentin realizes that "It didn't work." By falling in love with Sutpen's daughter, Judith, Bon sets in motion a chain of events that proves the ruination of the design.

Ellen Coldfield Sutpen is favorably disposed toward Charles Bon as suitor for her daughter's hand. Her son, Henry, dearly loves Bon, loves him with the selfless sort of love that Sutpen has repressed in his relationships with everyone, women or otherwise (89). The fact that the sort of love Henry holds for Charles is feminine in its depth and character sheds light on Henry's role as compensatory instrument of a daimonic power that is feminine but also potentially destructive. For this close friendship sets the stage for the violent events that destroy Sutpen's "design." After the war, Bon arrives at Sutpen's Hundred bent on marrying Judith. Henry (now knowing who Bon is), in what appears to be a complete reversal, succumbs to the voice of his father's "Southern" male-authoritarian principles and kills Bon in order to protect his sister from miscegenation and incest (96-104).

A murderer now, Henry flees, leaving Sutpen without the "respectable" male heir necessary to the "design." Ruthlessly, Sutpen tries to get his sister-in-law to "breed" with him, promising to marry her if the result is male. Rosa Coldfield refuses, and Sutpen seduces the 14-year-old granddaughter of his "white trash" foreman, Wash Jones. When Milly has a female child, Sutpen reacts in an unfeeling, crassly masculine way: "'Well, Milly: too bad you're not a mare...Then I could have given you a stall in the stable'" (286).

Wash himself—representing the feminine, or at least his daughter—parallels the Furies in the myth, for the revenge he takes on Sutpen for the comment is of an essentially feminine and impulsive nature. Indeed, his killing of Sutpen with the rusty scythe is fueled by suddenly aroused daimonic emotional elements deep within Wash's own psyche. Time, too, like the daimonic forces of compensation, has caught up with Sutpen (cf. Sullivan 198).

An outrageous coda, a final emblem representing Sutpen's insane tragedy, is the tableau involving his last male descendent: Jim Bond, a miscegenated idiot babbling in the burnt-out ruins of Sutpen's plantation house at the end of the first decade of the twentieth century. Charles Bon fathers a son by a New Orleans morganatic octoroon bride. In another eruption of daimonic compensatory forces out of the unconscious, Sutpen's grandson, Charles Etienne de Saint Velery Bon pays back, as it were, the cruelties involved in Sutpen's "design" by marrying a coal-black, brute-like woman whom he flouts recklessly in the face of the respectable Southern community, the approval of which Sutpen has craved from his youth onward. Jim Bond, the "bondslave," is the fruit of that match. The wheel has come full circle: the ultimate result of Sutpen's quest for "Southern" respectability, Jim Bond, a direct descendent of the rejected first wife, has been enslaved by the demon of insanity.

Sutpen's "design" is an *idée fixe* generated out of archetypal compulsions during his meditation in the cave to recuperate from the trauma he suffered at the hands of the slave of the respectable plantation owner. The psychic inflation brought on by the "design" blinds Sutpen to a vast portion of life, causing him to ignore and deny the demands of the anima within himself, the feminine principle in his social environment, as well as the volatile daimonic factor, especially in the lives or those related to him by blood or social ties. Sutpen goes far enough in the masculine heroic direction of "design"-building to suffer the inevitable *enantiodromia*, or reversal of fortune, of the tragic hero. Like Orestes, he murders the feminine, the mother, in the name of the father, thus suffering punishment by the Furies in the form of the daimonic revenge of the neglected element—the feminine; but, unlike Orestes, he never comes to self-knowledge, is never acquitted of his crime, as Orestes is in the Athenian court (Barrett 277-78).

Faulkner's work has a veritable panorama of characters parallel to Sutpen displaying hubris or some kind of debilitating imbalance in the psyche and frequently pursued to their ends by the Furies of daimonic retribution. It includes, of course, for the most part, Southern characters. The form generally taken, as well as the specific causation, relates to that character's being a Southerner at a given point in history. Yet, primarily, Faulkner's work is universal in its essential quality and only Southern by accident. His insight into both neurosis and psychosis in the nineteenth- and twentieth-century world of his fiction has clear depth both when seen in terms of the classical Greek tradition—with its heart in myth, perennial and ubiquitous throughout the world—and in terms of the insights of modern clinicians like Jung and May.

Notes

[1]May defines the daimonic as "any natural function which has 'the power to take over the whole person. Sex and eros, anger and rage, and the craving for power are examples.... When this power goes awry and one element usurps control over the total personality, we have 'daimon possession,' the traditional name through history for psychosis" (120). Since the daimonic is associated with eros, because of Sutpen's ignorance of and denial of the value of love, the daimonic is both that which he has repressed in himself and what he has suppressed in others. The daimonic is frequently associated with the feminine (see Barrett 278-80). Sutpen and Orestes have both wronged the daimonic. Yet the matter is somewhat complicated. Though here I usually refer to the daimonic as the repressed element which keeps returning, in a certain sense, the masculine power drive is also daimonic, according to May's definition. However, in that sense, the daimonic in Sutpen has been possessed by the desire for the artificial trappings of the rational persona, thus making the daimonic in the other sense more appropriate in referring to that deep element which revenges itself upon Sutpen for his denying of it both in himself and in others.

[2]The anima is the feminine aspect of the male psyche. Jung also uses the term for the archetype, or pattern in the unconscious representing the feminine side (see Jung, *Archetypes* 54-74).

[3]According to Connolly, "Most of the 60's and 70's studies are devoted to the two general topics of 'What went on at Sutpen's Hundred' and 'Who is a reliable narrator and who is not?'" (255-56). Occasionally, Faulkner critics mention Greek terms, giving no real explanation of the matters in the novel to which they relate and putting no emphasis on a classical Greek definition of madness. For example, Scott calls the novel "almost Euripidean in power" with no further explanation, never even

mentioning psychological matters. Brylowski, in "Faulkner's 'Mythology,'" makes no reference to a connection between madness and mythology. He cites Fry, Cassirer, and Eliade—never Jung or May. His use of myth relates, for the most part, to what might be termed mythological "parallels."

⁴Though Adams mentions the presence of mythical patterns of a biblical, classical, or medieval nature (181) in Faulkner's portrayal of Sutpen, he never discusses Sutpen's madness or even mentions Orestes or the Furies. Chavkin, focusing on an "alternative to Sutpen's 'Design,'" deals more with saner, mostly feminine characters, rather than with Sutpen himself, his madness, or any Orestian aspects. Radloff focuses on the design, but his study employs existential philosophy rather than psychology, with no reference to anything Greek.

⁵The persona is a consciously chosen self-image which one strives to make society believe is the real person. It is necessitated by the demands of the ego and its goals and ideals. Pushing the needs of the persona always means repressing some other element or elements.

⁶Psychic inflation involves a situation in which the ego is taken over by, possessed by or filled with, blown up with, a given content. In *Two Essays*, Jung speaks of cases of inflation in which it is "not the dignity of an office that causes the inflation, but very significant fantasies" (143). Sutpen's fantasy (the "design") holds that by duplicating the career of the rich planter, he can get revenge and somehow "fix things" or correct the insult he sustained as a boy.

⁷Yet, according to Brooks, "Sutpen is less 'Southern' than 'American'" (429, 426-28).

Works Cited

Adams, Richard P. *Faulkner: Myth and Motion*. Princeton: Princeton UP, 1968.

Barrett, William. *Irrational Man: A Study in Existential Philosophy*. Garden City: Doubleday Anchor, 1962.

Blotner, Joseph. *Faulkner: A Biography*. 2 vols. New York: Random House, 1974.

Brooks, Cleanth. *William Faulkner: The Yoknapatawpha Country*. New Haven: Yale UP, 1974.

Brylowski, Walter. "Faulkner's 'Mythology.'" *William Faulkner's "Absalom, Absalom!" A Critical Casebook*. Ed. Elizabeth Muhlenfeld. New York: Garland, 1984.

Chavkin, Allan. "The Imagination as the Alternative to Sutpen's 'Design.'" *Arizona Quarterly* 37.2 (1981): 116-26.

Faulkner, William. *Absalom, Absalom!* New York: Random (Modern Library), 1964.

_____. *Light in August*. New York: Random House, 1968.

_____.*The Sound and the Fury*. New York: Random House, 1956.

Jung, C.G. *The Archetypes of the Collective Unconscious. The Collected Works of C.G. Jung*. Vol. 91. 2nd ed. Trans. R.F.C. Hull. Princeton: Princeton UP, 1980.

_____. *The Development of Personality. The Collected Works of C.G. Jung*. Vol. 17. Trans. R.F.C. Hull. Princeton: Princeton UP, 1977.

_____. *Two Essays in Analytical Psychology. The Collected Works of C.G. Jung*. Vol. 7. Trans. R.F.C. Hull. Princeton: Princeton UP, 1966.

May, Rollo. *Love and Will*. New York: Dell, 1974.

Miller, David L. "Orestes: Myth and Dream as Catharsis." *Myths, Dreams, and Religion*. Ed. Joseph Campbell. New York: Dutton, 1970.

Radloff, Bernard. "*Absalom, Absalom!*: An Ontological Approach to Sutpen's 'Design.'" *Mosiac* 19.1 (1986): 45-56.

Scott, Arthur L. "The Myriad Perspectives of *Absalom, Absalom!*" *William Faulkner's "Absalom, Absalom!" A Critical Casebook*. Ed. Elizabeth Muhlenfeld. New York: Garland, 1984.

Slabey, Robert M. "Faulkner's Wasteland Vision in *Absalom, Absalom!*" *Mississippi Quarterly* 14 (1961): 153-61.

Sullivan, Walter. "The Tragic Design of *Absalom, Absalom!*" *South Atlantic Quarterly* 50 (1951): 556-60.

Swiggert, Peter. *The Art of Faulkner's Novels*. Austin: U of Texas P, 1962.

Vickery, Olga W. *The Novels of William Faulkner: A Critical Introduction*. Baton Rouge: Louisiana State UP, 1964.

Images of the Shaman
in the Works of Kurt Vonnegut

Lawrence R. Broer

George Bernard Shaw accounted for the savage unreason-ableness of mankind by suggesting that some alien world was using the earth as its insane asylum, dropping lunatics off at regular intervals. For such writers as John Barth, Joseph Helier, Thomas Pynchon and Kurt Vonnegut, Shaw's observation of madness at the center of human affairs becomes a disturbingly literal estimate of the human situation in the latter half of the twentieth century. The times are no longer out of joint; they are unimaginable—an ongoing nightmare of violence and unpredictability in which the writer's conception of his world changes from that of Matthew Arnold's "battle-ground" in "Dover Beach" to the lunatic asylum of Ken Kesey's *One Flew Over the Cuckoo's Nest*, Beckett's *Watt*, or Vonnegut's *God Bless You, Mr. Rosewater*. Responding to the recent writers' obsession with warpedness in what he calls "the literature of 'Extremis,'" Kurt Vonnegut explains, "we all respond with a sort of shriek to the ghastliness of news today...It is typical of people who have a gruesome history, who have seen many invasions, a large number of dead people, and many executions."[1]

While these "shrieks" of madness in contemporary fiction occur with important variations, two extremes persist: writers such as Beckett, Donleavy, Barth and Heller, whose bitterness leads to depressing or dispiriting fictions, and writers such as John Gardner, Norman Mailer, Bernard Malamud and Kurt Vonnegut, whose despair is balanced by an optimistic faith in the possibility of change or renewal. The former writers create characters incapable of ordering or coping with contemporary experience, "agitated spirits," as Saul Bellow's Mr. Sammler calls them, "casting themselves into chaos" (*Mr. Sammler's Planet* 136, 137), while the

Reprinted from *Sanity Pleas: Schizophrenia in the Novels of Kurt Vonnegut*, UMI, 1989, with permission.

latter seek to restore order and purpose through the affirmation of old values or the creation of new ones. I speak, of course, of polarities which represent reactions to a radical age whose norm is to breed such extremes. Tags such as "affirmative" or "negative" should be used guardedly. Personal sympathies may determine what one finds bracing or dispiriting, and the choice of our best writers to affirm or to deny is not always as clear-cut, as categorical, for instance, as John Gardner would have us believe.

Though hardly unique in reading Vonnegut as a pessimistic writer, Gardner has been more vociferous than most in accusing Vonnegut of "cold-heartedness and trivial-mindedness." Confusing the withdrawal of Vonnegut's often dazed and pliant hero into narcissistic fantasies and escapist daydreams with an absence of moral commitment on the author's part, Gardner claims that "Vonnegut's moral energy is forever flagging, his fight forever turning slapstick" (41-49). In this same vein, Kalidas Misra sees Vonnegut's vision as so dark, his characters so powerless, she uses *Slaughterhouse-Five* to describe a shift in the modern war novel from "hope to final despair" (76). Critics from David Goldsmith to Josephine Hendin have argued that the philosophic determinism of Tralfamadore in *Slaughterhouse-Five* represents Vonnegut's own sense of the futility of the human condition. It is the wisdom of Tralfamadore, they say, based upon the belief that human events are inevitably structured to be the way they are and hence do not lend themselves to warnings or explanations, that allows Billy Pilgrim and the author to adjust to their traumatic memories of Dresden.

It is usually these same critics who, seeing Vonnegut as a "facile fatalist," fail to understand the psychological function of Vonnegut's exotic settings and imaginary worlds, associating such fantasy creations as Tralfamadore, Titan, Mars, San Lorenzo or Shangri-la with frivolity and superficiality. The fact is that these escapist worlds warn against rather than affirm fatalist sophistries. Such mirror reflections of our own planet enforce Vonnegut's position that the insane world of soulless materialistic lusts for fame and money, of suicidal wars and self-serving religions, that we presently inhabit is a world of our own lunatic invention. The Tralfamadorian view of reality is the very antithesis of Vonnegut's position that artists should be treasured as alarm systems—specialized cells for giving warning to the body politic. The Tralfamadorians eventually blow up the universe while experimenting with new fuels for their flying saucers. They do not improve Billy's vision; Billy's conversion to Tralfamadorian fatalism, OR FATAL DREAM ("Tralfamadore" by anagram), ensures his schizophrenic descent into madness.

John Irving provides valuable counterpoint to the argument by Hendin, Roger Sale, Jack Richardson, John Gardner, et al., that Vonnegut infects his readers with despair and world weariness. Irving agrees that Vonnegut "hurts" us with visions of a ruined planet, evaporated sunny dreams (41-49). But Vonnegut's "bleak impoliteness" provokes us to be more thoughtful, creative and kind. Doris Lessing, too, reminds us that Vonnegut explores "the ambiguities of complicity," which causes the reader to think carefully about degrees of responsibility for violence and injustice (35).

The irony of viewing Vonnegut as a writer of "pessimistic" or "defeatist" novels is that no writer has been more self-conscious in serving his society as a "Shaman," a kind of spiritual medicine man whose function is to expose these various forms of societal madness—dispelling the evil spirits of irresponsible mechanization and aggression while encouraging reflectiveness and the will to positive social change. It is this almost mystical vision of himself as spiritual medium and healer that Vonnegut intends by calling himself a "canary bird in the coal mine"—one who provides spiritual illumination, offering us warnings about the dehumanized future not as it must necessarily be, but as it surely would become if based on the runaway technology of the present. In his novel *Bluebeard*, Vonnegut's artist-protagonist Rabo Karabekian describes his part in "a peculiar membership" with ancient historical roots—people telling stories around a campfire at night or painting pictures on the walls of caves. Its purpose is to cheer people up, inspire fellowship and open up minds that would go on exactly as before "no matter how painful, unrealistic, unjust, ludicrous, or downright dumb...life may be" (75, 75, 199). The historical role of Vonnegut's artist-Shaman is described by Mircea Eliade as someone proficient in speculative thought—a singer, poet, musician, diviner, priest and doctor—preserver of oral traditions in literature and of ancient legends (30).

Both roles—Shaman and canary bird—meet Vonnegut's major criterion for himself as artist—that writers are and biologically have to be agents of change, specialized cells in the social organism (*Wampeters* 238). Functioning as the projective imagination of the Life Force, Vonnegut, particularly in his later novels, shapes us a more benign and creative future—one in which human beings feel their common humanity at a deep and emotional level of being. Such a future community would have kindness, awareness, mercy, fairness, charity and mutual respect at its core, symbolized by gentle people sharing a common bowl. It is on behalf of this saner world that Vonnegut directs his satirical missiles, warning us with visions of apocalyptic fury in novels from *The Sirens of Titan* to *Galapágos* that we are a doomed species unless we learn to replace lunatic aggression and cruelty with gentleness and restraint.

In fairness, those critics who see Vonnegut as a fatalist are partially right. It seems that for a long while the author's fictional voice is dualistic—"split.... right up the middle" (as is said of Paul Proteus in *Player Piano*) into a self that affirms and a self that denies (226). It is the fierce combat of these warring identities, referred to by Freud in *Beyond the Pleasure Principle* as a battle between the forces of Eros, the life instinct, and Thanatos, the death instinct (78-110), which the tormented Howard Campbell in *Mother Night* calls "schizophrenic," and whose attempts at resolution constitute the psychoanalytic plot central to each of Vonnegut's novels and to his work as a whole. Wavering conviction as to the possibility of human progress once caused Vonnegut to remark that "Shaw's optimism in *Back to Methuselah* was science fiction enough for me" (145). Vonnegut commented that he suffered from "Hunter Thompson disease"—the affliction of "all those who feel that Americans can be as easily led to beauty as to ugliness, to truth as to public relations, to joy as to bitterness.... I don't have it this morning. It comes and it goes" (*Wampeters* 235). So come and go the efforts of Vonnegut's early protagonists, Paul Proteus, Malachi Constant, Howard Campbell, Jonah and Eliot Rosewater to overcome that fear, cynicism and will-lessness which impedes the spiritual growth of Vonnegut's prospective Shaman-hero. Significantly, Eliade observes that the Shaman—the primitive magician, the medicine man—is above all one who has successfully cured himself (31). Through his own psychodrama he knows the mechanism, the theory of illness, the instability, that threatens the human soul (216). The Shaman's personal illness—"the manifestation of a psyche in crisis" (xi)—is a sign of election, of superior psychic energy and awareness of dangers in the world. Far from lunatic, the Shaman's so-called "psychomental maladies," tendencies toward morbid sensitivity, taciturnity and meditation, reflect the kind of propitious nervous constitution that provides intimate contact with the spiritual world and the capacity to heal (26, 31).

On the one hand, the protagonist's idealistic voice encourages him to maintain youthful idealisms: to nurture a drive for awareness, self-possession and moral responsibility, and to pursue dreams of a more just and harmonious social order. On the other hand, the protagonist's lunatic experience breeds a potentially incapacitating despair which undermines his drive for autonomy and social reform. A paralyzing fatalism prompts him to forsake all hope of improvement in the human condition. Hence arises that compulsive search for refuge from life's storms which causes the protagonist to drug himself to reality—to dream dangerous fantasies of perfect peace and harmony which may relieve him from dealing with painful experience, but which threaten to condemn him to the "existential gangrene" spoken of by R.D. Laing (82). The preface to the novel *Slapstick* establishes that the protagonist's battling voices are indeed Vonnegut's own. Vonnegut identifies the loss of that youthful socialist self who believed in improving labor unions to achieve economic justice. On the other hand, he says that the need to resist the pull of his defeatist self was necessary to life itself. If he is to go on living, he says, he had better follow the lead of idealistic labor leaders like Powers Hapgood (iii).

The problem, then, is that while a majority of critics heed the more audible and visible nihilistic voice in Vonnegut's protagonists—the self filled with "lie down and die"—they miss or ignore altogether its Shaman twin—the efforts of a healthier, yearning, creative self to brave the life struggle, to develop the awareness and courage to act against self-imprisoning cat's cradles and to determine its own spiritual identity in a world of mechanistic conformity and anonymity. Vonnegut's first schizoid hero, Paul Proteus, appears partially successful at best in resisting the system of machines that threatens his sanity. The problem is that despite his inherent resistance to, as he puts it, "carrying out directions from above," Paul ultimately lacks the strength of will and the courage to follow a partially awakened conscience and to act against the totalitarian machinery which he himself helps to administer. As soon as his positive voice asserts itself, the pessimistic voice nullifies it, creating a kind of spiritual stalemate. While we leave Paul Proteus in limbo, the element of hope in Paul's last name, "Proteus," signals a potential for growth realized by future heroes, each of whom becomes increasingly successful in combatting defeatism, in struggling against tyrannical systems of control, and in becoming a self-healer and then a healer of others. The denouement to Paul's psychodrama is still to come—not in *Player*

Piano and not until the dialectical struggle between hope and despair that begins with Paul is worked out in a process of exorcism and renewal through such extensions of the Vonnegut hero as Malachi Constant, Howard Campbell, Eliot Rosewater, Billy Pilgrim and Kilgore Trout.

Each of these characters is more successful than Paul Proteus in achieving moral awareness and combining this awareness with existential responsibility for his actions. Each confronts the dark side of his personality and attempts to practice the moral imperative described by Malachi's spiritual twin, Unk, in *The Sirens of Titan* as, "making war against the core of his being, against the very nature of being a machine" (300). Yet, tormented by the fear that he is no better than a robot in a machine dominated world, each moves back from the threshold of complete moral awakening that will allow the Shaman to emerge. The lingering pessimism that is Kilgore Trout, or Billy Pilgrim, remains. No resolutions are possible for Vonnegut's protagonists until Vonnegut has found some way to achieve an "equilibrium" based on the belief that people can successfully resist becoming appendages to machines or, as is said of Billy Pilgrim and people in general in *Slaughterhouse-Five*, "the listless playthings of enormous forces" (164).

In opposing the standard view of Vonnegut as fatalist, Kathryn Hume objects as well to the notion that Vonnegut's work is static or repetitious—repeating rather than developing, as Charles Samuels says ("Heraclitean Cosmos" 208). Hume sees that Vonnegut's "heavy reliance upon projection makes his books unusually interdependent," "a single tapestry" ("Self-Projections" 178). She infers the spiritual progress of Paul Proteus by noting, "the artistic and personal problems he (Vonnegut) takes up in one story are directly affected by those he did or did not solve in the previous story." Nowhere is Hume's insistence upon the intensely personal nature of Vonnegut's work and upon continuity and progress at the heart of Vonnegut's vision more pertinent than in the case of *Slaughterhouse-Five* and *Breakfast of Champions*—novels Vonnegut says were conceived as one book, and which Peter Reed identifies as the "central traumatic, revelatory, and symbolic moment" of Vonnegut's career (172, 173).

A striking paradox of *Slaughterhouse-Five* is that it presents us with Vonnegut's most completely demoralized protagonist while making what is to this point the most affirmative statement of Vonnegut's career. The former heroes' gains in awareness and moral courage fail Billy Pilgrim entirely—by design—for Billy like Kilgore

Trout in *Breakfast of Champions* becomes Vonnegut's scapegoat, carrying the author's heaviest burden of trauma and despair but whose sacrifice makes possible Vonnegut's own "rebirth." Vonnegut is careful to dissociate himself from Billy as from no character before—signaled by the fact that the author speaks to us directly in the important first chapter about the impact of the war on him, and that with references such as "I was there," and "that was me," he personally turns up in the narrative four times.[2]

In *Breakfast of Champions*, Vonnegut invites us to contemplate a portrait of his more embittered and cynical Trout-self—that "unhappy failure" who represents all the artists who searched for truth and beauty without finding "doodly-squat!" (37). Although Vonnegut happens to be describing his fictional counterpart Kilgore Trout in this instance, their lives are in many ways so similar as depicted in this novel that what is said about the one often applies to the other. Trout is given an iron will to live but a life not worth living. He is given Vonnegut's Shaman-like conscience and artistic goals but a pessimism so great that it negates his artistic mission and vitiates his moral zeal. Trout, in fact, has been turned into a proper Tralfamadorian, believing there is only one way for Earth to be—the way it is. Hence Trout reacts with bitter irony to the coordinator of the Midland City Arts Festival who implores him to bring humanizing new truths and hopeful songs to awake and restore the spiritually dead of his town. "Open your eyes!" exclaims Trout. "Do I look like a dancer, a singer, a man of joy?" (233). Through obvious parallels to Trout, the author tells us that his mounting fear and despair actually made him ill—that his machine-induced nightmares were dreadful enough to result in a state of suppressed schizophrenia that led him to contemplate suicide (his mother's fate) as a solution. He was driven into a void, "my hiding place when I dematerialize," to distance himself from potentially overwhelming horrors (294). Twin forces of hope and despair were at work in his soul, struggling for control of his creative imagination. But they balanced one another and cancelled one another out, creating a kind of sterile ambivalence, or spiritual stalemate, out of which either irresolution or nihilism emerged as the dominant effect. It was his pessimism that compelled him to fashion the character of Kilgore Trout to bear the brunt of his own cosmic misery and futility. Vonnegut had fractured his own mind, the character Vonnegut tells Trout, and so, for the sake of wholeness, the poisonous Kilgore, the voice of Thanatos, the will to self-destruction, must go. Determining to cleanse and renew himself for the years ahead, Vonnegut sets

Trout free, a symbolic act which amounts to the author's repudiation of his most pessimistic voice, and which allows the protagonist's Shaman identity to assert itself. In effect, this constitutes what Eliade calls the "initiatory essence" of the Shaman's preparation for Shamanism (64)—a ritualistic descent into self, a symbolic death and resurrection that transports him into that secret society Vonnegut refers to in *Bluebeard*.

It is on such a healthy note that Vonnegut announces the birth of "a new me," preparing to give us protagonists who not only resist fantasized nirvanas, but who develop the necessary moral sense and faith in human improvement to create for themselves and for others that "humane harmony" lacking in the world around them. We experience the first fruit of the author's spiritual rebirth in his novel *Slapstick: Or Lonesome No More*. His subject here is the same—the damaging excesses of the machine upon the human spirit—and he writes of desolated cities and the depletion of nature, of loneliness and spiritual death—but he writes in a voice that is more persistently affirmative than ever before. Dreaming up numerous improvements for mankind, and putting great emphasis on his old idea of the karass from *Cat's Cradle*—bringing together people without great wealth or powerful friends into membership in extended families whose spiritual core is common decency, Vonnegut confirms in this book his optimistic faith that human beings can be anything we want to be. Because people are just families rather than nations, even wars become tolerable; the machines no longer fight and there are no massacres. As Kilgore Trout says in *Breakfast of Champions*, we are free now to build an unselfish society by devoting "to unselfishness the frenzy we once devoted to gold and to underpants" (25). *Slapstick* bears out that the paranoia that permeates the metafictional writing of the sixties and seventies gradually transforms to more positive forms of fantasy—fabulatory extravaganzas, magic realism. The potentially creative paranoia of Paul Proteus, his stifled gift of invention, gives way to renewal and celebration. The two forms of fantasizing—Paul's and Wilbur's—are contrasted through the desirable social vision of extended families, and the dynamite bouquet represented by Wilbur's delusional visit with a Chinese man the size of his thumb, a dangerous retreat from fear and guilt.

Like Wilbur, the protagonists of *Jailbird, Deadeye Dick, Galápagos, Bluebeard*, and *Hocus Pocus* also become agents of illumination and spiritual healing, characters with restored souls and the creative potency to, as Vonnegut says in the Shaman-like prologue to *Slapstick*, "bargain in good faith with destiny." Each overcomes a crisis of personal identity to become either a literal physician healer like Wilbur, whose work as a pediatrician is symbolically appropriate to curing his own childhood afflictions, or a creator who resolves both personal and social fragmentation by creating fantasies that encourage communal bonding rather than narcissistic withdrawal. There are no Titans or Tralfamadores on the mental horizon of these Shamans, no panaceas or womblike hiding places from complex human problems. Their social visions require no bloody revolutions, no sacrificial messiahs, no deterministic structures and no Godlike figures on whom to thrust moral responsibility. They settle for companionship, fair-mindedness and common decency. With the help of three powerful female guides who personify psychic healing and creative optimism, Walter Starbuck of *Jailbird* fulfills the hero's long frustrated drive for human service as executive vice president of the RAMJAC Corporation, by achieving concrete reforms and putting merciful people in positions of power and influence. Accepting his Shaman-like role, he declares, "I was in an extraordinary position theologically with respect to millions of employees" (230). The redemptive significance of Walter's ascending creative self is conveyed through the wedding gift Walter gives to his wife Ruth, a wood carving of an old person with hands pressed together in prayer. It is, he stresses, a multi-dimensional creation ("my invention") whose attitude of hope and love he himself has designed (28).[3] The next incarnations of Vonnegut's Shaman hero, Rudy Waltz, Leon Trout, Rabo Karabekian, and Eugene Debs Hartke will move even closer to that final artistic identity by which they merge with their creator, Kurt Vonnegut.

Rudy Waltz of *Deadeye Dick* demonstrates the regenerated hero's creative potency and healing power through his work both as a pharmacist and dramatic artist, learning, as he says, "to be comforted by music of my own making" (188). In a double sense, Rudy, the Waltzer, the scat singer, the writer, becomes his own creator. Climactically the identities of Rudy and Vonnegut connect first in a mirror image of one another and then in the image of an artist-priest with power to raise ghosts from the grave. Eliade tells us that the Shaman is often invited to funerals to prevent the soul of the deceased from returning (181). Here the function is reversed. In the novel's epilogue, which occurs at the mass grave of those killed by the neutron bombing of Midland City, the gifted metaphysician Hippolyte Paul De Mille offers to raise the ghost of anyone Rudy thinks should haunt Midland City for the next few hundred years. Rudy tells him to go ahead; then he declares, "And I, Rudy Waltz, the William Shakespeare of Midland City, the only serious dramatist ever to live and work there, will now make my own gift to the future, which is a legend" (239).

In *Galapágos*, the work of the protagonist Shaman functions still more purely—as the projective imagination of the Life Force, a directing instrument of the evolutionary process that would help us avoid the kind of sooner-or-later fatal technological horror that occurs in this story. The Shaman now assumes the ultimate role of priest and healer by guiding the destiny of the universe itself. As its title suggests, the setting of *Galapágos* is that of Darwin's *Origin of Species*. With the benefit of nearly a million years of hindsight, the narrator's ghost, which has survived from the year 1986 to the year One Million A.D., tells of "the suicidal mistakes" nations used to make during his lifetime (140). Suggesting that nature's directions in the year 1986 have been anything but felicitous, the end of life in its present form begins with the introduction of an irreversible disease in which creatures invisible to the naked eye try to eat up all the eggs in human ovaries (162). Military scientists finish up the job by bringing on an apocalyptic nightmare that changes forever the course of human destiny. Yet, as a welder of human souls as well as ships like the Behia d'Darwin, Leon's evolved will and conscience compels him to complete his research into the human mind and heart, joining ranks with Rudy Waltz to discourage the suicidal impulses of a world verging on absolute sterility and annihilation. Rejecting the fatalism of his father, the noxious Kilgore Trout, Leon achieves the wholeness and the will to declare, "Mother was right, even in the darkest of times, there was still hope for humankind" (259). The mother's optimism informs Leon that mechanistic structures—ticks of the clock such as his father's pessimism, lovelessness and apathy, the stockpiling of weapons of destruction, evolution itself—all are imaginative constructs open to revision. Noting that "The Galapágos Islands could be hell in one moment and heaven in the next...." (16). Leon realizes that it is we who are responsible for our creations, that it is we, as a character says in *God Bless You, Mr. Rosewater*, who "are right now determining whether the space voyage for the next trillion years or so is going to be a heaven or hell" (18).

Rabo Karabekian, the hero of *Bluebeard*, represents the main regenerative force in the author's spiritual evolution and the end product of the hero's metamorphosis into the consummate Shaman.

It is Rabo, overcoming personal fragmentation to become a healer of others, who asks of his two schizophrenic friends, Paul Slazinger and Circe Berman, "And which patient needed me most now in the dead of night?" (195).

Rabo Karabekian is furthest indeed of all Vonnegut's protagonists from belonging in a prison or asylum.[4] The question of Paul Proteus's sanity posed 50 years ago in *Player Piano* has been answered with an unequivocal assertion of restored mental health. The vigor of Rabo's narrative alone, the energy of Eros, tells us so. But it is the amazing painting in Rabo's potato barn that climaxes and confirms his achievement: a harmony of self and society, body and soul, man and artist, that makes him not only sane but happy—Vonnegut's most emotionally fulfilled hero. At age 71, high time! Soul clap its hands and sing. Rabo subtitles his autobiography "Confessions of an American Late Bloomer"—it might have read, late blooming Shaman—or "Always the Last to Learn" (194).

Notes

[1]Gary Harmon, "The Scene with Kurt Vonnegut, Jr.: A Conversation." This is a transcript taken from conversation that took place at Stephens College, with Jack Lazebrik as the moderator and a group of students joining in the questioning.

[2]John Tilton says that to analyze the narrative mode of *Slaughterhouse-Five* is to analyze its primary subject—its author. Tilton presents a thoroughgoing argument that Vonnegut and Billy are very different people. See *Cosmic Satire in the Contemporary Novel* (Lewisburg: Bucknell University Press, 1977: 78, 89, 103).

[3]It should be noted that the Shaman is typically a disrupter of order, necessarily isolated from the tribe so that, paradoxically, alienation is part of his role as a healer. The phenomenon of alienation is an inevitable part of the Shaman's psychic life, keeping critical distance between himself and existing social institutions and conventions.

[4]The protagonist of Vonnegut's 13th novel, *Hocus Pocus* (1990), is literally imprisoned for alleged crimes against the State, yet judged insane by his own attorney, he keeps faith with the Shaman's belief that the greatest use a person can make of his or her lifetime is to "improve the quality of life for all in his or her community" (176). As a "sort of non-combatant wiseman" (91), Eugene Debs Hartke learns not only that such mechanisms as Tralfamadore can be resisted, but that they can be reconstituted through the fabulating power—the "hocus pocus"—of creative imagination.

Works Cited

Bellow, Saul. *Mr. Sammler's Planet*. Greenwich: Fawcett Crest, 1969.

Eliade, Mircea. *Shamanism: Archaic Techniques of Ecstasy*. Trans. Willard R. Trask. New York, Pantheon, 1951.

Freud, Sigmund. *Beyond the Pleasure Principle*. Trans. James Strachey. New York: Bantam, 1967.

Hume, Kathryn. "The Heraclitean Cosmos of Kurt Vonnegut." *Papers on Language and Literature* 18 (1982): 108-24.

____. "Vonnegut's Self-Projections: Symbolic Characters and Symbolic Fiction." *The Journal of Narrative Technique* 12 (Fall 1982): 177-90.

Irving, John. "Kurt Vonnegut and His Critics." *New Republic* 181 (22 Sept. 1979): 41-49.

Laing. R.D. *The Divided Self*. New York: Random, 1969.

Lessing, Doris. "Vonnegut's Responsibility." *The New York Times Book Review* 4 (Feb. 1973): 35.

Misra, Kalidas. "The American War Novel from World War II to Vietnam." *Indian Journal of American Studies* 14.2 (1984): 73-80.

Reed, Peter J. *Writers for the 70s: Kurt Vonnegut, Jr*. New York: Warner, 1974.

Shaw, Bernard. *Back to Methuselah*. Baltimore: Penguin, 1961.

Tilton, John. *Cosmic Satire in the Contemporary Novel*. Lewisburg: Bucknell UP, 1977.

Vonnegut, Kurt. *Bluebeard*. New York: Delacourt, 1987.

____. *Breakfast of Champions*. New York: Delacourt, 1973.

____. *Deadeye Dick*. New York: Delacourt, 1982.

____. *Galapágos*. New York: Delacourt, 1985.

____. *God Bless You, Mr. Rosewater*. New York: Dell, 1970.

____. *Hocus Pocus*. New York: Putnam's, 1990.

____. *Jailbird*. New York: Delacourt, 1979.

____. *Mother Night*. New York: Avon, 1967.

____. *Player Piano*. 1952. New York: Dell, Inc. 1971.

____. *The Sirens of Titan*. New York: Delacourt, 1959.

____. *Slapstick*. New York: Dell, 1978.

____. *Slaughterhouse-Five*. New York: Dell, 1971.

____. *Wampeters*. New York: Dell, 1976.

Stephen King's *Misery*:
Manic Depression and Creativity

Carol A. Senf

Pyrokinesis in *Carrie* and *Firestarter*. Vampires in *'Salem's Lot*. The wendigo in *Pet Sematary*. A haunted hotel in *The Shining* and a haunted automobile in *Christine*. These works and their preoccupation with the paranormal or even supernatural have caused best-selling novelist Stephen King to be identified as a writer of supernatural horror. However, despite King's obvious interest in the supernatural, many of his works focus on a more ordinary kind of horror—madness.

For example, Jack Torrence in *The Shining* is an alcoholic who breaks his two-year-old son's arm during a period of uncontrollable rage and, apparently possessed by the brooding evil of The Overlook, attempts to kill both his wife and son. John Rainbird in *Firestarter*, who has a shoe-collecting fetish as well as marked homicidal tendencies, positively looks forward to killing Charlie McKee, the novel's eight-year-old heroine. Frank Dodd, a policeman who murders young women, appears in *The Dead Zone* and *Cujo* while "Strawberry Spring" and "The Man Who Loved Flowers" (*Night Shift*) also feature serial killers; and "Nona" (*Skeleton Crew*) focuses on a young man whose dead mother encourages him to go on a murder spree. The religious obsession that King examines in Carrie White's mother (*Carrie*) and Johnny Smith's mother (*The Dead Zone*) finally becomes full-fledged madness in "The Revelations of Becka Paulson" (*Rolling Stone*). After falling while cleaning house, she starts to hear scandalous information from the picture of Jesus on her television set. Following his instructions, she wires the television to electrocute her adulterous husband and then commits suicide. "Paranoid: A Chant" (*Skeleton Crew*) probes the persona's feeling of being persecuted. Finally *IT* features two of King's most disturbed and disturbing characters, Henry Bowers and Patrick Hockstetter. Bowers, finally committed to Juniper Hill—an institution for the criminally insane—after he kills his alcoholic father, hears voices (that he believes come from the moon but that are actually the voice of the supernatural force designated as IT) telling him to kill others; and Hockstetter (identified by King's omniscient narrator as a sociopath) keeps dead flies in his pencil box, uses an abandoned refrigerator to kill stray animals and suffocates his infant brother while their mother naps. Many of these works suggest the connection between madness and the intervention of supernatural or paranormal forces instead of focusing on madness as a condition of ordinary human life.[1] However, in *Misery*, his 14th novel (not counting the five he wrote under the name Richard Bachman), King expands his generalized interest in all forms of extreme behavior to focus on madness *per se*.

Misery is particularly horrifying because it has no hint of supernatural agency, only madness horrifying in its intensity and its impact on the two individuals involved. (Also atypical of King, who seems to enjoy placing his exceptional individuals in the midst of their community, *Misery* features only these two characters.) Annie Wilkes discovers the best-selling novelist Paul Sheldon in his wrecked car and uses various drugs to restore him—not to health exactly since he can no longer use his legs, but to the ability to work. Moreover, King makes it clear that Annie is not just eccentric but certifiably crazy, for she periodically loses her ability to function even within the isolation she has created for herself. Not only does she neglect to tell the authorities (even when they come to see her) that she has found Sheldon, but she keeps him a prisoner in her home until he completes a novel especially for her, cuts off his foot with a hatchet when she believes that he has attempted to escape, cuts off his thumb when he criticizes the second-hand typewriter she had bought for him, and finally kills the young highway patrolman who has come looking for him while Sheldon looks on helplessly. Most horrifying perhaps, she also keeps a record of the numerous other people she had killed, a kind of diary of her homicidal tendencies.

That King is interested in presenting more than shocking details, however, is evident from his use of accurate technical terminology. Most interesting to me, however, are the subtle connections King makes between artistic creativity and insanity, most specifically manic depression. (Links between insanity and creativity also exist in *Cujo*'s wayward poet Steve Kemp, Thorpe in "The Ballad of the Flexible Bullet" and *The Shining*'s Jack Torrance.) Annie Wilkes may be certifiably insane (and Sheldon's amateur diagnosis of manic depression seems likely), but Sheldon also alternates between feelings of depression when he cannot work and periods of intense elation—almost euphoria—when his writing is going well. Despite these similarities, however, *Misery* ultimately presents the creative artist, not as a madman who has lost control of his world, but as a creator and shaper.

Though it might be tempting to link King and Sheldon—both, for example, are popular writers rather than writers who have received a great deal of critical acclaim—familiarity with King's works *and* with his work habits suggests that King himself is *not* manic depressive. Furthermore, *Misery* opens with an acknowledgment to three medical people, including a psychiatrist, who helped "with the factual material." This acknowledgment suggests that King, instead of drawing on personal experience or making up material on Annie's madness, had actually checked details with people accustomed to dealing with such extreme behavior. Several of King's other works also suggest his research of unfamiliar fields. *Pet Sematary*, for example, thanks two people—one for providing medical information and another for providing insight into the nature of grief. Other works, including *'Salem's Lot*—clearly based on *Dracula*—and *The Shining*—both modeled on and dedicated to Shirley Jackson—are plainly derivative of earlier literature and film. (*Danse Macabre*, King's nonfiction study of horror literature and film, reveals his familiarity with both classic horror literature and the pulps; and Don Herron argues that King is so often derivative that one must look outside his fiction for "any sentiment other than the cliched" [151].)

Indeed the internal evidence of King's research and his interest in accurate clinical details are startling in *Misery*. For example, Sheldon reveals that he had researched the subject of madness to write one of his novels:

Because of his researches for *Misery*, he had rather more than a layman's understanding of neurosis and psychosis, and he knew that although a borderline psychotic might have alternating periods of deep depression and almost aggressive cheerfulness and hilarity, the puffed and infected ego underlay all. (50)

Paul is careful to keep reminding the reader of the cyclic nature of Annie's behavior as well as her extreme mood swings from violence and agitation to "waxy catatonia." (Here again the reader should note the use of a clinical term.) However, it is not until the novel is half over that he gives an actual diagnosis, using the language of the medical community instead of lay terms such as "dangerously crazy" or simply "insane":

He suddenly remembered a note on mental illness he had taken for the first *Misery* book, where much of the action had been set in London's Bedlam Hospital.... *When a manic-depressive personality begins to slide deeply into a depressive period...one symptom he or she may exhibit is acts of self-punishment: slapping, punching, pinching, burning one's self w/ cigarette butts, etc.* (157) (King's italics)

Sheldon's diagnosis reveals that he believes Annie is suffering from manic-depressive psychosis—described by some psychiatrists as bipolar affective disorder,[2] an episodic mental illness usually characterized by good social functioning between episodes. In fact, King has Annie experience all the characteristics of manic depression that Peter Ostwald associates with the disease in his study of the composer Robert Schumann: "severe, recurring depressive episodes" that are accompanied by "guilt and self-accusatory ideas...occasionally leading to self-destructive behavior" alternating with periods of manic excitement that "often resulted in creative overactivity" (303).

It is interesting to observe the accuracy with which King presents Annie's behavior and ultimate deterioration.[3] Researching manic depression (the rest of this paper uses this term, both because it describes the extreme mood changes that Annie and Sheldon experience and because it is the term that King's mouthpiece uses) convinces me that King very carefully laid out Annie's symptoms to correspond to this form of insanity. For example, he observes Annie's persecutory delusions, her confusion and memory loss during the manic phrase (she tells Sheldon that she doesn't remember killing the hitchhiker but that she regained consciousness enough to bathe what was left of him so that his murder could not be traced to her), her voracious appetite, her mood swings and the fact that her first attack takes place when she is only 11 years old. (According to Winokur, Clayton and Reich, "the onset of manic depressive disease is more frequently associated with an onset at a younger age than depressive disease" [19].) Even a relatively minor detail, such as Annie's devouring sweet foods like ice cream and sugared cereals without using cutlery, corresponds to a theory first expounded by Karl Abraham in 1911 that, in depressed people, the libido regresses to the oral and anal sadistic levels of psychosexual development. In fact, Winokur et al. note that "one characteristic of manic patients enshrined in nurses' lore" is their demand for a meal at "the time of admission whether it be day or night" (73).

More interesting than mere accuracy of detail, however, is the connection King makes between manic depression and creativity, for—like Annie Wilkes—Paul Sheldon also comes perilously close to manic depression at times.

This link between madness and creativity continues King's interest in the exceptional nature of the artist, an interest that emphasizes both the power and the limitations of the creative individual. A short work, "Word Processor of the Gods" (*Skeleton Crew*), gives the artist the literal power to create and destroy life. Ben Mears, the novelist in *'Salem's Lot*, undertakes the formidable task of killing the vampires who have destroyed his hometown. William Denbrough in *IT*, a writer of horror stories much like King's own, returns to Derry, Maine, to destroy the unspeakable evil that had killed his younger brother and had almost destroyed himself and his five friends when they were children. In all of these works, the creative individual is able to confront the unspeakable primarily because of his exceptional gifts. Even *Cujo*, one of King's most frighteningly realistic works, includes Vic Trenton, a commercial writer whose "Monster Words" can keep the monster in his four-year-old son's closet temporarily at bay. Only in "The Ballad of the Flexible Bullet," *The Shining* and *Cujo* (failed poet Steve Kemp, unable to control himself when Donna rejects him, destroys her home and—in a gross travesty of the creative process—masturbates all over the Trentons' bed) is creativity a liability, for the artist's extraordinary sensitivity also makes him/her susceptible to outside forces beyond the individual's control.

Though these earlier works often ask the reader to consider the artist's exceptional nature, only *Misery* and the previously mentioned *Shining*, *Cujo* and "Bullet" ask the reader to consider the link between madness and creativity. (Having Annie remind Sheldon and the reader of the fire at The Overlook which was set by its crazy caretaker is King's less than subtle reminder of the similarities too.) King asks the reader to consider the similarities between madness and creativity by drawing attention to similarities between Annie and Sheldon—especially to their cyclic behavior, their compulsiveness, their egotism and their hostility.

In *Misery*, King first links madness and creativity by emphasizing similarities between Annie and Sheldon. Both are writers. Sheldon writes novels, and Annie has prepared a book of her experiences—a collage of newspaper clippings arranged in chronological order—rather than original prose or poetry. Nonetheless, Annie's book shapes and records her experience, an inescapable pattern of homicides in which she "got a job, killed some people, and moved on." King further underlines the similarity in the two by having Sheldon, who initially pretends that the pattern can't be true, admit that the "Annie in him knew" (176-77) and finally come to identify with Annie:

In an act of self-preservation, part of his imagination had, over the last few weeks, actually become Annie, and it was now this Annie-part that spoke up.... And while what it said was perfectly mad, it also made perfect sense. (174)

These two brief passages would mean little by themselves, for they serve only to reveal the rather simple psychological tendency of captives to identify with their captors, slaves with their masters.

However, King reinforces the link between madness and creativity by having Sheldon observe his own cycle of mania and depression:

He laughed until his gut and stump both ached. Laughed until his *mind* ached. At some point the laughter turned to horrible dry sobs that awoke pain even in what remained of his left thumb, and when that happened he was finally able to stop. He wondered in a dull sort of way how close he was to going insane. (226)

Though the reader should note the connection, it is important not to equate madness and creativity, for Sheldon is under immense stress at this point. Not only has he been kept a literal prisoner for months and made a drug addict because of the extraordinary physical pain he suffers, but he also suspects that Annie will kill him once he completes *Misery's Return*. Such experiences would leave their mark on almost anyone.

What turns one human being into a homicidal maniac while another is able to live with his experiences—perhaps even to turn them into something socially or artistically meaningful—is, of course, a question that has fascinated both experts and laymen, including King. For example, he observes in *Danse Macabre* that sanity and insanity resemble one another:

If we were all insane, then all insanity becomes a matter of degree.... The potential lyncher is in almost all of us (I exclude saints...but then, most or all saints have been crazy in their own ways), and every now and then he has to be let loose to scream and roll around on the grass. (174)

King raises an interesting question here though he does not pursue it in *Danse Macabre*.

King indirectly raises the same question in *Misery* though he seems to have a somewhat different answer. Despite his occasional resemblance to Annie and his references to his own questionable sanity, Sheldon is not a madman; and the question of whether or not he is crazy would probably not occur to most readers. (There should be no question in anyone's mind that Annie is crazy though readers might disagree on the diagnosis since schizophrenia, manic-depressive psychosis, and even syphilis of the brain in its final stages often have similar symptoms. [4]) However, King does suggest that the creative process is cyclical for Paul and that the extreme mood swings of creative artists in some ways parallel those of manic depressives. For example, Sheldon's work on *Misery's Return* alternates between days of intense productivity and days in which he accomplishes almost nothing; and Sheldon notes that the compulsion to do something, which he calls *the gotta* and which corresponds to mania, had existed throughout his life as a novelist:

You didn't know exactly where to find *the gotta*, but you always knew when you did.... Even sitting in front of the typewriter slightly hung-over, drinking cups of black coffee and crunching a Rolaid or two every couple of hours...months from finishing and light-years from publication, you knew *the gotta* when you got it.... days went by and the hole in the paper was small.... You pushed on because that was all you could do.... And then one day the hole widened to Vista Vision width and the light shone through...and you knew you had *the gotta*, alive and kicking. (224)

The obverse, of course, is periods when there is no compulsion to work, periods when nothing happens. These periods correspond to the depressive phase of manic depression, when the person may fall into a stupor, experience paranoid delusions or contemplate (perhaps actually attempt) suicide. For example, Paul describes Annie's depressive phase and contrasts it with her manic phase:

Her eyes were dull.... he heard the creak of her favorite chair as she sat down. Nothing else. No TV. No singing. No click-click of silver or crockery. No, she was sitting there. Just sitting there being not all right. (156)

His own experiences—both during his confinement and after his escape from Annie—resemble this depressive phase. After his escape, he spends nine months in which, unable to write, he is filled with self-recrimination, paranoid dreams of Annie's return, and even desires to die:

Half an hour later he was sitting in front of the blank screen, thinking he had to be a glutton for punishment.... he was going to sit here for fifteen minutes or maybe half an hour, looking at nothing but a cursor flashing in darkness. (308)

This time, however, Sheldon's creativity returns: "The hole opened and Paul stared through at what was there, unaware that his fingers were picking up speed...unaware that he was weeping as he wrote" (310). This return to creativity—an episode that mimics the manic phase—concludes the novel.

   Through Sheldon, King suggests that creativity—like manic depression—runs in cycles. Even the prolific King, who—according to Winter—"tries to write every day except for his birthday, Christmas, and the Fourth of July" (13) has had periods in which it was difficult to write. Winter notes that King experienced a two-year dry spell after completing *IT* when he did very little original writing, and he quotes King as saying that he was "knocked over to learn that there was indeed life after *IT*" (15). Written in the aftermath of that experience, *Misery* may be King's testimony to the ebb and flow of his own artistic creativity.

   There are, of course, other similarities between artistic creativity and manic-depressive psychosis. One of these is the compulsive nature of mania. As Winokur et al. observe, people during the manic phase are often compulsive communicators—usually through excessive talking, though the compulsion may take written form:

This pressure to communicate also manifests itself in writing usually voluminous letters. During five of our 100 episodes the patients spent many hours working "on a book." In one example, the father of an index patient, himself manic, wrote plays during his mania and edited them afterward. One of his plays has been seen on television. (68-69)

   King has Sheldon characterize this compulsion as "the gotta" though he doesn't restrict it to the compulsion to communicate. Indeed King's "gotta" can be a compulsion to read or to learn as well as a compulsion to write.

However, if the compulsion to create characterizes both the artist and the manic depressive, so does the compulsion to destroy. Winokur et al. observe that people are particularly prone to violence during the manic phase:

Eighty-three percent of the manic episodes were characterized by hostility, generally verbal but at times physical, and 14% of the admissions were the result, in part, of assaultive or destructive behavior. In two patients this hostility reached homicidal proportions in that the patients expressed the desire to kill a close relative or friend, but no such attempts were ever made. (62)

Annie's book reveals that she killed both her father and her college roommate as well as countless patients at hospitals where she had worked. Through Sheldon, King reveals that artists have more socially acceptable ways of channeling their hostility. In fact, writers can kill off characters with impunity, and Paul is positively gleeful at escaping from his character Misery Chastain.

What enables writers and manic depressives to feel that they can control—even kill—other people is their egotism. Sheldon observes that "a borderline psychotic might have alternating periods of deep depression and almost aggressive cheerfulness and hilarity" but that under everything else lay "the puffed and infected ego...positive that all eyes were upon him or her, positive that he or she was starring in a great drama" (50). In fact, this ego makes the manic depressive believe that he/she can make important decisions for other people. After he observes Annie kill a rat, Sheldon observes that manic depressives believe they can make similar decisions for people as well:

This was how depressives got just before shooting all the members of their family, themselves last; it was the psychotic despair of the woman who dresses her children in their best, takes them out for ice cream, walks them down to the nearest bridge, lifts one into the crook of each arm, and jumps over the side. Depressives kill themselves. Psychotics, rocked in the poison cradles of their own egos, want to do everyone handy a favor and take them along. (160)

Both King, who—again according to Winter—admits that he "writes for an audience of one: himself" and Sheldon confess to having similarly large egos: "*The reason authors almost always put a dedication on a book...is because their selfishness even horrifies themselves in the end*" (279) (King's italics).

Much of *Misery* asks readers to consider similarities between the artist and the manic depressive. Despite these similarities, however, it seems sensible to conclude with some obvious differences, differences that are in fact more relevant to King's notion of the artist. Though artists are clearly exceptional people— different from the ordinary—they are not madmen. Indeed what makes them exceptional (at least this judgment is true of successful writers though not of Kemp or Torrance) is their ability to channel both their euphoria and their hostility. The differences between the artist and the madman are as extreme as the differences between Annie Wilkes and Paul Sheldon. Annie can only destroy life while Sheldon creates it—magically and memorably. (He notes, for example, that Annie isn't interested in the writer's tricks of the trade—in the ways he shapes his material; and her own book merely takes what others have written about her with little or no attempt to control or shape it.) The essential difference is that Sheldon—despite his mood swings and violent compulsions—is finally in control of himself and his destiny in ways that Annie is not. Though manic-depression psychosis may be a metaphor for the painful ebb and flow of genius, King suggests in *Misery* that it is an inexact metaphor at best.

Notes

[1]Looking at the link between insanity and King's use of the supernatural, Bosky suggests that King has always been more concerned with psychology than with the supernatural:

> In most of King's fiction, the part of the mind that leads toward sanity and integrity...and the part of the mind that leads toward obsession and dissolution are separate and in constant battle, but they indubitably spring from the same grounds. Supernatural intervention may aid one side or the other—particularly malefic forces influence the latter—but this can only occur because the character possesses these tendencies and yields the corresponding influences. (225)

[2]Blashfield notes that affective disorders constitute an area of major difference between the DSM-III (*Diagnostic and Statistical Manual of Mental Disorders*, a classification system published by the American Psychiatric Association in 1980) and the ICD-9 (*International Classification of Diseases*, the official classification system adopted by the World Health Organization in 1978):

The ICD-9 maintains the distinction among manic-depressive psychosis, psychotic depression, and neurotic depression.... the DSM-III organizes affective disorders into major affective disorders, affective personality disorders, atypical affective disorders. Within major affective disorders, the DSM-III emphasizes the bipolar/unipolar distinction. (275)

[3]According to Webb and her colleagues, "The two building blocks of Affective Disorders are the depressive syndrome and the manic syndrome. Each syndrome has at its core the disordered mood" (83).

Woodruff and his colleagues provide a more detailed discussion of mania and depression. For a diagnosis of mania, a person must have the following characteristics:

A. Euphoria or irritability.

B. At least three of the following symptom categories.... 1) Hyperactivity (includes motor, social and sexual activity). 2) Push of speech (pressure to keep talking). 3) Flight of ideas (racing thoughts). 4) Grandiosity.... 5) Decreased sleep. 6) Distractibility.

C. A psychiatric illness lasting at least two weeks with no preexisting psychiatric conditions.... (200)

A diagnosis of depression also requires certain definite characteristics:

A. Dysphoric mood characterized by symptoms such as the following: depressed, sad, blue, despondent, hopeless, "down in the dumps," irritable, fearful, worried, or discouraged.

B. At least five of the following criteria.... 1) Poor appetite or weight loss.... 2) Sleep difficulty.... 3) Loss of energy.... 4) Agitation or retardation. (5) Loss of interest in usual activities.... 6) Feelings of self-reproach or guilt.... 7) Complaints of or actually diminished ability to think or concentrate... 8) Recurrent thoughts of death or suicide.

C. A psychiatric illness lasting at least one month with no preexisting psychiatric conditions....

[4]According to Woodruff and his colleagues, one of the big differences is that patients with affective disorders "do not develop the formal thought disorder characteristically seen in schizophrenia." Nonetheless they admit that "the distinction between mania and schizophrenia can be difficult" (17).

Works Cited

Blashfield, Roger K. *The Classification of Psychopathology: Neo-Kraepilinian and Quantitative Approaches.* New York: Plenum P, 1984.

Bosky, Bernadette Lynn. "The Mind's a Monkey: Character and Psychology in Stephen King's Recent Fiction." *Kingdom of Fear: The World of Stephen King.* Eds. Tim Underwood and Chuck Miller. New York: NAL, 1986: 209-40.

Herron, Don. "King: The Good, the Bad and the Academic." *Kingdom of Fear: The World of Stephen King.* Eds. Tim Underwood and Chuck Miller. New York: NAL, 1986: 129-60.

King, Stephen. *Danse Macabre.* New York: Berkley Books, 1981.

____. *Misery.* New York: Viking, 1987.

____. "The Revelations of Becka Paulson." *Rolling Stone* 19 July - 2 Aug. 1984. The story eventually appeared in revised form in *The Tommy-knockers.*

Ostwald, Peter. *Schumann: The Inner Voices of a Musical Genius.* Boston: Northeastern UP, 1985.

Webb, Linda J., Carlo C. Di Clemente, Edwin E. Johnstone, Joyce L. Sanders, and Robin A. Perley. *DSM-III Training Guide: For Use with the American Psychiatric Association's Diagnostic and Statistical Manual of Mental Disorders.* New York: Brunner/Mazel, 1981.

Winokur, George, Paula J. Clayton, and Theodore Reich. *Manic Depressive Illness.* Saint Louis: C.V. Mosby, 1969.

Winter, Douglas E. *Stephen King: The Art of Darkness.* New York: NAL, 1984.

Woodruff, Robert A., Donald W. Goodwin, and Samuel B. Guze. *Psychiatric Diagnosis.* New York: Oxford UP, 1974.

The Class Flew Over the Cuckoo's Nest:
A Theme Course on "Madness in Literature"

Branimir M. Rieger

Origin of Theme Courses at Lander University

When Lander University revised its general education curriculum in the early 1980s, the concept of a theme or idea course devised for sophomore literature was part of the overhaul. In addition to the already entrenched, traditional survey courses in English, American and World Literature, it was decided that a fourth option, a theme course, would be a welcome alternative for both students and teachers. This fourth course could also be used to satisfy the sophomore literature requirement, and would include a more non-traditional approach. It would give teachers a new and exciting idea course to prepare and teach. However, the course was still to contain a mixture of English, American and non-Western literature from different centuries. This was to prevent someone from teaching a course like "Anti-Serbian Metaphors in the Modern Croatian Novel." So, while the new course was an alternative course and contained a non-traditional approach to a survey course in literature, it nevertheless had boundaries and limitations and was meant to expose the student to important concepts from different countries and ages.

The course was called "Literature and Experience" and was described in the catalog as follows: "A thematic approach is used in exploring the continuity and development of human experience as reflected in significant works in both English and American literature and in other world literature in translation. Such various themes may be explored as the nature of man as expressed in literature, man's relationship to the natural world and his changing under-standing of that relationship, or man's search for understanding of the supernatural." While faculty offered sporadic courses on the nature of the hero, man and nature, and man and animals, I was the only one who was "crazy" enough to offer the madness course on a regular basis.

221

My First Theme Course: "The Rebel in Literature"

My teaching background and my disposition for experimentation made me a perfect candidate to construct our first theme course. As I searched for ideas, I recalled that I had recently enjoyed teaching Dostoyevsky's *Notes from Underground* and Kafka's *The Metamorphosis* in an honors course in fiction. Both works had appeared in the text I used, *Nine Modern Classics*, edited by Barnett, Berman and Burto. I had also recently come across Albert Camus's essay, "What is a Rebel?" Therefore, the combination of Dostoyevsky, Kafka and Camus gave me the core for my first theme course, "The Rebel in Literature."

Rebels in literature were worthy of study because rebellion is a recurring response to the human condition and to authoritarianism. Using Camus's essay as a core essay, the course focused on the nature of rebellion, and the writer's portrait of a specific character, a rebel, who acted against conventional rules in his society. Rebellion is a theme or idea that is not peculiar to one culture or age. Camus's definition that a rebel is a man who says no was particularly useful in discussing rebels from different ages. While there is an anthology called *The Rebel: His Movement and His Motives*, edited by John Cole and F.L. Schepman (Prentice Hall, 1971), I did not use it because I concentrated on whole works in paperback form. The books I used in the "rebel" course were: Sophocles' *Antigone*, Shakespeare's *Hamlet*, Dostoyevsky's *Notes from Underground*, Kafka's *The Metamorphosis*, Camus's *The Stranger*, Kate Chopin's *The Awakening*, Ellison's *Invisible Man*, Orwell's *1984*, Plath's *The Bell Jar*, and Ron Kovic's *Born on the Fourth of July*.

The course, "The Rebel in Literature," showed that there were individuals outside of mainstream society who were forced to rebel or take unconventional actions by choice, necessity or force. These "underground men" or rebels were used by their writers to show how the dominant values of a culture were irreconcilable with the characters' personal lives, political or moral convictions, and social consciousness. Some of the values these characters rebelled against were social hierarchy, the sanctity of personal property, gender rules, fervent nationalism, racial oppression, absolute morality, indiscriminating respect for the law and the wisdom of the status quo.

Time for Change

I taught this course a number of times with some success and the course seemed to be popular with students. I even changed the course title a number of times, calling it "The Underground Man in Literature," "The Loner in Literature," or "Alienation Through the Ages." But I also sensed that a change in my focus was needed. Since some student reaction to the Dostoyevskyan or Kafkaesque characters in the course was "Hey, these guys are a little weird," it seemed obvious that weirdness seemed the next logical, or illogical step, especially since there could be more discussion about the mental stability of these characters. But since "Weirdos in Literature" would not be a very impressive course title on a syllabus turned in to a Dean or Department Chairperson, the term "madness" seemed to offer the most challenging opportunity. While I kept some of the basic readings from the rebel course, I also focused on psychological terminology to give the course more of an interdisciplinary approach.

"Madness" Frequent Topic of Writers

The theme of my "new" course was "madness" in all its many individual and social forms. Writers have always examined humanity's contradictory motivations. Endowed with a sensitivity for psychological observations, the writer charts the geography of the inner landscape of the characters' minds with a power and precision unmatched by the more objective methods of psychological science. For many writers, the most compelling features of man's psychological terrain are the deep-shaded valleys of desire, the hidden caves of fantasy and the dark abysses of madness. Pathological experience, in its myriad forms, has long obsessed the artist. My "Madness in Literature" course examined literary works in which some strains of individual or collective madness may be observed. The works I used included: *Oedipus, Antigone, Hamlet, Notes from Underground, The Metamorphosis, Candide, The Stranger, The Bell Jar, The Awakening* and *One Flew Over the Cuckoo's Nest.*

A General Education Course

I stress to my students that the course fulfills the general education requirements by the use of thought-provoking readings, but has as its ultimate focus the lives and concerns of human beings who, like us, struggle to find meaning in their lives and make sense out of chaos. Consequently, a variety of readings were selected from the cultures of Europe, England and the United States, particularly classics dealing with universal concerns. The course stressed that while most of us are not clinically mad, most people have some of the tensions and frustrations of the literary characters.

Two Approaches Used:
Psychological Examination and
Consideration of Various Aspects of "Madness"

The first approach tries to understand literary characters through the descriptions of emotional responses, as used in psychology. The second approach considers whether certain characters are "mad" or different or non-conformist, and why the writer took pains to describe the particular character as someone very unusual in terms of sensitivity, moral conviction and individuality.

First Approach: Psychology and Literature as Complementary Disciplines. Psychology and literature can be complementary disciplines. Each probes the complexities of human perception, emotion and behavior; each assesses the impact of environment and personal relationships on an individual. Each contributes, in its own way, to an understanding of personality. Great literary works frequently complement psychology by depicting characters whose emotional turmoil may reflect some disorder. Literature often presents fierce emotions characters cannot control, or which are in tremendous conflict with each other.

Adjustment to life's pressures can produce dynamic changes. Both literature and psychology chronicle people changing. The level of adjustment or adaption is influenced by two factors: the characteristics one brings to environmental situations (skills, attitudes, physical condition), and the nature of the situations with which one is confronted (conflicts or disasters). These personal and environmental characteristics jointly determine the ease with which the individual survives, is content, prospers or falls by the wayside. Using some of the terminology from psychology, this course studies mankind's personal and social adaptation or lack of it in selected works.

Second Approach: Various Aspects of Madness Considered. The second approach examines certain individuals who have been considered outside the mainstream of society, either by choice, necessity, force, tensions or illness. These "mad" people have been used by the writers to show how the dominant values of a culture have often been irreconcilable with the individual's personal life, especially one's political, moral or social convictions. The readings and class discussions show the various ways these supposedly "mad" persons try either to reconcile or divorce themselves from the prevailing beliefs of their societies. But since the course is not one on criminal psychology, the readings are not intended to be displayed as case studies of "sick" or demented mental patients. The course deals with strong individuals who are thought "mad" or different or non-conformist or rebellious by their societies. Students debate whether the characters are "mad," since the readings emphasize the characters as social beings at odds with other human beings. The use of both approaches insures that the term "madness" is not used in a limited sense, but includes a wide variety of possible human behavior and explanation of that behavior either in general terms, or in specific psychological language.

Some Psychological Terms Used in Discussions of "Madness." While the primary goal of the course is a literary appreciation of the works, psychological terms broaden students' outlooks on "madness." Some of the terms are standard psychological terms, while others come from the newer *DSM-III-R* (*Diagnostic and Statistical Manual of Mental Disorders*), the manual of mental disorders published by the American Psychiatric Association. The terms that have been used in my class include the following: loneliness; depression; isolation; anxiety; frustration; unhappy childhood; identity crisis; unipolar depression; bipolar depression; manic depressive; psychosis; manias; phobias; psychotic; McNaghten rule; paranoia; schizophrenia; neurosis; demented; self-doubt; despair; stress; brainwashing; aggression; suppression; repression; regression; hallucination; nihilism; anarchism; existentialism; coping strategies; psychoanalysis; lovesickness; rational; irrational; shock therapy; shattered idealism; romantic; naturalistic; realistic; mother surrogates; father surrogates; sources of depersonalization; feeling of powerlessness; inferiority complex; superiority complex; Oedipus Complex; Electra Complex; deviant behavior; melancholy; suicide.

Oral Reports on Terms and Study Sheets

Each student is required, at the beginning of the semester, to prepare and give an oral report, and pass out to the class a one-page study sheet on one or more of the above-mentioned psychological terms. These are assigned in the first class period, and the sheets and oral reports are due on the third class meeting. From all the written study sheets I produce a booklet for each class member so everyone will have notes on standard psychological terms to refer to throughout the course; these terms are used throughout the semester in discussing the literary works on the reading list. In addition to these terms, I provide an outline of the major theories of Freud, Jung, Laing and Horney, and often invite a psychology instructor to discuss the theories of these psychological pioneers.

Madmen, Fools or Heroes?

It is also helpful to discuss some famous personalities, evaluating them as madmen, fools, or heroes. Or are they outlaws, heretics or saints? Some people that have provided interesting discussion are: Jesus, Moses, Thoreau, Caesar, Attila the Hun, Napoleon, Henry VIII, Hitler, Robert E. Lee, Jane Fonda, Muhammed Ali, Nixon, Carter, Reagan, Bush, Clinton, Perot, Khomeini, Qaddafi, Lincoln, Castro, Sirhan Sirhan, Lee Harvey Oswald, Jack Ruby, David Berkovitz ("Son of Sam"), Richard Hinkley, James Jones, Charles Manson, Squeaky Fromme, Jeffrey Dahmer, and David Koresh. Are they madmen, fools, or heroes? If there are differences of opinion in the class, what accounts for those differences? Do these figures have more vices or virtues? If they have obvious faults, odd behaviors, or eccentricities, does that make them clinically mad? Sometimes the same person can be a madman to one student and a hero to another. It is also useful to distribute Louis Kronenberger's essay, "Cranks, Eccentrics, and Individuals," which describes three kinds of nonconformists who stubbornly refuse to fit into homogenized American culture. Such class discussions help to point out that staunch individualists have often been considered mad by certain segments of society.

Differences between Analysis of Real People
and Literary Characters

After establishing the proper psychological background for students to use when analyzing literary characters, I also warn them of the dangers of going too far with this approach. Handouts on demented literary characters like the narrators of Browning's "My Last Dutchess" and Poe's "The Cask of Amontillado" establish some obvious examples of disturbed characters. But the mentality of other characters is not always so clear-cut. Faulkner's "A Rose for Emily" shows that Emily Grierson may be crazy, but what clues in the text about her background help to explain her unusual behavior? Frequently students will assert factors or conditions about Emily's condition that are not found in the story. Prospective literary critics need to understand that there are limits in treating literary characters as if they were real people. I read excerpts of A.C. Bradley's critical approach to Shakespeare, where he analyzed characters like Lady MacBeth as though they were independent of the text. While it is fun to brainstorm and come up with theories for characters acting in certain ways, I insist students find reasons in the text for their assertions. The criteria for commitment to a mental institution in

South Carolina are also reviewed because this also helps to distinguish clinical mental illness from literary madness.

Books Discussed in the Course

Discussions of the readings can either focus on certain strains of supposed madness in the literary characters, or on application of one or more of the psychological terms to them. Sophocles' *Oedipus Rex* addresses the values the Greeks placed on rational thought, as well as the inherent limits of rational thought, especially when dealing with Fate and the gods. Discussions also focus on topics such as Oedipus' irrational pride as his possible madness or fatal flaw, and the futility of struggling against the will of the gods. Sophocles' *Antigone* brings up the themes about the "madness" of disobeying the establishment, the mentality of tyrants, and martyr complexes. Shakespeare's *Hamlet*, supplemented by viewings of the Derek Jacobi or Mel Gibson film versions can provide lively debates about Hamlet's sanity. The examination on *Hamlet* asks the students to discuss the possible sanity or madness of *Hamlet*, as if they were participants in deliberations on a murder jury.

Dostoyevsky is a forerunner of modern psychology and his *Notes from Underground* reveals the role of the irrational in behavior, long before Freud. With prodding, students are able to look for the various psychological reasons offered by Dostoyevsky for the protagonist's inability to love or be loved: the Underground Man knew no love as a child; he tried to dominate potential friends; and he was incapable of compromising his narrow view to attain even temporary bliss. Sensitive students comprehend that Dostoyevsky exaggerated his Underground Man because he despised the "madness" of blind belief in the optimism of nineteenth-century philosophers.

Kafka's *The Metamorphosis* contains numerous psychological ideas, but alienation is a recurring theme in his works; this may have been partly caused by traumatic events in his life: he was a Jew in a Gentile world; he was a German speaker in Prague; he was a victim of tuberculosis; he was estranged from his domineering father; and he was a literary man in a bourgeois society. Camus's *The Stranger* introduces students to a philosophy which believes man's existence is madness or absurdity. Chopin's *The Awakening* and Plath's *The Bell Jar* both deal with the traditional gender roles assigned to women, and the anguish the main characters suffer because they are viewed as irrational by their respective societies. Voltaire's *Candide* explores the mass philosophical delusion that eighteenth-century society is the best of all possible worlds, and satirically comments on the progress that "ignorant armies" have brought to Europe. Kesey's *One Flew Over the Cuckoo's Nest* indicts supposedly modern treatments of mental illness. Other books used include Beth Henley's *Crimes of the Heart*, Faulkner's *The Sound and the Fury*, J.D. Salinger's *The Catcher in the Rye*, Alice Walker's *The Color Purple*, F. Scott Fitzgerald's *The Great Gatsby*, and Tennessee Williams' *Cat on Hot Tin Roof* and *The Glass Menagerie*.

Student Reports on Outside Works

Each student has to prepare an oral and written report on a book, not on the required reading list, which deals with some aspect of madness. I provide them with an outside reading list of books that they might pick, but the final choice is up to them. They are not required to choose only "classic" literature, and are free to select modern horror writers like Stephen King or Clive Barker. The reports do not have to contain clinical objectivity but rather some general, possibly original, observations on possible madness, society's standards for evaluating madness, and a brief discussion of the character's "madness" by application of one of the psychological terms. The students are then asked to locate and use four descriptions of their particular term (like paranoia) in a book, two journal articles, and one *New York Times* article. They then need to apply what they have gathered on this one term in their research from these four sources, which will be descriptions of some form of medical madness, to their literary character. Book reviews on their assigned books are not allowed in the report, and this exercise allows them to apply psychological terminology to literary situations without a critic telling them what they should think about the book. In this way, they are using psychological criticism to illuminate their book for themselves and class members.

These reports do not have to be on novels. The multiple personalities described in Flora Schreiber's *Sybil* have produced excellent reports. A recent report on the madness of army life in Heller's *Catch-22* complemented the discussions of war in *Candide*. There have been other reports on the psychopathic killers in Capote's *In Cold Blood*, compulsive behavior in Judith Rossner's *Looking for Mr. Goodbar*, the mother's influence in Lawrence's *Sons and Lovers*, social madness in Sartre's *No Exit*, deranged narrators in Poe, and the real madness of mass murderer Ted Bundy in Ann Rule's book, *The Stranger Beside Me*. I insist students find logical reasons in the text to support their conclusions. The whole experience of applying these terms has opened new ways of looking at literature to students.

Conclusions

This course studies fictional characters whose distorted perceptions, intemperate emotions or peculiar behavior can be examined for certain "disorders." Characters like Oedipus, Antigone, Edna, and the Underground Man, who are considered mad by their contemporaries, are often found to be highly intelligent individuals ahead of their times. Students become aware of how the unreasonable constraints of restrictive societies are sometimes to blame for characters' plights.

My theme approach on madness allows students to gain an increased appreciation for literature. The literary works also offer some insights on the problems of madness in its legal, medical, moral, and social contexts. The frequent heated debates demonstrate the thin line between sanity and madness, and are pivotal if students are to become independent learners.

The "Madness in Literature" course is a successful way of getting students involved in the study of literature and life: questioning, reflecting, probing, wondering, and sometimes rebelling. This course explores psychological problems inherent in the human condition. It has helped my students develop strategies for defining their values and approaches to solving their problems in a sometimes confusing world. In a world of future shock, such skills are imperative.

Contributors

Nancy Topping Bazin wrote *Virginia Woolf and the Androgynous Vision* (1973), the first book to explore the interrelationship between Woolf's art and her mental illness. The author of articles on Woolf, Gordimer, Lessing, Emecheta, Head, Wharton, Piercy, and Atwood, Bazin also co-edited *Conversations with Nadine Gordimer* (1990). Dr. Bazin teaches at Old Dominion University.

Lawrence R. Broer, was educated at Florida State and Bowling Green State University. He is presently Professor of English at the University of South Florida. Professor Broer is the author, co-author, or editor of five books, including *Hemingway's Spanish Tragedy* (University of Alabama Press, 1973), and *Sanity Plea: Schizophrenia in the Novels of Kurt Vonnegut* (UMI Research Press, 1989). He has contributed essays to numerous anthologies of literary criticism and authored 70 articles and critical papers on modern and postmodern literature. Broer served as a Fulbright lecturer at the University of Paris in 1981 and 1984, and received both the Faculty Award for Excellence in Teaching at the University of South Florida in 1986, and the Theodore and Venette Askounes-Ashford Distinguished Scholar Award for 1989.

Michael Cohen is Professor of English at Murray State University. In addition to *Hamlet in My Mind's Eye*, which won the SAMLA Studies Award, Cohen has also written *Engaging English Art* (Alabama, 1987) and *Sisters: Relation and Rescue in Nineteenth-Century British Novels and Paintings* (Fairleigh Dickinson, 1994). He lives on Kentucky Lake with his wife and two sons.

Robert de Beaugrande, University of Wien, Austria.

Thomas C. Fiddick teaches history at the University of Evansville in Indiana. He has written one book, *Russia's Retreat from Poland, 1920,* published by Macmillan and St. Martin's Press, while recently contributing a chapter on Lenin in Greenwood Press's *Statesmen Who Changed the World*. He has also written a psychological study of the Russian anarchist, Bakunin, for the *Psychohistory Review*, and is working on a psychological comparison of Hitler and Stalin.

Michael Fleming is chief psychologist of inpatient services at Dr. Solomon Carter Fuller Mental Health Center, Boston, and adjunct Associate Professor of psychology and psychiatry, Boston University. His book, *Images of Madness: The Depiction of Insanity in the Feature Film*, with co-author Roger Manvell, is the first systematic historical inquiry into the interaction of film and psychiatry.

Kenneth L. Golden has published articles on a number of works of modern literature in regard to myth/psychology. His 1992 edited volume *Uses of Comparative Mythology: Essays on the Work of Joseph Campbell* was published by Garland. His critical volume *Mythology and Science Fiction* will be published by Mellen in 1994. Dr. Golden has taught English at the University of Arkansas and Memphis State University.

Peter H. Goodrich teaches English literature and technical writing at Northern Michigan University in Michigan's Upper Peninsula. He has published an anthology and several articles about Merlin and related medievalisms, and is currently editing a casebook of Merlin scholarship.

James R. Huffman is Professor of English and Coordinator of American Studies at the State University of New York College at Fredonia. He has published articles on literature, psychology, American studies, and popular culture, and is currently working on a book tentatively entitled *In Sickness and in Health: A Psychological Approach to U.S. History and Culture*.

Martin S. Lindauer received his Ph.D in experimental psychology from The New School. In addition to perception, he works in several areas of the psychology of art. He recently retired from SUNY at Brockport, and now lives and writes in San Francisco.

Barbara Tepa Lupack, formerly Academic Dean at SUNY/ESC, now directs a small literary press and edits *The Round Table*. Her books include *Plays of Passion, Games of Chance: Kosinski and His Fiction; Take Two: Adapting the Contemporary American Novel to Film*; and *Inmates Running the Asylum: Insanity as Redemptive Response in Contemporary American Fiction*.

Roger Manvell, was Professor of Film at Boston University. He wrote numerous books on film history and was the Editor-in-Chief of *The International Encyclopedia of Film*.

Carol A. Senf, Associate Professor at the Georgia Institute of Technology, studies Victorian literature and popular culture. *The Vampire in Nineteenth-Century English Literature* (1987) was published by Popular Press. *The Critical Response to Bram Stoker* (Greenwood) was published in 1993. She is currently working on two projects—Stephen King's women characters and changing attitudes toward children.

Alisa von Brentano, born in Germany, attended The University of Heidelberg School of Journalism and has a Ph.D. in Literature from the University of Tennessee, where she taught for 17 years. Currently an art dealer, she is completing a book on Melville and Marlowe and revising for publication an autobiography about her childhood in World War II Germany.

Paul Youngquist teaches English at Penn State University. He is the author of *Madness and Blake's Myth* as well as articles on Blake, Browning, and Mary Shelley.